Conjuring the Commonplace:

A Guide to Everyday Enchantment & Junk Drawer Magic

Laine Fuller & Cory Thomas Hutcheson

Conjuring the Commonplace: A Guide to Everyday Enchantment and Junk Drawer Magic © 2023 by Laine Fuller & Cory Thomas Hutcheson

All rights reserved. No part of this book may be used or reproduced in any manner whatsoever, including internet usage, without written permission from Laine Fuller & Cory Thomas Hutcheson or 1000Volt Press except in the case of brief quotations embodied in critical articles and reviews.

First edition, 2023

ISBN: 978-1-7347422-7-5

Interior illustrations and some cover illustrations by Cory Thomas Hutcheson

Although the publisher and the author have made every effort to ensure that the information in this book was correct at press time, and while this publication is designed to provide helpful information in regard to the subject matter covered, the publisher and the author assume no responsibility for errors, inaccuracies, omissions, or any other inconsistencies herein and hereby disclaim any liability to any party for any loss, damage, or disruption caused by errors or omissions, whether such errors or omissions result from negligence, accident, or any other cause.

1000voltpress.com

About the authors:

Laine Fuller is the co-host of the *New World Witchery* podcast and *Myth-Taken: A Buffy the Vampire Slayer Podcast*. She has a bachelor's degree in English from Tennessee Tech University. While this is her first book, she's no stranger to writing and even won a first-place prize in a college short story competition. When she's not working witchcraft, you can find her spinning, knitting, quilting, painting, or spending time with her husband, her daughter, and her two cats.

Cory Thomas Hutcheson is the co-host of *New World Witchery*, a podcast and website dedicated to uncovering and recovering traditional North American folk magic practices. He is also the author of *New World Witchery: A Trove of North American Folk Magic* (Llewellyn Publications, 2021). Cory has his doctorate in American Studies with specializations in Folklore & Ethnography and Religion & Ethnicity from Penn State. He also holds a graduate certificate in folklore and ethnography and has had his academic work published in *Midwestern Folklore* and *Contemporary Legend*, among other journals. He is a contributor to the *Oxford Handbook of American Folklore* and *Folklife Studies* and *American Myths, Legends, & Tall Tales: An Encyclopedia of American Folklore*. He has written for popular occult publications, including *The Cauldron* (UK), *The Crooked Path Journal*, and *Witches & Pagans*.

Dedication & Acknowledgments

This book is dedicated to my friends, from whom I am constantly learning more about magic. And myself. Thank you for being a part of the magic. – CTH

I'd like to dedicate this book to my husband, who has supported me in more ways than I could name. I'm going to love you as long as the grass shall grow. I'd also like to thank my daughter, who makes me laugh every day and amazes me with her kindness and empathy. And finally, my mother, who fostered my love of books, reading, and especially writing. – LF

Collecting lore means getting to talk to a lot of wonderful people. It would be impossible to share that lore with you minus the contributions of some very specific wonderful folks, however. To that end, we want to say a mighty thank-you to our editors, Victoria and keifel at 1000Volt Press, who have been advocates for our work from day one and more supportive than we could have hoped for. We've also been extraordinarily lucky to have support from all of our listeners and Patreon supporters while we worked on this little book. Thank you all for making it possible for us to take this step, gather this lore (sometimes directly from you!), and share the little magic of the everyday for over a decade. And of course, thank you to Laine for being a constant inspiration, a constant source of laughter, and a constant source of support (that part's from Cory, by the way).

Cory is the best co-author I could have ever asked for. Throughout this whole process, he was supportive, inspiring, and knowledgeable. I don't know what I did to deserve his friendship, but I consider myself incredibly lucky to have it. Thank you again, Cory. Your friendship has meant so much to me over the years.

I'd also like to acknowledge the people who supported me while I worked on this book. My husband, who was more than support, he was like scaffolding. My mother, who finds every way she can to help me, even when struggling with her own health. My amazing friends Amy, Christina, Bre, Marelle, Sara, Kristin, and Wendy who all helped me through writer's block of the most brutal sort, in one way or another. AthenaBeth, who has the uncanny ability to text when I least expect it and often most need it. And I also must thank Victoria. Not only for her support of Cory and me over the years, but for her feedback, guidance, and lore!

Praise

"Conjuring the Commonplace is a cozy and comprehensive guide to magical tools that are already nestled in your home. Cory and Laine guide you on a delightful journey through the surprising terra incognita of junk drawers and hall closets, pointing out magical uses for everything from humble pennies and old rags to your favorite teacup or coffee mug. As relaxed and welcoming as a chat with an old friend around a kitchen table, this book is brimming with advice about how to turn every moment magical."

Dee Norman, author *Burn a Black Candle: A Grimoire of Italian-American Magic*

"Grab your dish towel, covet your spice rack, be mindful of where you sweep, and don't let things fall to the floor because Conjuring the Commonplace is afoot! We often hear how magic and divination are all around us, but it's the where and how that is rarely explained, until now. Dwell in your dwelling –like never before– with this distinctly damn near definitive book on household magic!"

Christopher Orapello - Artist, witch, coauthor of *Besom, Stang & Sword*, and cohost of *Down at the Crossroads* podcast

"This book is such a treasure and is a compendium of how I do my own work. A need arises, the tools to solve the issue are always at hand and the witch gets to work. What's in my pocket? What's in my quilting bag? Then a ramble through the garden. Done and dusted! What's in your Drawer of Miscellany? Everything you need for magic. Read this book—it will inspire your practice and unleash your creativity."

H. Byron Ballard, witch, author of *Small Magics: Practical Secrets from an Appalachian Village Witch*, and forensic folklorist

"Laine and Cory weave folk charms and rituals together into a seamless tapestry of magical traditions. Their work takes us back into our own home as a source of power--a place that many of us have forgotten in our practice. Repurposing household items for magic and healing is at the heart of so many folk cultures and it's refreshing to see these traditions treated with such kindness and excitement. It's clear to tell that this is a passion project for both of these fantastic storytellers. This practical and comprehensive guide will no doubt find its way onto the shelves of beginners and seasoned practitioners alike."

Brandon Weston, author of *Ozark Folk Magic: Plants, Prayers & Healing* and the *Ozark Mountain Spell Book*

Table of Contents

Dedication & Acknowledgments	5
Praise	6
Introduction	9
About This Book	13
1. Coins	15
2. Keys	23
3. Matches	29
4. Towels, Rags, & Other Soft Goods	35
5. Knife, Fork, & Spoon	43
6. Teacups & Bowls	53
7. In the Ice Box	61
8. Bottles, Cans, & Jars	69
9. In the Pantry	77
10. Washing Up	85
11. Cobwebs, Dust, & Dirt	93
12. Brooms	101
13. Ribbons, Strings, & Cords	107
14. Needles & Pins	113
15. Buttons	121
16. Desk Set	127
17. Cards, Toys, & Games	137
18. Sticks and Stones	145
19. In the Weeds	155
20. Fido and Fluffy	161
21. Purses and Wallets	169
22. Broken Things	175
Conclusion	183
Additional Notes, Resources, and Valuable Knick Knacks	185
Spell Concordance	187
Index	189

Introduction

When you hear the word "magic," does it conjure up images of ancient wizards in towers peering into orbs, summoning crackling bolts of lightning and riding fire-breathing dragons? Or do you envision unruly schoolchildren sending sparkling ribbons of light out of the end of intricately crafted wands to turn each other into toads, cats, or ferrets? Or is it something else? Something a little plainer, but somehow warmer and more inviting? For us, magic is "home." It's a feeling that wraps around us, makes us feel alive and in love with the world we inhabit. It's the cozy, everyday enchantment that bespells us and that we use to bespell our lives.

Magic inhabits the physical spaces of our homes, sometimes in the most mundane of places. This connection between the physical space and the feelings it evokes is probably familiar to you. If you have ever walked into an old jailhouse, an empty building that is usually bustling with people, or a parking lot that's just a little too dark, you know the way it can give you chills up your spine or goosebumps on your skin—or can make you completely comfortable and at peace.

Our homes can make us feel things too. When we have had a long day, or have been away on a long trip, there's nothing quite like walking through our front door. That sensation of being "home" permeates our skin and bones, melts away the outside world, and says "welcome" to us. Similarly, you probably know the feeling of walking into someone's home where you feel alien, like an intruder in the space. That is because the home is one of the most magically attuned places we can be. Yet a great deal of magic seems to be associated with those strange stone towers or ancient ruins. We like to think of magic as something exotic and unusual, but for most of human history that has not been the case. Instead, magic is a part of the everyday experience of everyday people trying to accomplish everyday things, albeit through extraordinary means.

This book is our invitation to you, then, to step across our own little "Welcome!" mat and into the imagined home we've conjured for you. It's a chance to fall in love with magic by touring the house with us, seeing the way everyday objects like buttons, spoons, teacups, and string all hold onto a magical history and offer us new ways to work with enchantment today. There's nothing wrong with outlandish staves and ethereal crystal balls, but so often people look for magic in those strange objects and skip right past the marvels in the broom closet, the bewitchment in the sewing kit, or the magic in the mudroom. We are here to remedy that by going through all these "everyday" objects and discovering the mysteries in a matchbook or the spectral in a bit of string. In short, we are asking you to come and rifle through the junk drawer with us and see what sorts of spells, sorceries, and splendors we can find together.

But first, we need to ask a few important questions...

What is folk magic?

If we wanted to be a bit impish, we could just say "the magic of the folk." But then you'd put the book down and walk away with a snort of disgust, and we already like you too much to let that happen. So let's talk about who the folk are and why they might need magic in the first place.

"The folk" can be any group of people who share a common identity or goal. These groups can pop up around location, occupation, ethnicity, something as small as "everyone named Aaron," or something huge like religion. For the vast majority of our history, many people have shared a general lack of power and resources in common. Thus, the "folk" are often groups that are subject to the authority and whims of more elite groups. Those elite groups have wealth, political control, and sometimes even military might in their corner—and that brings us to why the folk turn to magic. When you are cut off from the sorts of advantages that those in power have, you use what you have and what is available to you. And magic? Well, that's everywhere! The folk are very crafty people, and they know how to turn an old well into a powerful source of enchantment, or how to twist a bit of string just so to make sure that they aren't going to starve this year.

So what about the "magic" bit of that "folk magic" stuff? That gets into a whole mess of metaphysics and spiritual philosophizing that can be better explained by those with more letters after their names than we have. For our own purposes, though, we think of magic as a force that connects the world—its physical and non-physical aspects—and allows us to change it in ways that aren't always logical or rational. For example, when we make a wish on the first evening star, we have no reason to logically think that a little pinprick of light that started billions of miles away somehow being visible at just the right moment will grant us a favor, but we might do it anyway because it feels like the universe is paying attention to us while we are paying attention to it. It becomes almost a language we speak without words, but rather with symbols, gestures, intentions, and objects. It's not sparks flying from wands so much as a subtle sense that we've shifted things just a little bit. We've started a chain reaction that will ripple out from us to the wider world—and hopefully bring back the results we want. We light a candle or flip a coin, we hold our breath in a tunnel, we cross our fingers behind our back, and sometimes we get what we're after. Like magic!

The folk have spent a long time developing all kinds of methods for making those little shifts occur. Sometimes they do it for personal gain, like when ancient Romans would etch curses into sheets of lead and bury them to make someone give them their towel back at the baths or make a particular charioteer a little unlucky in the next race. Sometimes it comes from a place of need—a person protecting their milk from bewitchment so they won't go hungry, trying to determine the right match for a marriage, or even looking for healing when the current medical technology doesn't deliver the results they hoped for.

Of course, when the folk use their magic, those who are in power tend to get nervous. This fear leads them to call folk magic by a different name: witchcraft. In contemporary times, however, even that word has been reclaimed, and we find that witches are no longer fearful fairy tale creatures bent on destruction, but real people who have chosen a magical existence as a part of their spiritual identity (which makes witches their own type of folk, after all).

This book does touch on witchcraft here and there. In some cases, we offer spells that might be classified as "witchcraft" by one group, but as "cures" or "charms" by another. In other cases, we also have folklore about how to protect yourself against "witchcraft," which is usually meant as "curses" or "hexes" in those particular passages. It's important to remember that witches come in a lot of flavors, and the word "witchcraft" has a long and complex history. We tend to like witches, ourselves. They're pretty wonderful in our experience, but this isn't a book exclusively for or about witches. It is, instead, for everyone who has ever wanted to live in a slightly more enchanted world. It is our perspective that if you live in any kind of home, you probably have a lot more magic around you than you think you do. We want to show how everything around us also has a long and complex history, one frequently tied up in the mystical, esoteric, and enchanting.

But isn't all that mystical stuff found in secret shops in hidden alleyways? Like crystal balls and rune-inscribed daggers? That brings us to the next important question...

Why use everyday objects?

The fancy objects—wands and athames and altars and chalices—those are all perfectly valid magical tools. If the folk are doing magic, though, they have not historically had access to the shiny bits, and they have had to make do with what's at hand. Thus, in folk magic, most of the wonders are tucked into pretty ordinary things. A gnarly tree at the roadside gets tied with bits of ribbon or string, and that's enough to make wishes come true (or at least to tilt the wishing in your favor). An old horseshoe or a penny from the year you were born are just as rich in magical lineage as any glistening amethyst orb in a metaphysical shop. The other nice part about commonplace things is that because they are so ubiquitous, they are constantly undergoing reinvention, and each group of folk will often add their own tweak to the magical lore and history.

We often like to free-associate with everyday objects to find new ways to use them in magic. Sometimes there are certain "universal" symbols, like a heart for love or a crown for power. But finding your own personal association with an object can be very powerful. We know several witches who use small trinkets in their bespoke divinatory systems that may not make sense to anyone but them—and doesn't that seem to hold much more power? A chess piece may symbolize logic, strategy, or playfulness when read purely based on those "universal" symbols. Maybe you were in the chess club, though, and so a chess piece can indicate school and education for you. But it also might mean something to do with Laine's father in her own system, as he's the one who taught her to play chess, or it could mean her brothers, who played countless games with her growing up. For Cory, a chess piece like the king or bishop might symbolize power or bureaucracy since for him it conjures images of royalty and a certain level of upper-crust fanciness, while a queen or knight might feel more like the realm of the intellect because they require thinking about the board differently.

What sort of objects are you drawn to? Do books, knives, old oil lamps, or just any bits and bobs strike your fancy? The wonder of using everyday objects is that they're easily accessible, and almost every object in your home has some sort of history with you. Think about its place in your home. Was it a gift, or did you buy it? Was it a purchase of necessity, or one of want? Another upside to all this, if it matters to you, is that it can be hidden in plain sight. This is one of our favorite features of folk magic: it can sit on a bookshelf or a kitchen counter and seem completely inconspicuous. While that may not matter to some, we find that most witches don't feel one hundred percent comfortable advertising to their neighbors (or even some family and friends), "Hey! A witch lives here!" So these everyday objects can—and do—fill your home with the marvelous, while looking like just another wooden spoon or pair of dice. No one ever has to be the wiser! Bwahahaha!

About This Book

At this point, you hopefully have a sense that we're not going to bite. Well, not hard, anyway. We want this book to be welcoming and friendly for you, to make you feel—quite literally—at home. In inviting you across our proverbial doorstep, we intend to take you through the various rooms, cupboards, drawers, baskets, bins, and more in a fairly "typical" home so that you can get to know all the sublime and spellbinding friends that are just waiting to meet you. If your flavor of magic is rooted in the domestic, this book will help you. If you feel like a well-made meal or a sturdy spring cleaning is an enchanted act, this book will help you. If you like to curl under blankets on a cold day with something warm in a mug and a favorite book, this book will help you (mostly because it will give you something to read while curled up with your cuppa).

We've tried to make this book a little more organized than your typical junk drawer, although you'll find no shortage of odds and ends inside. We begin with a few of the objects you might have tucked away in your typical "catch-all" space: buttons, matches, and keys. These serve as a jumping-off point for the rest of the tour. We go through the kitchen and laundry room looking at the pantry, icebox, laundry supplies, brooms, and more. We even show you some of the wonders you can work with dust, dirt, and cobwebs. (You don't have to have a clean home to enjoy the folk magic here—come as you are!) From there we look at some additional sewing notions, toys and games, and even the writing desk for inspiration. Then we wander just a little bit outside, looking at the backyard trees, stones, leaves, and more, and even spending some time playing with the magical pets in your life. Finally, we end with a chapter on "Broken Things," in which we examine the chipped cups and shattered glasses to see that even when things are imperfect and undone, they can still hold onto their enchantment.

There's a lot here, but we hope we've made it a little easier to explore. We've done our best to untangle the strings and sort the spoons from the forks for you, while leaving just the right amount of mess to make it fun. You'll be able to find spells here, yes, but you'll also be gaining insights into how you can create your own magic based on your own home and all its (supposedly) inanimate denizens. Once you've befriended your broom and unpacked your Mary Poppins-purse of bewitching baubles, we think you'll find that you can't stop seeing magic everywhere. And that will be truly enchanting.

So please, come on in. We've been waiting a long time for you, and we're so glad you're here.

1. Coins

Making Change with Magic

Who hasn't worked a little magic with coins in their lives? From having a "lucky penny" to tossing coins in a wishing well (or Trevi Fountain in Rome, if you've been lucky enough to pay it a visit), coins are among the most common and useful magical tools. They are versatile and offer a lot of ways to work a spell, and there's something about them that just feels magical. Jingling a pocketful of change, or getting a bit of foreign currency, or spinning them around to have lunch table battles in school, coins are everywhere. So let's dig into a bit of the magical lore behind them and see how to put them to good use. A quick note: while we will address currencies from around the world, we will mostly focus on the coins found widely in the United States, as that is the region the authors know best.

Denominations of Destiny: Using Different Coins for Different Purposes

Virtually all coins have some magical lore attached to them. Ancient Roman coins held the image of the demigod emperor, and ancient Chinese coins were often imprinted with key Taoist symbols. Indeed, many Chinese coins were minted specifically for fortune-telling and as good luck charms, even when they had no monetary value (although that did not stop them from occasionally being circulated with regular currency). The face value of the coin is not a primary indicator of what sort of magic it can be used for. The symbolism on the coin often supersedes the cash equivalence of the tiny metal disk. The different denominations of coins, though, do frequently have different magical uses, because the symbols on those denominations are often unique.

Pennies - Pennies are probably one of the most ubiquitous coins. A bit of popular lore is often circulated about how pennies actually cost more to make than they are worth. There's some truth to that, although most modern pennies have very little copper, so the difference in value becomes significant only when looking at millions of pennies minted. But there's something rather enchanted about the idea of a coin that has no real value, yet still remains in circulation.[1] They are the coin most likely to be lingering in your car's coin tray or between the cushions of your sofa, too, and they seem to like living in those "lost" spaces. That may be why they are often a good coin to use in working with the dead. They evoke images of placing copper coins over the eyes of the deceased so they can pay the ferryman, Charon, to cross into Hades in Greek mythology. People practicing folk magic in the Southern United States—both Hoodoo and Southern Conjure—are likely to use pennies to pay for "graveyard dirt," soil gathered from the grave of a relative or other cemetery denizen to use in spellwork involving anything from love to vengeance. Prices range from three to ten pennies in most cases, and in folk practice pennies are often buried at the gravesite (although it is worth noting that all coins can leach metals into soil and surrounding environs, so it would be just as savvy to drop them into a donation box for cemetery upkeep).

Pennies are also imprinted with useful symbols. The "wheat pennies" found in the U.S. in the early twentieth century have associations with bounty and prosperity, and they were kept near the door to the home or in the pantry to ensure that food and good fortune would always be in the house. The "Indian head" penny was engraved with a side-facing portrait of a person wearing a Plains tribal headdress (possibly inspired by Blackfoot or Ojibwe designs).[2] In some forms of Southern folk magic, those pennies would be nailed up around the doors of homes where activities occurred that were not quite on the right side of the law; moonshiners or smugglers, for instance, would have been likely to add these "scout" pennies to their homes as a way to keep the law away or provide magical warning when the local sheriff wandered too near. A more modern design includes a shield shape on the back of the penny, and it works equally well for protection from the law and other harmful influences. For example, Cory frequently places shield pennies with their shields facing up along his dashboard as way to keep his automobile off the radar of any lurking lawmen. And there's always the nursery rhyme about pennies and luck: "See a penny, pick it up/All the day you'll have good luck!"

Nickels - Nickels feel like the overlooked middle child of coin denominations. They have more value than a penny, but while pennies are everywhere, nickels tend to crop up less often and usually don't get particularly memorable designs. One image that has remained popular, however, is the "buffalo nickel." This design, minted in the late nineteenth and early twentieth centuries in the United States, depicted an American bison (popularly called a "buffalo," although it's a distinct species) on one side and an image of a Native American man—likely Lakota Sioux or Cheyenne—on the facing side. Similar to the "Indian head" penny, these nickels could be posted as "scouts" for protection from the law, but they also seem to be used for their bison imagery. The bison is a strong, powerful animal and, as such, can work as a ward against unwanted intruders. This is especially true because the bison circle around their young when under attack from predators or hunters, creating a barrier of strong adults to guard them. Thus that symbolism transfers well to the nickel. Carrying one in your pocket or wearing one made into a bit of jewelry might also offer that kind of protective enchantment.

Other nickels also have a bit of lore about them. During the Depression era, many transient people traveled around looking for work, often forming unofficial camps. While frequently derided as "hobos" or "tramps," these nomadic workers developed a sophisticated culture, including a series of signs and symbols to communicate with each other. Another aspect of their culture was the "hobo nickel," coins that were carefully defaced with knives, iron nails, or other implements to alter the images on them and turn faces into skulls or other figures. These did not have intrinsic magical value, but they represented a sort of folk art form. Nickels frequently have very large heads compared to the overall area of the coin, and the materials used to make them (mostly copper with some nickel added in) are easily shaped and carved. This makes them ideal for anyone who wants to play with a bit of sandpaper and a penknife to turn them into something more magical. The traditional skull could be used to ward off evil or pay for favors from Otherworldly denizens (see later in this chapter on the magical role of defaced coins). One could even carve a whole batch of nickels into a divination set!

Dimes - Dimes have a good bit of lore regarding their magical possibilities. The ones minted before 1965 in the United States are made mostly of silver, which makes them a marvelous coin for lunar magic, protection, and work involving things like dreams or psychic awareness. The most famous of these dimes was the "winged Liberty" dime minted from 1916 to 1945. While the classical figure of Liberty is the intended image on the facing side, most people assumed it was designed to look like the Roman god Mercury, and so the dime became known as the "Mercury dime." That dime has a long history of practical use in African American folk magic, such as Hoodoo, where it is frequently drilled or punched with a hole (often using a small nail and a hammer), and then tied on a red string to be worn around the ankle or waist. The dime would then absorb any harmful spells or curses that the wearer encountered, tarnishing or turning black when it had successfully deflected such a hex.

The Mercury dime also works well for any sort of magic involving travel, due to Mercury's association with roads, highways, and movement (he was the messenger of the gods, after all). Cory has long kept a Mercury dime hung on a silver chain in his car to help him travel safely, especially on his regular commute of an hour or more. The silver in the coin can also be used to ward off harmful creatures, including witches with ill intent or devils bent on one's destruction. A good way to work with a silver dime is to slip it under the sole of your shoe and let it deflect harm as you walk.

Quarters - People love quarters. They are the coins that can get you a pack of M&Ms™ from a vending machine, they are the ones used to claim "next" on an arcade game. (Does anyone do that anymore?) Quarters feel like the "fun" coin, and there are a lot of ways to use them magically. They can be carved like the "hobo nickels" and turned into talismans and tokens fairly easily. Their silvery hue makes them effective in lunar and water-based magical rites. Cory likes to use a spell adapted from one of Scott Cunningham's books, which may be derived from Ozark lore, involving catching the light of a full moon on a quarter at the bottom of a bowl of water.[3] He says a small chant to the effect of "as you wax, so wax my fortunes; and as you are full, so are my pockets" while washing his hands in the lunar-and-quarter-infused water, then letting them air dry. It is good for inviting small windfalls of money over the course of the next month—nothing life-changing in terms of cash, but a little extra to help make ends meet.

The other wonderful perk of using quarters in the modern age is that the U.S. Mint began issuing all sorts of state quarters throughout the beginning of the twenty-first century. Many states have great designs on them, including symbols such as plants and animals, which can be good for bringing those influences into a magical working. For example, the Kansas state quarter has a picture of an American bison on it, which could be used much as the "buffalo nickel" is used (North Dakota also has these big, shaggy creatures on its quarter). Washington's state quarter features a salmon, which is associated in Irish folklore with wisdom and knowledge. Thus, it might be a good one to use if you're creating a pocket charm or talismanic piece of jewelry for doing well in school or in intellectual work. North Carolina, Ohio, and Indiana all have images of vehicles on them, which make them good for travel workings. Massachusetts features a minuteman volunteer soldier, and Connecticut has the Charter Oak, both good for steadfastness and protection. Tennessee has a range of musical instruments, which might make it good for making crossroads deals for musical talent and fame. And, of course, Georgia features the famous peach, which can definitely be about bounty and fruitfulness, but which also has a hint of playful sexiness in this age of emojis—so that could be a fun way to use it.

Tokens of Appreciation: Other Coins and their Magical Uses

A few years ago, we sent out some care packages to supporters who were helping to keep our show afloat. In that bundle we added a batch of subway tokens. Why? Because tokens are often excellent for magic, since they are not actually "money," but they represent access to something: travel (in the form of a subway or ferry token), excitement (as in an arcade or amusement park token), or luck (as in a casino or gambling token). Worked into a charm bag or worn as a necklace, these tokens can become simple amulets that don't draw too much attention.

Foreign currency, too, can be incredibly useful. Some coins from countries such as China have holes in them, because they were carried on long strings at one point in time. Now most Chinese coins don't have holes, but there are still ceremonial coins produced for Taoist rituals and offerings that do—and even esoteric symbols such as the *bagua* or I Ching trigrams. A wide variety of animals appear on coins from various nations: kangaroos on the Australian dollar coin, an eagle and snake on some Mexican pesos, or a rooster on the French twenty-franc coin. You can even find English commemorative coins with dinosaurs on them!

Sing a Song of Sixpence: Coins in Folklore

Coins may be mundane, but that doesn't mean you can't squeeze a good story out of them! A number of folktales include coins as a key theme.

Probably the best-known tale involving a coin is the story of "Wicked Jack," found in various forms throughout England, Ireland, and the Appalachians. In that tale, sometimes called "Wicked John" or "Stingy Jack," a scoundrel of a man (Jack, of course) meets with the Devil, who comes to claim the sinful man's soul and take him away to hell. There are a lot of versions of the story, so it very much depends on who's telling it, but Jack always finds a way to trick the Devil and put him in a tight spot. One version specifically says that the Devil obliges Jack a final drink at the local public house, but Jack says he doesn't have any money to pay so the devil can't take him away until his debts are settled. Old Scratch then transforms himself into a coin, intending that Jack use the coin to pay for the drinks, but the clever rogue grabs the coin and shoves it into a bible, trapping the Devil inside. Only when he agrees not to take Jack off to hell does the cunning man release him. That diabolical promise comes back to haunt Jack, who finds that he's too wicked to get into heaven after his death, and too clever to get into hell. He winds up walking the earth with only an ember of hellfire to light his way in a lantern made from a turnip—the origin of jack-o-lanterns!

We mentioned earlier that some coins, like the silver Mercury dime, are valued in folk magic for the substances that make them up. There are a number of tales where a silver coin—usually a dollar or half-dollar—is melted down to be turned into that most famous of evil-fighting weapons: a silver bullet! A story from Appalachian Virginia tells of a witch who had been plaguing a local man with ill luck and health. He feared he might never be right again, but then a neighbor recommended he speak with a witchmaster, a sort of local cunning man who knew how to counteract witchcraft. He tells the man to make an image of the witch and then shoot it with a bullet made of silver, which the man crafts by melting down a coin. As soon as he does so, the witch is horribly injured despite being miles away, and the man is freed from her curse.[4]

In our years of exploring folk magic, we've come across many bits of lore that pop up over and over and in different ways. It's become almost an inside joke between us that—in places we wouldn't always expect—there's always a tip for getting rid of warts! But one of the most common ones we come across is the idea of using coins to get rid of them. For Laine, who had them on her hands as a child, a coin-based method was used.

She was taken to the seventh son of a seventh son, a common example of someone "born with the power." He was an older man who was likely friends with her grandpa. He dug around in his pocket and produced a handful of change—mostly pennies, if memory serves. He asked Laine to pick the shiniest penny out of his hand, and she did. Soon, her warts went away, and she's never dealt with them again. And then, years later, when chatting with her brother, she came to find out he had his warts dealt with in the same way, by the same family friend. This is connected with a similar method, called "buying the warts" from someone. If you happen to be afflicted with warts and want to be rid of them, you can ask someone to buy them from you for a small fee. Even just a penny will work! Some people will rub the warts with the coin before the "transaction" is considered complete, but other tales say that just buying them is enough to get rid of them.

Finally, there's a Dutch story that tells of fairies discovering that the Dutch have invented money and they decide to have a bit of fun with them. In the tale of "The Mouldy Penny," the fairies follow the misadventures of three brothers, each given a silver penny to begin their fortunes. The first brother tries to hoard it and hides any and all money that comes his way, leaving his wife and children with little food and less clothing to make do. The fairies hide away his penny so that it will molder and rot, much like his soul. Another brother spends his penny at a gin-house, and winds up stone dead, with his wife's money going after him to pay for his funeral. The wisest brother, however, uses his penny to help pay for the things his family needs, while also seeing to his business carefully. When he gets an increase, he doesn't hoard it away, but instead spends it on the local orphans to buy them clothing and food as well. He lives a long and happy life, full of pennies that shine because he keeps them moving (and thus they never gather any mold), and like his penny, his reputation remains sterling long after he is gone.[5]

A Miscellany of Minted Magic

Before we leave our little coin tray of assorted magics behind, we thought we'd mention a few other little bits of folklore associated with coins and magic:

- An old English holiday custom involves putting a coin—usually a silver sixpence, which seems plenty magical—into a Christmas pudding. Whoever finds the coin gets good luck for the coming year. (See also our chapter on the Pantry for more on this tradition).
- Another bit of European lore involves finding trees at sacred sites (often near forests or wells believed to be fairy-frequented or enchanted) and pushing coins into the trunk. While the custom is fairly old and widespread, it's best not to do it to a living tree since the coins can eventually kill it.
- English folklore tells of a custom of begging twelve pennies from twelve people of a different sex, then trading those pennies for a silver coin left in a church offering. That coin would then be carved, molded, or melted into a ring worn to prevent fits.
- As an alternative to the pick-up-a-penny rhyme, if you drop a coin you should step on it and say "money on the floor, money at the door!" to ensure that more money will come your way.
- Of course, many people know about leaving teeth under pillows to be traded for shiny silver coins. (What does the tooth fairy even use those for, anyway?)
- Wishing wells are another classic form of coin magic. While there are some wells that feed into surface or ground water supplies that you should avoid tossing pennies into, a number of fountains are designed to allow people to toss in coins (and the coins even help pay for their upkeep). The Trevi Fountain in Rome is probably the best-known of these, and it's said that if you toss three coins over your shoulder into the waters, you'll one day come back to the Eternal City.[6]

Coins can provide all sorts of magical inspiration, and what we've covered here is only a wee fragment of what exists out there in the world. But the next time you jingle a pocket full of change or find a penny on the sidewalk, maybe you'll think of a bit of magic as well!

NOTES

1. There is a long, ongoing debate about whether the United States and other countries with similar currencies should keep pennies in circulation. A coin shortage in 2020 exacerbated that discussion, and many people believe that pennies have no place in a modern "cashless" society (although it's worth noting that there are still plenty of people who do operate on a cash basis and who get left out of these conversations). A good overview of the issue can be found through the National Public Radio program, *Planet Money:* https://www.npr.org/sections/money/2020/07/14/890435359/is-it-time-to-kill-the-penny

2. The "Indian head" penny is a problem for a few reasons. Its name is not the preferred nomenclature for Native or Indigenous peoples, for example. Additionally, while the headdress is designed to look a bit like the Plains tribal adornment, the design used would not typically have been worn by women in a tribe, and the figure depicted is modeled on a European American woman. The "Indian head" on the buffalo nickel, on the other hand, is more clearly modeled on a Native American in traditional dress, although it, too, has its controversies.

3. The Ozark lore states that "It is always a good idea to be touching silver when you see the moon" (from Vance Randolph's *Ozark Magic and Folklore* (Columbia Univ. Press, 1947), pp. 330). Similar lore exists in several other collections, such as *Folk-Lore of Adams County, Illinois,* by Harry M. Hyatt (Alma Egan Hyatt Foundation, 1935), p. 192.

4. See Hubert J. Davis, *The Silver Bullet: And Other American Witch Stories* (Jonathan David Publishing, 1975).

5. You can find "The Mouldy Penny" in the collection *Dutch Fairy Tales for Young Folks*, collected by William Elliot Griffis (Thomas Y. Crowell Company, 1918).

6. Many of these coin traditions are outlined in an article by folklorist Icy Sedgwick entitled, "Money Folklore: Coins, Wishes, & Fairy Gold." Available at https://www.icysedgwick.com/money-folklore/

2. Keys

Unlocking the Magic

For as long as she can remember, Laine has found the ideas of secret doorways—hidden down long passages, a caretaker patrolling the corridors with a large set of skeleton keys dangling from their hip—so intriguing. She loves the idea of something secreted away and all the power of being able to access it living in a single piece of carefully shaped iron.

We blame this key obsession on one of her favorite books, *The Secret Garden* by Frances Hodgson Burnett. The first time she read it, she was captivated by every page; they seemed to whisper secrets and emanate magic. From the robin showing Mary the key buried in the earth, to the children forming a circle and chanting their intentions, she was bewitched. For years, she reread this book at least once a year, and it always kept that mysterious character about it. And now, she can't help but feel a bit of that same thrill whenever she uses an old skeleton key in her own magic.

For us, keys have come to represent a great deal. We see them as symbols of gaining knowledge, not just about the world around us, but as an insight into the self as well. We also like to use keys as a reminder of the Witches' Pyramid: to know, to dare, to will, and to keep silent.[1] The "to keep silent" part has always been particularly interesting to Laine, as her understanding of it has evolved the most over the years. At first, "to keep silent" seemed to simply remind us of the importance of knowing when to keep your mouth shut, lest your magic is robbed of its power or you accidentally reveal someone's involvement in witchcraft. But as we've practiced more and more, it's also come to symbolize the idea that we can keep parts of ourselves secret. Some people give and give until they have nothing left for themselves, or as we've commonly heard it, "You can't pour from an empty cup."

Did you grow up with teachers or parents asking for quiet by miming a zipping motion across their mouth, locking it, and throwing away the key? Or, as preschool teachers we have known would say, "Zip it, lock it, put it in your pocket." And so it is with a key: we can do just that! It's a little reminder carried with us that we should think before we speak, put ourselves first, and keep silent when needed.

This connection to secrets and silence and hidden things is well-rooted in a variety of folktales. For example, there's the well-known fairy tale, "Bluebeard," in which a murderous fiend tells his new wife she can visit any room of the house but one. He gives her a key to the door anyway, and when she inevitably opens it, she finds the bodies of his previous wives. She accidentally drops the key into some blood, which stains it and later reveals her secret, nearly condemning her to the same grisly fate![2]

Things associated with keys also have links to magical secrets and strange goings-on! There are stories of witches slipping into homes at night through keyholes, for example, either by becoming incorporeal spirits temporarily (often aided by pungent and intoxicating "flying ointments" or "witch greases") or by shrinking down and riding on the back of a wee beastie such as a beetle or moth.[3] Keyholes also imply peeping and spying, discovering secrets that are hidden. So keeping the plate from an old-fashioned keyhole might be a good way to see things hidden around you in a magical sense. One could even make a pendant from such a keyhole and use it like a "hag stone" to see otherworldly creatures like fairies or imps. If you cannot find a keyhole plate, looking through the gaps of an old skeleton key with a big, looping head might also work.

Keys have historically been used in protection magic. The Museum of Witchcraft and Magic in Cornwall, England, has a few examples of old iron keys paired with a hag stone that were used for protection of the family's farm, passed down for several generations.[4] While Laine personally associates keys with symbols of protection, we have many other uses for keys, such as:

- To access something—whether that be a tangible object or a more abstract idea, like gaining knowledge or control over a situation.
- To hold power over another person, particularly in a courtroom. Imagine a jailer's keyring or how influential people are given the "keys to the city."
- To open doors—of opportunity! We can use keys to literally open doors, but I love to use keys for matters of luck, in hopes that they will open the way to opportunities that I might have missed without a little extra nudge.
- To help with communication—a map key is an explanation of symbols that gives you the "key" to unlocking how to read the map. Use keys to foster better communication between yourself and another, such as a romantic partner, a new boss, your teenager, or perhaps your students if you're a teacher of some sort.
- You could create a fascinating "wishing ladder" by collecting keys from places you've visited and leaving a space on the ladder for your next key as a way to keep your roads open and facilitate future travel.
- Hotel key cards may not seem particularly romantic or glamorous, but they do have one advantage: they are often very easy to write on or mark up. Combining something with the power of a key and the ability to draw a sigil or symbol of power on them means you could easily create all sorts of interesting spells with these. While some hotels do have recycling programs, most generally don't care if you keep them when you check out, so it's a good way to put them to use without throwing away ecologically damaging plastic. (But please recycle them if you can!)

Many of these could simply involve keeping a skeleton key handy. (Cory keeps an old one he found in an antique shop attached to his regular key ring.) There's no reason it has to be single-purpose! You can absolutely use the same key for multiple magical applications. As the proverb goes, "The used key is always bright."

"Entreat Me Not to Leave Thee": Keys, Books, and Divination

Because of their strong connection to things hidden and things revealed, keys also have a lot of folklore connecting them to divination. One of the best-known and most widely circulated versions of key-based divination involves using a Bible. There is a tremendous amount of biblical magic out there, and a rather impressive number of Christians or semi-Christian people throughout history have seen the Bible as being as much a book of magic as one of faith, although they might not phrase it exactly that way.

The overall method seems to derive from a folk Catholic practice that was outlined in Reginald Scot's 1584 treatise on magic, *The Discoverie of Witchcraft*. In this book, Scot lampoons the "popish" superstitions of the Catholics and cites an example of their folk magic involving a scriptural text (a psalter) and a skeleton key:

> "Popish preests (saith he) as the Chaldceans used the divination by sive & sheeres for the detection of theft, doo practise with a psalter and a keie fastned upon the 49. psalme, to discover a theefe. And when the names of the suspected persons are orderlie put into the pipe of the keie, at the reading of these words of the psalme (If thou sawest a theefe thou diddest consent unto him) the booke will wagge, and fall out of the fingers of them that hold it, and he whose name remaineth in the keie must be the theefe." (Ch. 5)

The psalm cited, the 49th, is full of memento mori imagery, reminding the singer that death comes to all, and none escapes God's eye. Scot's mention of this form of bibliomancy is brief, though, and a more thorough description of the method can be found in Draja Mickaharic's *Magical Spells of the Minor Prophets*, in which the author (a proponent of folk magic, especially the folk magic of European American immigrants) describes doing the same sort of divination as found in Scot's work. He emphasizes that the key must be protruding from the top of the book, and it must be bound up tightly—although he notes that one can do this using string or rubber bands in a nod to the practicality of folk magic. This method involves determining which direction means "yes" and which means "no," and then asking simple questions and seeing which way the book moves. Mickaharic says this is very effective, and that "the first time I did this, the bible actually jumped from my fingers when the question was answered with a no."[5]

The Bible-and-key method is also backed up by practices within the Pennsylvania German "hexenmeister" community (the name means "witch master," basically magical workers who protect and defend against evil magic). In Chris Bilardi's hexenmeister manual, *The Red Church*, he provides an almost identical system for inserting a key into the Bible, binding it, and suspending it while asking questions. He is more specific about which books to use, however: "Take the key and place it into the Bible. Some traditional places to put it are the Book of Ruth (Chapter 1), the Gospel of John (any of the Four Gospels, really), and the Epistle of James."[6]

The use of the book of Ruth and the key is fairly common in folklore and is found everywhere from the Carolinas to Ontario. The basic method involved slipping a key into the Book of Ruth at Chapter One, especially so that the tip of the key touched the verse that read "Entreat me not to leave thee" (verse 16). The Bible would then be bound up tight, often with red thread, and two people would hold the book suspended in the air between them with the key dangling between their fingertips. One would then ask to reveal the name of their future beau, belle, or beloved, and they would alternate saying letters of the alphabet. The key would twist and the book drop when they got to the initial of the future lover.

Of course, the Bible is but one book you can use for this sort of divination. The connection here is to link the key with a particular passage by binding it against those words and then letting the book-and-key guide you to answers. Choosing a different holy book would be perfectly fine, or even selecting a favorite book of poetry that connects to your spirit in some way. For example, Cory is rather madly enamored of both Edna St. Vincent Millay and Anne Sexton (both of whom had some very witchy poems). Slipping a key up against Millay's "First Fig" or Sexton's "Her Kind" would be a great way to ask for some divinatory aid. And, of course, there would be all kinds of magic in sliding the key between the pages of *The Secret Garden*, perhaps during Chapter Eight: The Robin Who Showed the Way.

Beyond the *ex libris* bookish divination methods, keys may also provide divinatory experiences solely based on their presence. For example, one manual of dream interpretation widely found in early twentieth-century African American communities states that a dream of finding a key means that you will be able to get others to do work for you and bring you profit or benefit.[7] There's also no reason that you couldn't create an incredibly effective diviner's pendulum by dangling a nice iron key from a strand of hair or a sturdy ribbon (which would make it an excellent bookmark if you want it to do double duty).

Another contemporary update to key-based divination might involve collecting keys from various times in your life, then putting them all into a bag (or even on a key ring). If you need information about something from your past that is surfacing again but you can't quite figure out what the lesson or connection might be, you could then "pull" a key at random and see if it can reveal to you the time, place, or even person that is having renewed influence on you (such as an old roommate or someone from your childhood home or neighborhood).

A strange final connection for keys in folk magic has to do with necks. In a number of folk cures, applying a key to the back of the neck was used to stop nosebleeds (because of the cold metal potentially causing constriction in the blood vessels). This became the basis for also wearing keys on a green string around the neck to prevent nosebleeds in some folklore.[8]

Another connection between keys and necks comes from the eerie comics series (later a Netflix show) *Locke & Key* by Joe Hill and Gabriel Rodriguez. In that story, a young boy discovers that his family home—inherited from an eccentric and occult-minded ancestor—has a series of keys that can unlock different portals to other places. The boy and his family eventually learn that the keys can also be inserted into the back of their necks (where keyholes magically appear when the keys get close) to allow them to enter each others' minds. This sort of revelation of inner worlds and thoughts very much resonates with the lore of keys as secret-keepers (or revealers), although in a much creepier way than Mary's robin in *The Secret Garden*!

However you use your keys, we hope that these little bits of metal look a little different to you now. They contain entire worlds, you know, waiting only on you to give them a little twist.

NOTES

1. A common belief among Wiccans and pagans, originally put forth by Eliphas Levi as the "Four Words of the Magus" (*Transcendental Magic Its Doctrine and Ritual*, 1896).
2. An excellent collection of Bluebeard tales can be found in *The Classic Fairy Tales*, edited by Maria Tatar (W.W. Norton, 1999 [2017]).
3. In one story found in *The Silver Bullet & Other American Witch Stories* by Hubert J. Davis (Jonathan David Publishing, 1975), a witch named Rindy Sue Gose from Virginia uses a witch grease to make her skin "draw up" and shrink down so that she can ride a little beetle she keeps in a bottle around into her neighbors' houses (pp. 16-19)
4. For more information, contact the museum through their website: https://museumofwitchcraftandmagic.co.uk/.
5. See *Magical Spells of the Minor Prophets*, by Draja Mickaharic (Lulu Printing, 2010), p. 125.
6. See *The Red Church, or the Art of Pennsylvania German Braucherei*, by Chris Bilardi (Pendraig Press, 2009), p. 303. Similar lore is recorded in *The Frank C. Brown Collection of North Carolina Folklore*, Vol. I, p. 585.
7. See *Aunt Sally's Policy Player's Dream Book* (reprint) (Lama Temple, 1984), p. 79.
8. See *Folk-Lore of Adams County, Illinois*, by Harry M. Hyatt (Alma Egan Hyatt Foundation, 1935), pp. 125.

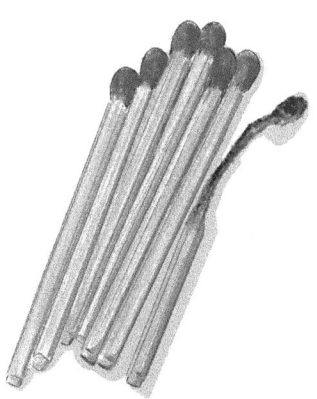

3. Matches

For Seeing in the Dark and into the Future!

There's something oddly nostalgic about finding an old matchbook from a hotel in the 1970s, or a bar you frequented in college. Just holding it in your hands can feel like a way to travel back in time or soar far away and reminisce. The magic of the matchbox, though, goes far beyond a swift trip down memory lane. Matches were necessities in a former age, providing quick starts to stove fires or a light for a cigarette back when smoking was in vogue. There's still something romantic about getting that match to flare up on the first strike, then lowering the little head of flame to the wick of a candle in a dark room.

Because of their ubiquity and relatively cheap price, matches also make for good folk magic. They make for quick enchantment, erupting into existence quickly when lit, then fading after only a moment or two. They are also like little people, each with its own "head" and a matchstick body, which make them ideal for figural magic. It should be no surprise then, that they often take the place of a person in magical rituals of divination. They are called upon to answer questions, particularly about affairs of the heart or issues of safety.

Here are some examples of match-based magic aimed at finding out if they love you, or if they love you not:

- Hold a match until it burns out. The direction it bends is towards your next love (or true love). This could easily be done in a group as a sort of "spin the bottle" type game.
- You can name a match for someone you love and light it. If you can hold it until it burns out completely, then they love you back. If it breaks or goes out before it burns to your fingertips, though, they do not love you true.
- You can throw a burned up match over your shoulder. If it doesn't break, then the person you're thinking of loves you.

The flame kindled by a match can also invite insight into the affairs of the heart. A few more fiery love divinations that fit well into match lore:

- If you can make a good fire, you'll be sure to find a good love.
- Dreaming of fire means a marriage to follow soon.

And as a bit of cindery spellcraft, if you take a burning piece of wood from the fire, name it after someone, spit on it, and put it back in the fire, the person will come to you.[1]

Beyond offering answers to questions of romance and courtship, the use of matches in divination could answer questions of a more dire nature. In Brandon Weston's *Ozark Folk Magic*, the author details a mountain magic ritual used when a person is under the effect of a curse or magically induced illness. A healer would hold up matchsticks and name them for the various ne'er do wells and wicked witches of the local area—sometimes working their way through practically the entire population! The match is then struck against its scratch surface (called a comb) exactly once. If it lights, then the healer knows who is responsible for the illness and can send it back on them.[2]

Of Fiery Walls and Alleviating Lucifers: Protecting and Healing Spells with Matches

Beyond their divinatory powers, matches are also attributed powers of defense. Fire is certainly good at keeping away the things that wish to harm you, as anyone who has ever fended off a mummy with only a torch in hand can attest. (That might be only Brendan Fraser and us.)

One form of magical protection involves the use of "fiery wall" oils, frequently infused with sharp, strong-smelling herbs. The oils are used to anoint a person, object, or place to keep evil away. Matches, however, can easily offer a simple way to create a similar effect. All you need to do is take a box of matches and face each direction, striking a match and telling the flame to protect you as it flares up. You might pray the part of Psalm 22, which says "be not thou far from me, O LORD: O my strength, haste thee to help me" (verse 11), if that falls within your belief system. Or you could state something direct and memorable like, "Fire and flame fend off my foes from the North" as you face that direction, then repeat for each other cardinal direction, letting the match burn down as far as you can before shaking it out. You would also likely want to repeat the charm with a match above your head and one at your feet, saying, "Fire and flame fend off my foes from Above" and "from Below." Then burn a seventh match directly in front of your heart. As it burns down, ask its flame to surround you in protection from any woes or ill wishes. If you wanted to add a little extra zip to the working, you could dip the base of the match in an oil like Fiery Wall of Protection—just be careful as oil is usually flammable and will burn your fingers if you let the flame reach it! If you want to protect your home, you could do this same ritual on each side of your house or apartment building and end by doing match-lightings at the front and back doors (or other relevant entrances, as we know from folklore that witches and Santa Claus love to sneak in through the chimney).

There are other ways that matches can be used to ward off misfortune. One Louisiana belief notes that crossing a pair of matches and sprinkling them with salt during a storm will make the rain and thunder dissipate, if you feel that you are in danger from it.[3]

Matches are also deployed to diminish illness in some places. That same Louisiana lore notes that wearing a pair of matches crossed in your hair is thought to ward off headaches. Attaching a pair of matches to a barrette would be fairly easy for those purposes, although it might garner a strange glance or two.

Ozark lore notes that "counting down" rituals can often use matches to gradually remove ill effects from a person. A verbal charm is said, which diminishes with each repetition, and a match is struck then thrown into a glass of water on every turn.[4] Probably the best known version of this is the "Abracadabra" charm in which a person says the word ABRACADABRA but takes away a letter each time as they strike and discard the match by the person they are trying to heal:

```
A B R A C A D A B R A
  A B R A C A D A B R
    A B R A C A D A B
      A B R A C A D A
        A B R A C A D
          A B R A C A
            A B R A C
              A B R A
                A B R
                  A B
                    A
```

A mysterious charm found within a Hungarian family in Pennsylvania recounts that in the case of a particularly colicky and fussy baby, a woman was summoned who used a needle floated on top of a glass of water, and who then would burn matches while saying "some kind of saying" to remove the baby's illness and discomfort. The family believed the baby had been exposed to too many strangers and was experiencing discomfort, so a woman would come and treat it. The person sharing the story said, "I think it involved a needle, on top of water, and a burnt match. She wouldn't give the baby anything to eat or drink. She just did all this stuff. It was like witchcraft."[5]

And, of course, there's wart-charming lore with matches. As anyone studying folklore for very long finds out, Folklore from Spanish California claimed that warts could be bought with matches as a cure for them. (See the chapter on Coins for more on wart-curing practices.)

Burning Out: Hotfooting, Bad Luck, and Fire Safety

They say where there's smoke, there's fire, but in magic where there's fire, there's usually also the potential for cursing. Think of a person wronged by an ex-boyfriend lighting a pile of love notes and photos in a trash can after the relationship ends, and of the feelings of anger and hurt that can be kindled alongside the flame in that moment.

One tradition found in the practice of Hoodoo involves "hotfooting" magic, which usually requires laying down "hot" ingredients like cayenne pepper in someone's path so they will walk over them. The end result is to send them bad luck or make them leave town in most cases, but "hotfooting" can also refer to the rather dangerous prank found among the sort of rapscallions from Depression-era film shorts like the "Little Rascals." That version involves sticking a match butt-end into the stitching around the sole of someone's shoe, then lighting it and letting it burn until they notice. While we do not advocate that particular "prank," if you need to make someone leave you alone or skedaddle out of town, match heads do often contain sulfur, which makes for a powerful cursing ingredient. Taking a few match heads and mixing them with cayenne pepper and black mustard seeds (also known for having hexing properties) then sprinkling that where you know a particularly unfriendly foe will be wandering might be a good way to "spark" their decision to pull up stakes and depart.

There are also a few bits of lore about matches that refer to bad luck, most especially indicating that a single match should not be used to light more than one or two objects. In particular, lighting a third item from a single match's flame is thought to bring misfortune or even death. Candles are sometimes part of this lore, but cigarettes are most frequently referenced, and the third person to light their smoke from one match is believed to have a death wish. This may well stem from wartime lore in which keeping a match lit long enough to get a third cigarette glowing was a good way to draw enemy sniper fire. Still, it can't hurt to play it safe and limit just how many times you share that match's fire around.

Speaking of safety, we should note here that when you are using matches, it is your responsibility to be safe. They are, in fact, incendiary tools and can cause—surprise—a fire! Doing spells and magic with matches is all well and good until suddenly you're standing among the smoldering ruins of your Victorian manor house. (Right, Rebecca?) All jokes aside, please never leave a flame burning unattended, and always have a safe way to extinguish any fire within easy reach when you use any kind of fire-based magic.

The Littlest Match-Girl: A Matchstick Poppet Spell

Did you, like us, grow up with the trauma of *"The Little Match Girl?"* Hans Christian Andersen's tale of a poor little girl trying to sell matches and ends up lighting them for a bit of warmth. With each strike of the match, a beautiful scene is illuminated, showing a feast, an ornately decorated Christmas tree, and lastly a scene with her deceased grandmother. Not wanting the last scene to fade away, she strikes the entire bundle of matches and begs her grandmother to take her to heaven with her. The next morning, people find the Little Match Girl dead, clutching a bundle of burnt matches, but with a smile on her face. Despite the macabre content of the story, it speaks to the power of love and hope and to the benefits of charity. The story endures.

We've already noted that matches resemble people with their tiny heads, but you can take that a step further by creating a small poppet and a little house to do spellwork using a match and matchbox. After all, why not give your Little Match Girl a home, rather than leaving her out in the cold like Andersen's story?

To make the figure, start by writing a name on the matchstick (or you can simply bless it with the name, or even baptize it, which has the added bonus of making the match wet and less flammable). Then wrap it in a scrap of cloth or a bit of yarn to give it "clothes." Take its matchbox and empty out all the other matches (save them for other spells, of course), and tell your little match-poppet you're making it a home. You can draw little symbols inside the box, add sprinklings of herbs, stones, or other curios to the box. Make them represent the things you want to surround the person after whom you've named the match. So, for example, if you name it after yourself and you want to have a run of good luck, you might put a lucky penny from the year of your birth and a four-leaf clover in the box. Keep the match inside the box, taking it out periodically—once a day, week, or month, depending on the level of involvement you need with the spell—and repeat what you want to happen to the doll. Change out its "furnishings" periodically, adding new things to represent the effects you want and taking out the old ones as needed.

This is a good way to have a number of small working spells that you can keep in a purse or pocket, or even on a bookshelf in your home. It also works well if you want to create "spirit dolls" to work with particular spirits, and it allows you to create a little spot for them even if you don't have much space. If you don't have a matchbox, but a matchbook, that can still work. Just draw symbols, sigils, or designs representing the things you want to affect your match-poppet on the inside cover of the matchbook.

Another way to add matches into your workings is to use an extinguished match head to write on scraps of paper with your intentions or aspirations. I've successfully used this method for love spells and for prosperity spells. Like the Little Match Girl, strike a match and imagine as clearly as possible what you want. Whether that be money, companionship, or even just more time for yourself each day, imagine it strongly until the match burns out. After it's cooled, write on a small piece of paper what you hoped for as the match burned, with that same match. If you're really feeling the pyrotechnics, light the petition paper on fire as well! Drop it in a fire-safe area (I like to use a cauldron) and again imagine what you want to make happen. Ending the spell with an act of charity would be a wonderful way to end this spell. As you donate to an organization you're passionate about, pay for the person behind you in the drive-thru, or even just pay someone a compliment, that will seal your intentions.

NOTES

1. Most of these love divinations with matches are found in the Frank C. Brown collection of folklore, especially Volume VII, Superstitions, pp. 393–3 and 594–97. While Brown's work is usually cited as *The Frank C. Brown Collection of North Carolina Folklore*, the entries are from throughout the United States.
2. From Brandon Weston, *Ozark Folk Magic* (Llewellyn Publications, 2020), p. 64.
3. From "Louisiana Superstitions," by Hilda Roberts. *Journal of American Folklore* v.40 n. 156, 1927, pp. 144-208
4. Weston, *Ozark Folk Magic*, p. 203.
5. From "Belief Tales and Superstitions," by Linda Lingle, 7 Nov. 1978 (in the Center for Pennsylvania German Studies archives, in a class collection project at Pennsylvania State University-Harrisburg with Dr. Yvonne Milspaw)

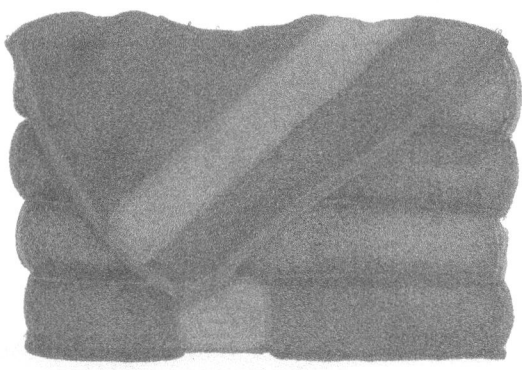

4. Towels, Rags, & Other Soft Goods

Scraps of Sorcery in the Linen Closet

Are you the kind of person, like Cory, who could fall asleep on a burlap sack? Or do you need 800-thread-count Egyptian cotton sheets to feel relaxed? Are you somewhere in between? When you do the dishes, do you pre-soak and scour with a sponge before putting essentially spotless dishes into a dishwasher, or do you basically show them a picture of the faucet and toss them in with industrial-strength dish detergent?

False dichotomies aside, there's a lot we learn about ourselves from the daily soft goods we use. The rags we use to wipe down counters might be old T-shirts repurposed into bar mops, or they could be matching ones from a domestic goods shop, or maybe they're an odd assortment collected over the years as presents or purchased on a whim or in a moment of need. The towels we use after a shower or bath and the sheets we tuck into at night also have something to say about our ideas of utility, luxury, and style.

These textiles are also just a little bit magical—or a lot magical, in some cases. Someone's old pair of long johns can be a great source of spell materials, and in many belief systems a rag can do anything from rubbing off a wart to predicting the future. In this chapter, we'll look at some of these beliefs and practices associated with dry goods and linens, and maybe we'll beat a little dust out of the rugs of forgotten magic along the way.

Dropped, Stolen, and… Milked? The Strange Magic of the Dish Towel

If you grew up immersed in British humor and science fiction, you probably already know where your towel is and just how important that scrap of fabric can be, thanks to Douglas Adams' *The Hitchhiker's Guide to the Galaxy*. In the world of folk belief, towels are remarkably prescient tools for discovering what might be coming your way, and they take on a level of importance not unlike that experienced by galactic stowaway Arthur Dent on his adventures.

Dish towels (and rags) quite literally do the dirty work of wiping and washing and removing spots and grub from our utensils, plates, bowls, and counters. A person working in their home would likely know where their towel is because it's always with them—thrown over a shoulder, tucked into a back pocket, or even draped over an arm or pulled through a belt loop. The towel's intricate involvement in everyday life makes it something of a busybody, ready to inform its bearer about grapevine gossip.

One of the most common bits of lore about dishrags says that when they are dropped, they presage someone's arrival. Depending on where you are, who you are, and when you are, that someone could be any of the following:

- A "dirty" person (literally in need of a bath, or a person with dubious morals)
- Someone "cleaner than you" if the towel is white
- A woman if it falls into a clump
- A man if it falls open and spread out wide (a "manspreading" towel, if you will)
- The opposite—a woman when spread out and a man if in a heap
- A hungry person
- A friend from far away
- Someone wearing a white shirt
- General unspecified "company" of some sort

Much of the lore is obviously a little contradictory, which means that the best thing to do is observe and remember or record who shows up at your door after dropping a towel to make sure you know how to interpret it.

There are also a few rituals that go along with dropping a towel, too. For some, dropping the towel to the floor meant bad luck, and so they would take a pinch of salt and toss it over their left shoulder. Still others would turn the bad luck around and use the opportunity to their advantage, as some lore says that stepping on or over a dropped towel allows you to make a wish.

Another bit of lore talks about what happens if you and someone else share a towel (and not in the sexy saving-water-in-the-shower kind of way). There's a little rhymed saying that goes with this belief that says:

"Wash and dry together,

Weep and cry together."

This means that if you both accidentally use the same towel, whether drying dishes or hands or anything else, you'll eventually have a falling out and quarrel with one another to the point of tears. Still other variations on this saying, though, seem to say the opposite:

"Wipe together,

Friends forever."[1]

In general, there seem to be more that say washing your hands in the same water as someone else is the real bad luck, but that wiping on the same towel will actually strengthen your bond.

Some of the most common lore about dishrags involves turning a little bit criminal. In numerous folklore collections, there are entries discussing the power of a stolen dishrag to cure warts. Wart cures are incredibly common within folk magic, with remedies varying from having the wart "bought" by the seventh son of a seventh son to rubbing the wart with half a potato. Rags have been credited as a particularly useful way of accomplishing this task, provided you knew what to do with them. In most cases, you were told to steal a dishrag, usually from someone you know and often from your "mother's kitchen." The rag should be dirty or already used, and then you rub it over the wart(s) you wish to see gone. Next you'd dispose of the rag, burying it in one of the following places:

- In the ground (anywhere)
- Under a flat rock
- By the kitchen door
- Under the eaves of the house where there's a leak
- Beneath the rain gutter downspout
- On the north side of the house before breakfast
- Under the steps to the house

In all of these cases, the aim was to put the rag in a spot where it could rot away. That process would eventually rot the wart off the person who had it. In most cases, this was expected to take a matter of days or weeks, although it could take months.

There are any number of more efficient medical wart cures you could try today, including having them "frozen" off using a cryogenic fluid. The mechanics of the magic, though, might still be useful! If you're not afraid of snagging someone's old dishrag when they aren't looking, you could potentially use it to rid yourself of any number of inconvenient conditions, habits, or even people. For example, you could take a stolen rag, rub it over a photo of an ex, and bury both in a place where they'll rot, which will make sure they won't be a preoccupation or distraction for you any longer. Or you might have a desire to stop cravings for sugar or sweets for some reason. Use the rag method to rub a particularly tempting dessert, then plant the cloth under your downspout and see if it gets rid of any excess cravings. Just remember to buy a new dishcloth or two to replace what you've "borrowed."

A final bit of lore about dish towels has them used for theft, rather than being stolen themselves. Folktales from a number of places discuss the use of a dishrag as a means for witches to steal dairy products from their neighbors. In most cases, the mechanics aren't specific, but they seem to involve a witch or group of witches hanging an old towel from various objects: an ax handle, the back of a door, a windowsill, or a gate post. The magical thieves would then wring the towel, and eventually it would begin producing milk, which they could squeeze into a bucket just as if they were milking a cow. Several tales mention witnesses who would attest to a neighbor's cow "drying up" because of this spell, and one even mentions seeing a cow's udder visibly shrink while the magic was being performed. In some cases not only fresh milk, but butter and cheese could be stolen in this way![2]

Most likely, the idea here was that a rag or towel can be made malleable and wrung in much the way a teat on a cow's udder can be squeezed, but the towel would probably have been used to wipe or touch the cow first in some way. This connects to a little bit of New Testament biblical lore in which the apostle Paul's handkerchief (sometimes also rendered as an apron or towel) was touched to other cloths to pass on miraculous healing powers—a belief that supports contemporary Catholic folk beliefs about saintly relics possessing wondrous abilities.[3]

Could you use this method today? Well, there are obviously ethical implications for stealing you'd want to consider, but assuming you're the kind of witch who likes to steal from the rich and give to the poor—a sort of sorcerous Robin Hood—you could try rubbing a cloth over objects of wealth from people in your area: sports cars, the doors to expensive homes, the bows of yachts, etc. Then you might pick a place that you feel deserves better funding and place its name beneath the towel as you hang it on your windowsill (or ax handle should you have that handy). As you "milk" it, you could focus on the wealth in your community being directed to help your chosen cause, maybe with a little repeated rhyme or chant like "Those that have, freely give, or else be compelled to share/and fill the pail of [your target in need of choice] and render crooked ledgers fair."

Who knows, maybe it will be more effective than a bake sale for the local scout troop!

"Grandy" Rags and Complicated Relationships

"If you have a boy friend and another girl is after him, try and get some of her garments that has some of her monthly on and throw it in running water. As it fades out of the clothes, she will fade out of his mind."

This tidbit of lore, recorded by Harry M. Hyatt (*Folk-Lore From Adams County, Illinois*) in the mid-twentieth century from an African American contact, reflects a few important pieces of information. Firstly, it's worth remembering that dealing with bodily fluids is something that everyone has to do, even if we are often squeamish about it. Secondly, menstrual blood (the "monthly" referred to here) has deep folk magical ties. And thirdly, people have only been using disposable menstrual products for a short time, prior to which many people used old cloths or rags torn from otherwise worn-out clothing.

While I doubt most people are keeping their used monthly period products in their junk drawer, menstrual products do have important folklore connected to them, and it would be folly to miss discussing them somewhere in this book. So, since rags, towels, and cloth all have historical connections to this brand of magic, why not discuss them briefly here?

A warning: This does deal with body fluids and some rather squick-inducing uses of those. So if you are squeamish about these sorts of things, you can skip this section.

One very common piece of lore about menstrual blood is that it can be used to control a person's lover. In much of the lore, the person menstruating would add a bit of their blood to a partner's food or drink to keep them from straying and maintain fidelity. In at least one account, however, the blood didn't need to be added directly to the food. Instead the woman in the story burnt her rags to ashes and added the ashes into the food (which does make it a bit more sanitary, as you probably wouldn't notice a pinch of ashes in a cake the way you might notice a bit of blood in your coffee).

However, burning menstrual cloths—sometimes called "grandy" rags—could have negative consequences for the person they belonged to. In some lore, it would make the person "absent-minded" or forgetful. Instead, people were instructed to bury their cloths in the ground if they could not wash them, or else they were sure to court some bad luck, even to the point of death in one account. There is also contradictory lore, though, that says burning these cloths could actually stymie cramping and other feelings of illness associated with menstruation.[4]

Changing these cloths too frequently was once believed to increase the flow of menstruation, although that could just be a bit of lore designed to keep the laundry manageable. More significantly, if you did have a menstrual cycle, you also needed to keep track of your rags, cloths, pads, or whatever else you were using. Why? Because they could very easily be turned against you. There are several stories about people doing just that. One tale tells of a man who wanted to break up with his girlfriend after finding out that she'd been using the menstrual ashes in his food trick, and so he took a piece of cloth with her menstrual blood on it and put it in his hat. Then, he took her out on a boat for what she thought was a romantic little date. Instead, he waited until she saw a snake and tossed his hat onto her. From that time on, she couldn't stop seeing snakes everywhere!

Other stories talk about someone finding another person's monthly cloths and burying them to lead to sickness or death, and one particularly chilling bit of folk sorcery notes that a man can take his wife's bloodstained rags and bore a hole in a tree deep enough to cause it to start rotting. He would then hide the rags in the dying tree and plug it up, so that as the tree died it would kill her, too, with no one any the wiser. Not an ideal partner for life, we daresay.

Brutal, no? It's important to note that relationships are complicated business. A person trying to keep a partner close to home at certain points in history was often someone in a very vulnerable position. They may not have had any independent income or outside support beyond that partner, and keeping them from running off was as much about having a home and food to eat as it was jealousy or sex. On the other hand, what would justify magical murder? It's worth remembering that anyone can be a victim of abuse, and so perhaps a bit of lore like the tree-based death curse might stem from a situation where a partner sees no other option in getting away from an abuser. That's not generally what's happening in these stories, but it is always possible.

Magic is neither a good nor bad force. It is used by people for all sorts of purposes, and the circumstances of its use can be incredibly nuanced.

But I will say if you decide to make some poor ex have to see snakes everywhere they go just because you don't have the nerve to break up with them, well, you're probably kind of a jerk.

Home is Where You Hang Your Towel (Just Don't Leave it on the Doorknob, You Monster!)

Believe it or not, there's more folk magic to towels, rags, and cleaning cloths than just divinatory dropping, embezzled dairy products, and menstrual mayhem. Beliefs about these unassuming objects are vast. So we thought we'd close this chapter by sharing a few more bits of lore that seemed fun, weird, or whimsical:

- Someone stepping on a nail or rusty metal might diminish their risk of tetanus by wiping the wound with a rag and then either burning it (boring) or sticking it in a rat's hole so the rat would "run away" with the poison (much more fun)!
- Tetanus could also be prevented by wiping the wound with an old oily rag, then burning the rag and holding the wound in the smoke.
- A kerosene-soaked rag was sometimes tied around the neck of chickens to keep off a disease known as roup (coryza). This was occasionally extended to people, too, to prevent things like colds or whooping cough.
- Tying a strip of dishrag around a corn supposedly made it diminish or go away entirely.
- Newlyweds benefited when the first gift they received was a dish towel in a new home, which was thought to bring good luck and help keep the house clean.
- Similarly, newlyweds are told to make sure the first dishrag they use in a new home is one of their mother's old rags, which will ensure order in the household.
- There's a playground rhyme that goes "Silk, satin, calico, rags" while either counting off among a group of friends or skipping rope. The one the rhyme ends on is what that person will be married wearing.
- You can wipe your nose with a tea towel for good luck!
- Hanging a towel over a picture frame is bad luck, and hanging one over a mirror will invite death into the house.
- If you hear an owl hoot, tie a knot in your apron string or turn it inside out to prevent misfortune.
- You can also turn your apron inside-out or wear it backwards for protection from witches and evil.
- If you sew, you can make an apron on a Sunday and then hang it outside the house before a storm to prevent lightning strikes
- Washing the dishes may be a chore, but if you hang the wet towel on the back of the door when you're done, it invites good luck!

Importantly in this last bit of lore, the towel should be hung on the back of the door, and not the doorknob. In fact, the doorknob is the one place you should never hang a dish towel. One story tells of a woman who worked for a household, and when the woman who ran the house caught her hanging a towel on the kitchen doorknob, she flew into a rage. This brings terrible luck, and even death, to the house!

Which means, just as Douglas Adams said, you should always know where your towel is.

NOTES:

1. The folklore collections in which these towel-related tidbits appear include Vance Randolph's *Ozark Magic and Folklore* (Columbia Univ. Press, 1947), pp. 53-7; *Folk-Lore of Adams County, Illinois*, by Harry M. Hyatt (Alma Egan Hyatt Foundation, 1935), pp. 285-86; *The Frank C. Brown Collection of North Carolina Folklore*, Vol. VI, pp. 472-73, 536; and Patrick W. Gainer's *Witches, Ghosts, and Signs* (West Virginia Univ. Press, 2008), p. 124.
2. The story of the cow's shrinking udders appears in Randolph's *Ozark Magic and Folklore*, p. 270.
3. The biblical passage reads, "And God wrought special miracles by the hands of Paul: So that from his body were brought unto the sick handkerchiefs or aprons, and the diseases departed from them, and the evil spirits went out of them." (Acts 19:11-12, King James Version)
4. From Hyatt, *Adams County*, p. 111, and Randolph, *Ozark Magic and Folklore*, p. 304.

5. Knife, Fork, & Spoon

Stirring up Sorcery and Putting a Fork in Folklore

Etiquette fascinates people. The rules surrounding which fork goes where, the proper spoon with which to crack one's creme brulee, and the placement of a knife at the end of a meal can feel like the unspoken criteria of a dance competition. We are baffled, and maybe even a little resentful and frustrated, when we don't quite know what to do with that shrimp fork. For many, tableware etiquette is a mark of elitism and class supremacy, but books are still published on updated tableware rules even today. The Better Homes & Gardens website maintains articles for those who might be hosting a dinner party and just need to know where that bread plate is supposed to go!

We're not here to police your table settings, though. As we often say, "we ain't fancy" and we're just as likely to eat ice cream with a soup spoon as anyone else—or, frankly, a fork if that's all we've got. Because it's ice cream!

What we will do, however, is talk about the magical lore of the table. We often keep our good silver tucked away in a drawer for special occasions. Perhaps it isn't a "junk drawer" exactly, but we do know that the silverware, flatware, or "eatin' hardware" that we keep on hand can have many magical dispositions. So let's look at a few of the more—and less—common bits of folk magic and lore sitting next to your dinner plate. (Or is that a charger?)

"Do You Feel Like Forking or Spooning?" and Other Awkward Questions

Forks and spoons are the subject of folk beliefs, but the shape of the objects seems tied to stereotypes about gender in some cases. The tined and prickly forks often get associated with men, and the curvaceous spoons get linked to women. While this is obviously pretty reductive, there's no reason a person can't learn the lore and build their own understanding about who a particular piece of flatware represents. If you feel a spoon represents more masculine figures because you associate it with watching your grandfather stir big bowls of cookie dough for after-school treats, that's absolutely fine.

One of the most common folkloric sentiments is that a dropped fork or spoon is an indicator of a guest soon to arrive. While a lot of sources specifically mention that a dropped fork means a man will visit and a spoon means a woman is coming, there are occasionally slight variations in that lore, where the dropped items can represent either gender. A dropped fork can also indicate that the person victimized by gravity and butterfingers will be married in the coming year. Paired forks or spoons accidentally placed at a person's spot or in their cup, bowl, or dish can also predict coming fortunes. A pair of forks left at someone's place indicates marriage in the near future, while someone who accidentally gets a pair of spoons in their coffee cup might expect either matrimony or the birth of twins.[1]

There's also something to the name: *silverware*. In particular, if you happen to be lucky enough to possess silver pieces, there's much lore about that metal being effective against all manner of unpleasant creatures. Many know the superstition about killing werewolves or vampires with silver bullets, but even a silver pie server or butterknife can have a detrimental effect on creatures of the night. This seems to stem from silver's reputation as a "pure" metal, representing a freedom from corruption or evil. I'm not sure if this only applies to polished silver, however, so perhaps keep your werewolf-fighting salad forks quite shiny just in case. We hear toothpaste is quite good for this.

Speaking of silver and things one might put in their mouth, silver spoons also have associations with babies in folklore. You may have heard the expression that a person born to privilege is "born with a silver spoon in their mouth," but there are folk origins to that phrase. Silver spoons were used as teething agents for babies in some places. On the magical side of things, silver spoons could also be placed in a baby's hand to ensure that the wee one would be blessed with wealth and prosperity for the rest of their life. Given that a wealthy family might be the one to have the silver spoons, this may seem a foregone conclusion, but there doesn't seem to be any admonition against stealing such a spoon for these purposes. The one catch is that if the baby fails to grasp the spoon on its own when it is offered, they would then be destined to lose any fortune they might have.[2]

Wooden spoons also have a bit of magic to them. In some cases, they are given to a new bride for good luck in their marriage. Or they could be given to a young lady by a suitor who wanted to declare his love or even his intent to marry. These spoons would be intricately carved with common motifs such horseshoes, keyholes, and encaged balls and were meant to symbolize things like good luck, love, and fertility. There are examples of this in Wales as early as 1667, but the practice was common in Germany and Scandinavia as well. There are also examples of two spoons linked together, carved from one piece of wood, in Mozambique.[3]

Finding a spoon in one's path, however—whether wooden or metal—is bad luck. A person is advised not to pick it up in any circumstances or they will likely be inviting a curse or misfortune to come with them.

Forks and spoons have a bit of healing lore associated with them, too. Spoons seem to be a common tool for remedying nosebleeds, with numerous methods for applying them. They can be hung from the nose, dropped down the back of a shirt, kept under the tongue, or pressed against the roof of a person's mouth to stop an existing nosebleed.

Charms using lead spoons tied and worn around the neck prevent nosebleeds entirely, according to folk belief . In North Carolina lore, one treatment for a sore throat involves taking a fork and scratching each side of the neck, then holding the fork over one's head to remove the esophageal ache. Using a fork to apply a bit of soot in the shape of a cross over the neck is also thought to cure a sore throat.[4] If you happen to be having trouble swallowing your medicine or keeping it down, you can also turn over the spoon you used to drink it as a way of charming it to stay where it belongs.

Spoons have also taken on a new meaning with many that deal with chronic illness. Christine Miserandino, in an effort to explain living with lupus, crafted her "spoon theory." We recommend reading it in full on her blog at ButYouDontLookSick.com, but in short she tells of sitting with a friend at a diner, struggling to explain how she must plan her day based on a limited amount of energy and pain management (represented by spoons grabbed off a few surrounding tables) and how once they're spent on things like showering and cooking, she is done for the day. Laine suffers from a chronic illness and has often used the spoon theory to help explain her condition. Just with a quick search on etsy, we're able to find jewelry, pins, shirts, coffee mugs, and even Christmas ornaments referring to spoons and chronic illness. Carry a spoon with you (either pulled out of your own silverware drawer or perhaps a fancy one you found in the kitchen section of Goodwill) to always have a backup spoon on hand. For many chronic pain sufferers, this is a small way to feel in charge of their bodies again, even if only symbolically. Or, some use it as a small way to identify other "spoonies" in hopes of finding commiseration and understanding. Witches of course can take that one step further and perhaps enchant their spoon. Douse it in coffee ("liquid spoons," as one mug proclaimed) or perhaps anoint it with a success oil, rubbing it whenever you need a little boost to get through the day.

What to do with those enigmatic sporks, though? It may seem a silly question, but we do come up with new tools all the time, and sporks—while often made of plastic and not great for the environment—might be worth unpacking a bit. For example, sporks could be a way to interpret nonbinary or gender-flexible meanings. It would be just as valid for someone to simply select the cutlery that they feel best represents them in any given moment, though, so this may not be for everyone. It could also be that the spork can become a useful representation of readiness and preparedness. Its all-purpose nature means that you have a fork and spoon on standby for magical use.

Spinning Knives and Cutting Ties

While forks and spoons share a lot of lore, knives have a body of folk belief all to themselves. Perhaps it is the dangerous nature of the knife, or its versatile utility, but something about knives seems to inspire people when it comes to folklore and magic.

Probably the best-known bit of lore about knives involves how one acquires them. In general, tradition stipulates that no one should ever give or receive a knife as a gift, or else it will sever the ties between them. So giving a knife to a partner or a friend is a good way to cut that person out of your life. However, there's a very important loophole here: if you wish to give a knife as a gift, the other person only need pay you a penny for it. That way the knife is "paid," and there will be no harm done to the relationship. In fact, when we sent this book to our editor, she left us a note on our initial draft that she once worked for a kitchen supply chain store that always sold knives that were giftwrapped to include a little card that contained a penny—specifically to avoid any bad luck accompanying the purchase! Similarly, in Italian American folk tradition, a dying parent can pass on a knife to a child or inheritor: "In this case, the son or daughter does not pay the symbolic fee because the point of passing on the knife is to maintain the connection to ancestors through this object."[5] As an ancestral object, the knife can come to symbolize a family line, and a failure to pass it on would instead be a "cutting" of ties.

Much like spoons and forks, falling knives are seen as divinatory predictions of company. Sometimes they are associated with a particular person or type of company, such as a soldier or a preacher. More importantly, if the knife falls and embeds itself in the floor standing upright, the company is coming soon and with urgent news or needs.

The divinatory power of knives is not limited to falling on the floor, however. I recall that while working late nights at a movie theater, my friends and I would get out of the building very late, often at 2 a.m. or later, and find ourselves hungry and not a bit sleepy (the joys of night shift work at a young age). Instead, we'd head over to the 24-hour diner and have some snacks and coffee. Eventually we'd begin spinning a butterknife on the table and asking it questions. "Which one of us will move away first?" "Who will be the first to die?" "Who should try to sneak the phrase 'duck pants' into their next conversation with the boss?" Many years later I found that this game is essentially the same as one played at least since the nineteenth century in England, in which young people would spin a knife to determine future spouses or love interests, like a precursor to "spin the bottle." Equally of note, however, is a bit of lore that says a knife set to spinning accidentally or outside of this game context would point to the next person to die at the table, so spin at your own risk![6]

A stolen knife can be a powerful tool for magic such as wart removal, as recorded in this passage from Vance Randolph's *Ozark Magic and Folklore*:

> "A prominent Arkansas lawyer tells me that in his boyhood the essential thing was to cut big notches in a stranger's apple tree with a stolen knife, one notch for each wart to be removed. This was quite an undertaking, for knives were highly prized and hence difficult to steal. Even more serious was the fact that the people in the neighborhood were all acquainted, so that a boy had to travel a considerable distance before he could find a stranger's apple tree" (p. 130)

Knives like this could also be used to bore a hole in a tree to "plug" a problem by putting someone's hair or nail trimmings into the hole and sealing it up.

There are several taboos regarding knives:
- An old proverb says, "Stir with a knife, stir up strife" (i.e., stirring with a knife leads to arguments).

- Knives should not be used to cut bread, since bread should only be broken (including cornbread).
- A person cut with a knife should not wipe the blade, but jam it into the dirt to make the bleeding halt and healing work faster.
- Finding a knife in one's path is considered to be bad luck.
- Midwives are not supposed to touch scissors or knives while attending a pregnant person for fear of harming the baby or the birth, but a knife or pair of scissors can be placed under the bed by someone other than the midwife to "cut" the birthing pains.
- All sharp objects should be put away during a storm to prevent lightning strikes (including knives, scissors, etc.).
- Knives should only be given to someone else handle-first (a folk belief that also follows good Boy Scout practices).
- When one person opens a folding knife, only that person should be the one to close it or bad luck will follow.

One of the more interesting knife tales in folklore has to do with the practice of something called the "Dumb Supper." At the time this ritual was recorded, the term "dumb" referred to someone who could not speak, and thus this term—which is now certainly an offensive one and included here only for historical context—referred to a silent meal shared by young people hoping to see a future beau, belle, or beloved. In one version of the story, a young woman and her friends set the table for this silent supper, working backwards and without saying a word, and leaving an empty space at the table for the visiting specter of the beau. The young woman also sets a very nice deer antler-handled knife at the empty spot. During the rite, a wraith-like figure appears and sits, and only when someone screams does it disappear, taking the knife with it. Many years later, the young woman marries a man. She's forgotten most of the strange ritual by this point, but she sees an antler-handled knife at his side as they're leaving the wedding in their carriage and decides to tell her new husband all about this silly game she played. The husband, on hearing it, turns white with rage and screams that her "game" was a rite that dragged his soul through hell. He uses the knife to kill the poor girl, then disappears and is never heard from again. Chilling, brutal, and a good reason not to arm a spectral wraith with your best cutting implement.

One of the ways we've seen knives most magically useful has to do with "cutting the wind." This is hardly scientific, and we would emphasize that if a bad storm is heading your way you should follow all official and professional safety guidelines regarding sheltering, evacuation, and preparation. If you do feel you've followed those, and you want to add a bit of magical aid to your protection, you can try taking a sharp knife and facing into the direction of the oncoming storm (before it gets dangerous). Slice downward through the wind, asking that it spare your home, and then embed the knife in the ground with the sharp edge of the blade facing the stormfront. In at least a few instances, we've heard from people who have used this and felt it was a little extra comfort and protection during a storm, and we've even used it a time or two ourselves—while also paying very close attention to tornado watches and warnings!

Setting the Table for Magic: A Few Odds and Ends of Silverware Spellcraft

We mentioned etiquette at the outset of this chapter, and there is no shortage of magical rules when it comes to setting your place at the table. One way to think about table layouts and arrangements is as a sort of language, not unlike the flower language deployed by Victorians when sending bouquets. Instead of indicating "this fish knife is turned the wrong way toward the white wine glass because I am fishing for little white lies as compliments," however, the meanings here are usually more direct and simpler (the fish knife thing would totally work, though, right?).

Usually the basic rule is not to lay your knife and fork in a cross pattern on your plate. Doing this is seen as a cursing action. Just whom you're cursing is a bit open-ended. Some say that it would indicate you will have "many crosses to bear" in your life and thus you've cursed yourself. Others would say you are laying a curse on your host or your dinner companions. However, there is at least one version of this practice that is done intentionally as a way to prevent any witchcraft or evil in the home, so it works as a sort of counter curse.[7]

Some other rules about good magical practices at dinner parties include:

- Never have thirteen place settings or guests in total, or else you'll have bad luck (or the first to get up from the table will die).
- Don't rub chopsticks together or stick them directly into the food being served. Additionally, don't leave them sticking out of food while you're not using them, as this is bad manners and also considered bad luck in some places.
- Shaking a tablecloth out after sundown will bring bad luck.
- No one should sit on the table, or else it will result in a failed marriage (or perpetual singlehood, so if that's for you, sit away!).
- Taking the last piece of anything (unless it is specifically offered to you) results in a single life unless you kiss the cook.

Dining with the Dead: A Modern Magical Mealtime Ritual

While the ritual of a silent supper has divinatory roots, it has evolved over the years to be more of a form of ancestor work. With the lore of the wraith, specter, or phantom being called upon to dine, it is easy to see this ritual shift into calling upon a specific deceased person, particularly if one has ancestral connections to them. If you would like to call upon the dead, or have them call upon you, try our version of the Silent Supper.

Once begun, it should be noted that everything is to be done in silence until everyone at the meal has eaten. And while the lore has shifted to this type of ritual being done on Samhain night, there are examples of these divinatory dinners being held on St. Agnes' Eve (January 20), New Year's Eve, May's Eve, and Midsummer Eve.[8] We have conducted this ritual at Samhain and were happy with the results, so we're going to suggest that date, but feel free to try it at other times. If you're hoping to visit with your deceased father, conducting this ritual on his birthday might be of more significance than any other date, so use your best judgment.

Start by setting the table backwards. This could mean setting out silverware first, followed by plates and ending with the chargers and placemats, or simply walking around the table and to-and-from the kitchen backwards (or perhaps both!), but it is up to you. One change we would like to suggest is leaving out knives altogether from the table settings. Often in the lore, a knife is dropped by the spectral visitor and collected by the one conducting the ritual, only to be later killed by the same knife. Or, a knife is taken from the table and later used to kill the querent. Regardless, the result is the same, so we suggest leaving them off altogether. Be sure to set a place for the dead, either at the head of the table or decorated in some way—a candle, a picture, or a totemic representation of them. Next, everyone should sit, and while still in silence, invite the dead to join you by dropping a spoon on the floor next to you. A dropped spoon often suggests guests are soon to arrive, so this lets them know they are welcome. Serve the ancestor's plate first, then work counterclockwise around the table, starting with dessert, moving to the main course, then any appetizers, soups and salads. However, this doesn't have to be a seven-course meal affair. If it is one dish with a few sides, start with the sides before serving the main dish. The idea, of course, is that you are serving the meal backwards.

While the meal is being served, think about what you hope to accomplish with this ritual. Do you want an answer to a question? Guidance in your life? Or perhaps you simply want to spend time with that person who is no longer here. Focus on this while serving the food, and listen for your answer while eating. When you're done, to indicate this to everyone, flip your (hopefully empty at this point!) cup over and set it on your plate (because a flipped cup indicates the gathering is done). When everyone has flipped their cup, thank the dead for joining your dinner, and flip their cups over as well. The rest of the time should be spent talking about any revelations the diners may have had or sharing memories of the deceased.

Turning the *Tijeras*: Shears and Scissors in Everyday Magic

One final bit of kitchenware that is worth mentioning is the shears or scissors many people keep in their drawers. We usually have at least one pair used for heavy cutting of things like poultry, and such shears have a very deep magical history of their own. Shears—either used in kitchens or even the shears used to trim sheep—are a part of a magical practice known as *coscinomancy*. This involves taking a pair of shears and a sieve (a wire mesh strainer), then balancing the sieve on top of the open shears. Two people balance the sieve and shears between them, on their fingertips, and ask questions. When the sieve begins to rotate or turn, that is an affirmative answer.[9]

Most often this method is used to detect thieves, with someone asking something like, "Did Jimothy steal my favorite Kenner Star Wars action figure?" and proceeding to ask the same question about Rogbert, Bethabel, and Tiffadora until the sieve starts spinning when it gets to cunning old Ruprecht, revealing them as the sneakthief! However, like all good games, this one was repurposed by clever adolescents and turned into a game to help determine whom they might next be kissing, using the same question-and-answer method while working through a list of potential crushes.

Coscinomancy is very old—even cited in the works of Cornelius Agrippa dating to the sixteenth century—but it is not well understood. People have trouble deciding just how to hold the shears. I favor using the handle to support the basket of the sieve hanging down, umbrella-like, while each participant places a finger under the point and tries to keep it balanced. If nothing else, this makes the game a bit more fun, and there's something about putting the point of something sharp on your finger—that little rush of risk—while asking questions of the great beyond that feels . . . witchy!

Scissors also show up in Mexican American folk magic, sometimes termed *brujería*, in which a pair of open scissors is placed near spellwork to prevent any counter cursing and cut any hexes that might come towards the *bruja* while they work. There are a number of spells in *brujería* practices that involve using the scissors—often iron ones—to "cut" harmful magic or hurtful ties that are causing problems in a person's life. They can even be used in a form of *limpia* (ritual cleansing) and moved around a person's body carefully to sever any ties to spiteful spirits or bad luck.[10]

A final note: if you're having bad dreams, you can carefully wrap a knife or pair of scissors and keep them beneath your bed or your pillow as a way to stave off bad dreams, nightmares, or even the dreaded "hag riding" phenomenon (a folkloric name for the experience of sleep paralysis).

NOTES:

1. Much of the lore regarding marriage, visitors, and birth involving dropped or misplaced forks and spoons comes from English lore, by way of North American regional accounts. Early sources for the English folklore can be found in *A Dictionary of Superstitions*, by Iona Opie and Moira Tatem (Oxford Univ. Press, 1989), while North American variations are found in *Witches, Ghosts, and Signs* by Patrick W. Gainer (West Virginia Univ. Press, 2008), pp. 123–25; *Folk-Lore From Adams County, Illinois* by Harry M. Hyatt (Alma Egan Hyatt Foundation, 1935), pp. 70–100; *Ozark Magic and Folklore* by Vance Randolph (Columbia Univ. Press, 1947); and *The Frank C. Brown Collection of North Carolina Folklore*, Vol. VI, pp. 628–30.
2. Hyatt, *Adams County*, pp. 73-77.
3. "Lovespoons in Perspective," by Herbert E.Roese in *Bulletin of the Board of Celtic Studies*, 1988, Vol.35, pp.106-116.
4. Brown, *North Carolina Folklore*, VI, p. 284. In at least one account, the soot cross can also be made with a knife instead of a fork. The use of the soot cross over the neck is similar to the use of crossed candles over the throat found in some Catholic and Anglican/Episcopalian blessings associated with St. Blaise, whose early February feast day was a time to perform this charm.
5. The quoted passage is from Mary-Grace Fahrun's *Italian Folk Magic* (Weiser Books, 2018), p. 98. The general lore about giving and receiving knives is found in abundant sources, including those already cited in this chapter.
6. Opie & Tatum, *Superstitions*, p. 219.
7. The quote is from Fahrun, *Italian Folk Magic*, p. 82 and is heavily reflected in English and Scottish lore, going back as far as 1646, when one author called the "sticking of knifes acrosse" a form of a witch-mark, or curse, by the superstitious around him (O&T, referencing Gaule on p. 218). However, in *Adams County*, Hyatt notes: "I knew an old French woman about fifty years ago [1886] that lived east of Liberty, that always put her knife and fork and spoon crossing each other when she set the table to keep the witches out of the house."(p. 462)
8. Hand, Wayland D. "Anglo-American Folk Belief and Custom: The Old World's Legacy to the New." *Journal of the Folklore Institute*, vol. 7, no. 2/3, 1970, pp. 136–55. JSTOR, https://doi.org/10.2307/3813868.
9. Or, as it is described in Reginald Scot's *Discoverie of Witchcraft* (1584): "Sticke a paire of sheers in the rind of a sive, and let two persons set the top of each of their forefingers upon the upper part of the sheeres, holding it with the sive up from the ground steddilie, and ask *Peter* and *Paule* whether A.B. or C. hath stolne the thing lost, and at the nomination of the guiltie person, the sive will turne round" (Scot XII.xvii)
10. For an excellent breakdown of the use of scissors in *brujería*, see Laura Davila's *Mexican Sorcery* (Weiser Books, 2022), p. 51-60.

6. Teacups & Bowls

Saucers Full of Secrets and Mugs Full of Magic

Some of the simplest magic can be done with a nice warm mug. That's not just the spell that we weave when we sit on a porch with a hot cuppa during a crisp fall morning, although that certainly has some fairy dust to it. Simple remedies and recipes, too, can appear in a warm curve of ceramic between our hands. One of Cory's go-tos for a sick child is to make them a mug of honey-lemon "tea," something that soothes the throat and helps calm the body. It's the first thing his kids request when they have a scratchy throat or a runny nose!

Tea played an integral part in shaping American history. It became a large part of life around the 1720s—colonists sat down to tea twice a day, which often doubled as social affairs. It was said that to the Americans, tea was the utmost in hospitality. And that, "they all drink tea in America as they drink wine in the South of France."[1] Later came the Townshend Acts from King George III, which led to, of course, the Boston Tea Party, a hugely impactful event in starting the Revolutionary War. While there were protests against the taxes (many refused to buy or drink tea at all), the important ritual of teatime didn't stop, it was simply replaced. Colonists would serve coffee, hot chocolate, or even dried raspberry leaves.[2] Additionally, young women of the upper class were sent to lessons on dancing, music, embroidery, and etiquette. These etiquette lessons included how to serve tea—how to pour, whom to serve first, and importantly, how to politely accept and refuse. The encoded language of teatime thus provides us with a useful and historically-grounded way to work a little magic.

To politely refuse a cup of tea, one turned over their cup and placed their teaspoon across it. If this wasn't done, the host would assume that their guest wasn't done, and therefore it would be impolite to not offer again while their teacup remained upright. And of course, it was impolite to say "no" if the host had offered. So the guest would drink another cup, and the host would offer another, and around we go again. Imagine getting caught in one of these etiquette loops! We like to use this little ceremony to firmly (but politely) put a stop to those conversations that seem to just go in circles. If you're on the phone with your aunt who loves to talk your ear off, or if someone at work won't stop trying to talk politics with you, or maybe you need to put a stop to gossip, brew yourself a nice cup of tea, stirring only counterclockwise, focusing on your intent to put a stop to those two-hour-long phone conversations or that awful rumor that you know to be untrue. Drink your tea (or if you're like Laine and don't like most teas, pour it on a plant as an offering), and when you're done, flip your teacup over and place your teaspoon across it. I even like to declare "no thank you" to really get my point across.

While coffee took over as the hot drink of choice in America, tea holds a special place in our collective hearts. Even those among us who are not keen on the flavor of tea can admit to the allure of it all—the beautiful and delicate dishware, the meditative property of boiling the water and letting it steep, and the strong historical associations that many feel a connection to. While we may think of the eighteenth century, many strongly associate a fancy tea ceremony with the Regency Era (or more specifically Jane Austen), or the cozy vibes of the current Cottagecore aesthetic, or even a childhood tea set with the chipped cups that were always good enough for a teddy bear picnic.

As we make our way through the kitchen, we'll look at the coffee pot and the tea kettle and pull a few favorite "#1 Dad" mugs off the shelf. We'll see that the magic of a good cup of joe or a tasty infusion of tea can do all sorts of things, from telling fortunes to making instant edible spells.

The Dregs of Magic: Divining with Tea and Coffee

We were in New Orleans for an event related to our work in podcasting, and we had a few hours to kill. Laine's feet hurt that day, and Cory begins melting at temperatures above 72 degrees, so we decided to look for an indoor spot where we could rest and maybe have a little bit of magical fun. We came across a tearoom at the edge of the French Quarter near the Pharmacy Museum on Chartres Street (which Cory highly recommends). One of the services on offer involved having tea leaves read, and since it also promised air conditioning, we decided "why not?" Many of our adventures begin with a question like that.

We waited a bit and each went back to have our leaves read by a very nice woman, who also recorded our session for us. We drank our tea, and the woman took our cups and swirled them, then turned them onto a saucer and looked inside to begin interpreting the shapes formed by the little dark masses of tea leaves clinging to the ceramic bowl of the teacup. In the end, there weren't any particularly earth-shattering predictions, and nothing that really "came true," exactly, but it was a good bit of fun over a cup of tea.

If you ask people about fortune-telling, most will likely have heard of tarot cards or crystal balls, but a fair number also know about tea reading. In fancier language, *tasseomancy* involves using teas (or tisanes or infusions, as each is a different way of experiencing hot leaf-water) that are steeped to leave some of the plant material in the cup. The dregs are then read to interpret symbols that might prove relevant to the life of the person whose tea is being psychically dissected.

It doesn't just have to be tea. Cory once had an amazing reading from a Turkish friend while he was living in Prague, and she used a strongly brewed form of Turkish coffee that left some of the grounds in the cup. Any brewed beverage that is likely to have detritus from the brewing process left in the servingware can be interpreted. This practice relies on both a belief in "contagious" magic—enchanted effects spread through contact, as when your lips touch the tea and the cup—and an ability to understand symbolism and metaphor in the Rorschach-like tea "blots" being read (so good on you if you took some English classes or a Psych 101 and are ready to dive deep into symbolism).

Some of the symbols and meanings that might show up, according to folklore, include:

- A line going straight from the bottom to the top indicates a funeral in the coming year.
- A ring formed high up near the rim means good news or a letter.
- A ring near the bottom means a marriage.
- A letter is taken to be the initial of someone important, usually a future spouse.
- A long stem or line means a tall person coming.
- An ant, bee, or bat means a period of hard work to come.
- Symbols like crabs or arrows can be taken as astrological signs connected to people (such as Sagittarius or Cancer).
- A dog can mean a good friend (although in popular culture at least one film series has interpreted the dog as a bad omen related to the Black Dog Shuck of the British Isles).
- A rose or flower can be a new romance.
- A sun or leaf can indicate a new beginning about to come.
- Wings can be either a note to release yourself from bondage and do what you wish, or a warning that soon someone you love will be leaving (possibly dying, as the wings can be an angel's wings).
- A spoon or bowl means someone generous, while a fork or knife means someone untrustworthy.
- Finally, a question mark can mean that you need to change your plans, or that something mysterious will happen in your life soon.[3]

You can find whole books on these symbols, and you can use other symbolic interpretation guides like dream books to offer some insight. The best way to do this, though, is to start with a few basic ideas and then see what *you* think the symbols mean as you read them.

The method for preparing the cup usually involves having the mug of coffee or tea and a saucer. The drink should be prepared loose-leaf or poured over the grounds, although you can modify it a bit as long as there's at least some material at the bottom. The person asking the question drinks down to the last bit, leaving just enough that the grounds or leaves in the brew can move when the cup is swirled. The swirling is often a major part of the divination, as the drinker is instructed to swirl everything slowly exactly three times, setting the liquid and detritus in motion, then cover it with the saucer and invert it.

The reader waits a moment for everything to drip and settle, and turns the mug back over to see where the soggy bits of plant matter have ended up. From there, it's up to the reader to interpret the globs and streaks. Some will take note of the position in the mug as though it were a clock face, with a blob that looks like a person around the three o'clock position meaning that someone important will be arriving in the next three months, or something similar. Some divide the cup into four quadrants, representing the four directions, and interpret a symbol like a pig in the south as being a loss of fortune. Some pay more attention to whether the blots are near the bottom or near the rim of the cup, with the rim representing good things or good news coming, and the bottom more serious matters like a marriage or a death.

There's also a handful of coffee or tea lore that works when the cup is full! If your coffee has bubbles in it, drinking it all before they go away is thought to bring good luck or money. If you see tea leaves floating in your cup, counting them can tell you how many lovers you'll have left in your life. And finally, you shouldn't look into a boiling coffee or tea pot, or else you'll "boil away" your future chances at romance!

A Bowlful of Bewitchment

Reading leaves and grounds aren't the only ways to get your magical daily dose from a bowl or mug. There are several well-worn magical techniques that range from the very ancient to the much-more-modern that you can try with an I♥NY mug.

If you're still in the mood for prognostication without having to consult your dictionary of symbols to decide if that smudge of leaves is a pine tree (meaning starting new projects) or a penguin (meaning fun and frivolity), then you could always employ scrying. This is the technique of using a darkened surface, such as a mirror or a bowl of water, in the way you might use a crystal ball. You simply let yourself get lost in the surface and see what images form. This can be somewhat difficult the first time you try it, so a great way to learn how to do this work is to light a candle and put a bowl of water between yourself and the flame. Then, watch the flame's reflection on the surface of the water, and let your mind drift. What images surface? Do you get flashes of memory, or possibly little snippets of lives you don't remember living? Do you have specific emotional responses: an urge to cry or laugh or scream? Those responses can give you hints as to what you hope to learn about, whether that's the future generally or the course of a specific relationship. A dark bowl works best for this, but as with all things junk drawer magic–based, use what you have! If you still want that dark surface, you can add some ink or dark food coloring to the bowl. A mug can be just as useful for this.

There are some taboos about bowls, such as when you're stirring up a bit of cake batter. In that case you should only stir in one direction, because switching directions can bring bad luck. Some beliefs even indicate that you should only stir clockwise while baking in order to avoid stirring in any bad luck or illness by going in the "sinister" direction (counter-clockwise).[4]

Bowls also have some uses when not filled with delicious cookie dough or a nice crunchy autumn salad. For example, there are Tibetan singing bowls, usually made of brass or other metals, that can be played like an instrument. These are usually struck on the side with a wooden pestle, then slowly stroked on their outer rim with the pestle to begin making humming harmonic sounds that can get quite loud. I've seen bowls of this type from sizes that would fit in the palm of your hand to enormous ones carved out of quartz that are as big as a cauldron. (The sound on that one was astounding!) Rather than going out and buying a bowl like this, however, you can find bowls that already do something similar. Often Pyrex glass bowls have a resonance to them due to their thickness and design, and most ceramic bowls have a "ring" when lightly struck as well. If you put them on a still, firm, flat surface like a table and lightly strike their sides with a wooden spoon, bowls like this will often ring a bit like a bell.

How is this magical? Well, it's certainly good for getting you relaxed and in a state of mind receptive to magical influence and practice—which is one of the reasons the Tibetan bowls are so good at helping with meditation. But there's also a lot of lore about ways to remove harmful or unwanted spirits from your space using sound. At its simplest, this can take the form of opening all your windows and banging pots and pans until you have sonically "cleansed" the space. But bells are also thought to dispel unkind spirits and fairy creatures that might wish you harm. If you've ever seen the classic Disney movie Fantasia, the final scene is based on Mussorgsky's "Night on Bald Mountain" and shows a demonic Slavic god known as Chernobog leading a witches' sabbat. However, at the end of the night, the dawn's early rays shine and suddenly all the spirits have to flee their revels and return to the darkness and underworld. What causes this response? The sounding of the local church bells calling the nuns nearby to their morning prayers. So if you want to sonically cleanse your area, the ringing of bowls can be a great way to do so, and it's tied right into the folklore of bells and sound. (But maybe let the witches finish their last dance first. No one likes a party pooper.)

Finally, bowls don't have to do only nice things. A few years back, we hosted an event at the Penn Museum in which we had a tour guide take us through a number of Ancient Babylonian and Sumerian artifacts associated with magic and ritual. One set of these artifacts was a group of cursing bowls—also called incantation bowls or devil-traps, designed to either trap demons (who might then do your bidding), stop the evil eye, or hex up an enemy. The ancient form involves making a bowl with inscriptions around the inside in a spiral, then inverting it over an image or representation of whatever you wanted to trap inside.[5] Today you could easily use a wax crayon or grease pencil to make similar marks on the outside of a kitchen bowl, then write a person's name or the name of a particularly irksome demon down and "trap" it under the bowl. If you're not comfortable writing in Ancient Sumerian (I, too, skipped that class in high school), you can always write in whatever language is most comfortable to you. What should you write? Start at the outer rim and work down and inward in a spiral. Write exactly what you want to happen: "From this day forward, Donny will stop all cruel and selfish behavior, and learn to treat other people with respect and dignity, or else his tongue will shrivel up and his teeth will fall out." (It's a cursing bowl after all!)

Some bowls even have images of their targets drawn at the bottom of the bowl, but if you don't feel comfortable with drawing, you can write their name. On the paper, you'll write their name again and then draw four crosses, stars, or X-marks in the corners to signify that the person within them is bound to the spell.

Of course, once you've inverted the bowl, put it someplace safe and out of the way until the target has done what you desired. You wouldn't want to accidentally find a Sumerian curse at the bottom of your Cap'n Crunch, after all!

NOTES

1. Quote is given by Léon Chotteau in his book *Les Français en Amérique*, Paris, 1876, this source was found cited in *Tea Drinking in 18th-Century America: Its Etiquette and Equipage* by Rodris Roth.
2. From Roth, Rodris. "Tea Drinking in 18th-Century America: Its Etiquette and Equipage." *Project Gutenberg*, Sept 13, 2014, https://www.gutenberg.org/ebooks/46775.
3. These symbols are mostly derived from lore found in the books *Ozark Magic and Folklore*, by Vance Randolph, and *The Frank C. Brown Collection of North Carolina Folklore*, Vol. VI. Some symbols are found in sources such as the "dream books" used to determine lucky numbers, as well.
4. A sample of this lore is found in the archives of Pennsylvania Center for Folklore. A piece of lore collected from a Hungarian American woman living in Pennsylvania says, "If you're making a cake, and you stir it to the right for awhile, and then turn around and stir it to the left—you're not supposed to do that. You're supposed to keep stirring it in one direction all the time when you stir a cake, otherwise...it won't come out." Found in "Belief Tales & Superstitions," student project coll. by Linda Lingle (PSU-Harrisburg, 1978).
5. While the exhibit we saw is closed, you can still view many of these incantation bowls online in the Penn Museum's collection with additional curator notes: https://www.penn.museum/collections/object/82460

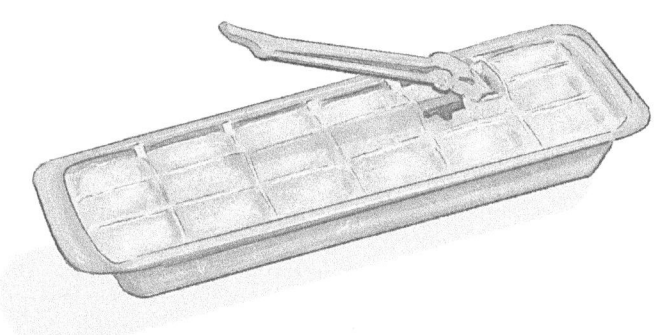

7. In the Ice Box

A Midnight Snack of Magic

The kitchen can have lots of magic hidden in the fridge and cupboards right beside the teacups, spoons, and dishrags. People have known for centuries that food is a magic of its own for its abilities to bring people together. Whether we come together in celebration, thanks, or even mourning, food can serve as more than just fuel for our bodies. Chocolate or coffee can stimulate us with caffeine, oysters can awaken our libido, and the smell of cinnamon can make a place feel more like home.

As we go through the kitchen, we'd be remiss if we didn't stop and focus a little on the refrigerator. Before the 1940s when they became common household appliances, they were known as iceboxes. Old iceboxes functioned by having a large block of ice deposited in the upper compartment, which then cooled the lower compartment as it very slowly melted. People would get weekly ice deliveries to ensure their goods stayed relatively cool and preserved, but of course the novelty of having a large block of ice on hand led to lots of creative uses, including some magical ones. Many icebox type spells have been updated to the modern day by using the freezer, while some have come about completely on their own since the advent of the fridge.

That Man Could Talk the Tongue Off a Wagon! A Tongue Spells for Talkers

A common type of spell involving freezers is a beef tongue spell. Yep, beef tongue. Judika Illes, in her book *The Element Encyclopedia of 5,000 Spells*, details a few variations of this magical working in her chapter on Courthouse Spells. Start by taking a slip (or slips) of paper and writing your legal opponents' names on them. Then place them into slits in the tongue, pin them closed, and freeze it all for at least a year.[1] Of course there are variations on this theme, but most end with a particular target on ice. With these beef tongue types of spells, the idea is usually that the ice will freeze the tongue of your foes, making it impossible for them to speak out against you. This is the general idea for most icebox spells, in that it will freeze someone out of your life.

Speaking of meat, we don't have to go much farther into the freezer to get more meat-based magic. Some of us have been the image of a nice raw ribeye placed on someone's newly blacked eye. While it was once believed raw meat (usually beef, but sometimes chicken or pork, including raw bacon!) had anti-inflammatory properties or the ability to draw out infection, we now know it basically just feels good because it's cold and can conform to the contours of the face. It seems in recent years the trope has gone from a steak to a bag of frozen peas since it feels just as good on the bruise without the risk of infection. Why not serve a meal of steak and peas to someone as a tongue-in-cheek sort of healing spell?

Ice can also tell us things even without a tongue. For example, one bit of North Carolina lore mentions that if a lump of ice falls in your glass while you're pouring from a pitcher, it means that your sweetheart is thinking about you.[2]

Ice to Meet You! (And Other Supervillain Catchphrases to Use When Casting Curses)

We can't leave the freezer without discussing ice and its role in magic. Scott Cunningham dedicates a whole chapter to ice in his book *Earth, Air, Fire & Water* where he mainly focuses on the transformative powers of ice—as it's a liquid that has been transformed into a solid. Many who work with ice magic tend to agree, but they also acknowledge the harsh qualities of ice that also give it properties of protection, banishment, or even death. But then again, the qualities of transformation and death are correlated in tarot, so we treat ice in much the same way. Ice magic can be powerful, but unforgiving.

With ice, the most common types of spells will involve freezing some water or letting the ice melt. Like with the beef tongue spell above, freezing is fairly straightforward in spellwork—you freeze the name or image of the thing you want to freeze out of your life or cool down. Melting makes your intentions slowly manifest, bringing things toward you. The ice starts as an unyielding solid and, if held too long against bare skin, it can be painful. But as the water starts to flow, the metaphorical blocks in your way are released.

Laine has used a version of a freezing spell to great success. She had a friend who was becoming a toxic presence in her life, but that person was also so wrapped up in her life that she couldn't deal with the stress of a dramatic friend breakup. She wrote their name on a slip of paper and placed it inside a cup of water and stuck the whole thing in the freezer. Slowly but surely, they were iced out of her life fairly painlessly, with none of the "How dare you?!" arguments she had expected.

You don't have to only work with ice just by melting and freezing it, though. You can fill a dish with water and freeze it—not all the way, you only need an inch or so. A wide-mouth dish gives you more surface area to work on, and a small cookie sheet is even better if you have the room for it to lay flat. Then use a utensil to trace words or symbols into the ice. We like to think of it as ice skating on the surface of a frozen lake, the blades tracing patterns in the ice. In fact, if we ever had the opportunity to do this spell on a large scale, on a lake with ice skates, we'd jump at the chance! Never mind that neither of us can skate and that we both live in the South. We'd still try.

A Box without Hinges, Keys, or Lid—Egg Magic!

As we move from the freezer to the fridge, we should stop at a staple in most American homes, the egg. There's a lot of lore around eggs and their various properties, usually having to do with dealing with foes, fertility, and cleansing. Anyone who's read J.R.R. Tolkien's classic *The Hobbit* will probably remember that "eggs" is the answer to one of the riddles in the contest between the titular hobbit Bilbo Baggins and the underground creature known as Gollum. But beyond their usefulness in puzzle games, eggs have a wide variety of uses.

Hoodoo practitioners have found several uses for eggs and their shells, including a popular method for cursing. Cutting off the end of the egg, or poking a small hole, then adding a name paper and cayenne pepper (and sometimes even graveyard dirt), will create an effective method of cursing someone when thrown over the roof of the house or onto the doorstep. Sometimes this method will go a step further and have you soak the egg in vinegar or war water to make it extra potent. Zora Neale Hurston also recorded an egg-based curse that's relatively easy to do (and only involves making your foe move away, rather than anything nastier):

> To Drive Away.
> Draw a picture of your enemy on an egg, with his name written twice at right angles so that it crosses itself. Throw the egg over the house and he must move.[3]

Eggs aren't only for baneful magic, as they are also used to cleanse yourself of negative energies coming your way. You can even use an egg to predict what's coming to you. This is very common for practitioners of *brujería*, who will perform a *huevo limpia* (egg cleanse) by rubbing a whole egg all over the body of the person they are cleansing, often accompanied by prayer, to rid them of *mal de ojo* (the evil eye) or just bad energy in general. After, crack the egg in a glass of water and interpret the shapes, much the same way you would the shapes of tea leaves. This is just a surface-level explanation, but there is much more information available on this practice.[4]

Eggshells are also ground up into a fine powder called cascarilla (not to be confused with the plant of the same name) and used for protection. One example we found of this was to press the cascarilla into a chalk stick shape and then to use it to write out a protective spell or symbols, or even to draw a protective circle. You can also sprinkle a bit on yourself before you begin your day or add it to a bath. If you make your own soap, you could add cascarilla powder to your soap for a protective boost every time you shower. It can also be used to protect your home. Sprinkle a protective line outside around your home, or at every door and windowsill to protect your house—and you inside it!

Many people who use eggs in their magic, whether that be the whole egg or just the eggshells, prefer to use only the eggs of black hens. This association likely comes from an 18th century French grimoire called *The Black Pullet*. The origins of *The Black Pullet* are questionable, but the story goes that it comes from a soldier in Napoleon's army who, while serving in Egypt, is rescued after an attack on their unit by a magician who emerges from inside one of the pyramids. He reveals to him the secret for hatching a black hen that could seek out treasure, particularly gold, giving the owner unimaginable wealth. There is also the belief that an egg from a black hen can cure poison (but we really recommend calling Poison Control first).

When Magic Goes Sour - Citrus Sorcery

Having had our fill of eggs, let's move onto something lighter—a nice, refreshing citrus. Citrus reminds Laine of summer days with friends, all slathering on coconut lime verbena lotion (it's okay if you were more of a cucumber melon type), eating oranges on the back porch, and putting Sun In® in our hair. If you weren't a teenage girl in the '90s, maybe you remember someone telling you to drink some 7UP when you were having a stomachache? The bubbles and the citrus were supposed to relieve those nauseated feelings.

Lemon and orange have also been common ingredients in cleaning products for hundreds of years for their abilities to break down grease. We talk more extensively about cleaners in our chapter on Washing Up, but it's worth mentioning here since citrus is so widely associated with being bright, spotless, and crisp. Because of this, most types of citrus smells evoke feelings of cleanliness and freshness, whether that is in a perfume or a cleaning product. One product that doubles as both is Florida Water. Florida Water started as an *eau de cologne* with notes of orange, lemon, bergamot, and neroli (orange blossom), and it is mainly still advertised as that in beauty stores and online. But if you find it in an occult store or a metaphysical shop, you might find it being picked up for several other uses, including purification for body and living spaces, offerings, and cleansing of ritual tools. This is especially popular with practitioners of Hoodoo and other African-derived and African American-derived systems. Florida Water is still made by the original patent holder Lanman & Kemp-Barclay, who list several uses for the formula on their website, including:

- Aftershave to reduce swelling
- Dab on bug bites to ease itching
- Spray as a room mist
- Mix with ice for soaking towels as cooling relief on the playing field or golf course
- Use in ceremonial rituals for cleansing, good luck, and protection[5]

So many uses packed into one small bottle!

Another happy use for lemons is to combat sadness and depression. After all, when life gives you lemons, make lemonade! The rind is a bright sunny yellow, and the fruit cut in half looks like the sun. Try shaving off some of the rind and carrying it with you, or put some dried slices on an altar or somewhere prominent in your home. And there's always food! Bake lemon cookies or tarts, perhaps, to work a little bit of kitchen witchery and brighten someone's day.

Lemons aren't all sunshine and happiness though. As the saying goes, with the sweet comes the sour. The sourness of lemon juice and their grease-cutting ability has given lemons strength in cutting you off from things in your life that no longer serve you. According to Zora Neale Hurston, they are also able to cut through emotional bonds, like a bad friendship:

To Break a Friendship.

Take three lemons and cut stem end off (squeeze some juice out). Write one name eight times one way on the paper and the other eight times across it. Roll it up and poke in the lemon, one in each lemon. Bury those lemons in the yard where the sun rises and sets on them. Every day at one o'clock pour one-half cup vinegar on the lemons. Those people will fight and part.[6]

We suppose that's definitely one way to sour a relationship.

Let's move on.

Magic on the Moo-ve—Dairy Divinations and Creamy Conjurings

Moving along through our fridge, we can't overlook the dairy! Milk is the first thing all mammals drink, and it represents life, maternity, and abundance. In the book of Exodus 3:8, the promised land of Canaan was said to be a "land flowing with milk and honey," also giving milk an additional meaning of divinity—both the Divine Mother and that it was seen in many cultures as food from the gods. Hindus also give special significance to milk; cows are sacred, and Krishna (a major deity and the eighth avatar of Vishnu) is often referred to as Makhan Chor or "butter thief." Milk, cheese, or butter—let's explore the legends in lactose.

Milk and witches have a long history together, and there are many stories of witches trying to steal milk or to spoil the milk of their foes.

- The tale of Granny Lotz in *The Silver Bullet*, an elderly woman whose neighbor "got after" her about forgetting to close her gate, which allowed his cattle to get loose. Because he ignores her age and persecutes her, she bewitches his cows to give bloody milk.
- A pair of stories entitled "How Witches got Milk and Butter" and "The Milk Witch of Wood County," from *Witches, Ghosts, and Signs*. In both tales, the witches are portrayed as poor members of the community who keep their families fed and healthy by magically stealing milk from neighbors. In neither case do neighbors take any retaliatory action, however, recognizing that the theft is occasional and non-debilitating, and that the witches seem to need it more than the dairymen do.
- Two stories in Ozark Magic and Folklore tell about witch-theft. In one case, two women "who lived all alone in a nearby farm" managed to siphon off milk from neighbors' cattle using an enchanted dishcloth. In another story, a woman refuses to sell some ducks (at a low price, admittedly) to a reputed witch, who tells her the ducks will be dead by the following Monday. Sure enough, the ducks die, and the witch is blamed for the deaths. It could be argued, of course, that the witch merely knew about the impending deaths and wanted to get some ducks on the cheap, ensuring a positive outcome for both parties, but that is not implied by the story.[7]

But how were people supposed to fend off this butter burglary? One way was a simple counterspell of placing a silver coin under a butter churn, which could help counteract the witchcraft and get butter to come unless the spell was severe. In that case, the milk was scalded in fire or whipped with switches to torment the witch that was spelling the churn. An informant cited in Gerald C. Milnes' *Signs, Cures, & Witchery* seemed to think that the coin should be heated to a high temperature and added to the churn, and that the presence of the words "In God We Trust" on the coin had something to do with its power, though that would only date the practice to the 1860s, when that motto first appeared on U.S. coinage.

Milk was seen as a symbol of health and livelihood. While it isn't really necessary to worry about milk theft anymore, perhaps we can take this information and craft an anti-theft charm. You could place a silver coin in a small container of milk as an act of protection. Or, if you suspect someone of theft, really go all out with the charm and whip the milk into butter with a switch of briars or brambles to "torment" the thief into returning your stolen item or to guilt them into turning themselves in.

Another use for milk was an extreme version of a souring jar. Usually you would write out a name paper and place that in a jar of vinegar, souring the life of your target. But we suggest a souring jar with milk instead, letting it curdle around the name paper of your target. Be careful with enclosed containers, though as spoiled milk emits gasses that can explode your container.

A Little Goes a Long Whey—Love and Cheese

In recent years, an excerpt from the book The Complete Book of Magic and Witchcraft by Katheryn Paulson has become quite popular through circulation on social media. It states, "You may fascinate a woman by giving her a piece of cheese."[8] Most share this because they find it funny. And removed from context, it is pretty hilarious. But when we've seen it shared, it has almost always been followed with the additional comment of "Sounds about right!"

If you're looking for a cheese-based love spell, perhaps try sharing your Babybel® with the object of your affection. I particularly like to suggest Babybel because of the red wax of the packaging for these small wheels of cheese. You can eat (or share) the cheese and then shape the wax into a symbol of your choosing. Maybe a heart with both of your initials carved into it? If you're a bit more devious, then sharing a cheese with someone, but keeping the wax (and maybe a smidge of their hair if you can manage it) might be enough to make a wee poppet for figural magic.

And, of course, Zora Neale Hurston also has something to say about cheese and love and magic:

> To Win the Love of a Young Girl
> Take equal parts of cheese, flour and salt. Mix together and place in the room where she sleeps and she will hasten to accept your proposal.[9]

As you can see, the icebox can be full of magic! Whether you choose to freeze your foes or make your desires known with dairy, we hope you found something fruitful in this chapter.

NOTES:

1. See Judika Illes, *Encyclopedia of 5,000 Spells* (HarperOne, 2009), pp. 226-228. Catherine Yronwode has some great resources for freezer spells crafted derived from Hoodoo practices on luckymojo.com.
2. From *The Frank C. Brown Collection of North Carolina Folklore*, Vol. VI, pp. 578.
3. From Zora Neale Hurston's "Hoodoo in America," in *Journal of American Folklore 44*, no. 174 (1931): 367.
4. Several excellent books have been published in the past decade or so dealing with Mexican and Mexican American folk magic, all of which mention *limpias* of various kinds. Some that we suggest include J. Allen Cross's *American Brujeria* (Weiser Books, 2021); Eliseo "Cheo" Torres and Timothy L. Sawyer's *Curandero: A Life in Mexican Folk Healing* (Univ. of New Mexico Press, 2005); Erika Buenaflor's *Cleansing Rites of Curanderismo: Limpias Espirituales of Ancient Mesoamerican Shamans* (Bear & Co., 2018); and Laura Davila's *Mexican Sorcery: A Practical Guide to Brujeria de Rancho* (Weiser Books, 2023).
5. See https://floridawater.com/pages/about
6. Hurston, "Hoodoo in America," p. 376.
7. These tales are found in *The Silver Bullet & Other American Witch Stories* by Hubert J. Davis (Jonathan David Publishing, 1975), p. 35; *Witches, Ghosts, & Signs* by Patrick W. Gainer (West Virginia Univ. Press, 2008), p. 167-68; and *Ozark Magic and Folklore* by Vance Randolph (Columbia Univ. Press, 1947), pp. 270-71, respectively.
8. Kathryn Paulson, *The Complete Book of Magic and Witchcraft*. New York, New American Library 1970. pg 97.
9. Hurston, "Hoodoo in America," p. 392.

8. Bottles, Cans, & Jars

Putting the Lid on Enchantment

Growing up, one of Cory's favorite times of year came in August and September, when "canning time" began. He'd spend hours with his mother in the kitchen, working to put up a bounty of jams, jellies, apple butters, and tomatoes—so many tomatoes—for the coming year. They would pull from their small farm's gardens for fresh produce, or Cory would be sent to the forest's edge along the property line to compete with the wasps and birds for wild blackberries and raspberries. (The trick is to go early in the morning before most other things are really up and moving.)

Even then, there was something magical about jars. Those quart-sized and pint-sized Mason or Ball jars would transform from a uniform emptiness to a suddenly radiant burst of reds, deep purples, rich browns, and even the occasional glowing golden yellow in years where they put up brandied peaches. Bottles and jars are possibilities, the magic of what can be. They can be transformed into so many things, used for everything from containing something that needs to be contained to creating a little world of magic where the spell-caster can stir up happiness and luck or trouble and woe, depending on their needs. This is some of the most reusable magic we have, as these sorts of spells can be done in a bottle, then cleaned out so the bottle can be ready for the next go-round of enchantment.

In the next few pages, we'll look at some of the history and folklore of bottles, jars, and even tin cans. We'll also look at a few of the more common applications for these handy tools. Oh, and don't worry if all you've got is an old jelly jar and not those fancy Ball canning ones. A well-rinsed baby food jar can become a wonderful home for magical work, even after the strained pears are long gone!

Keeping it All In—Bottle-based Containment Spells

You can put a lot of things in bottles. Maybe you've got a nice olive oil with some garlic and peppers in it sitting on your counter. Or maybe there's a jar full of axle grease in your garage for auto projects. Possibly you keep bottles of perfume in your bathroom or bedroom, or maybe you even have a little bottle of someone's homemade moonshine tucked into a liquor cabinet. (We're from the South; we don't judge.)

But what about the other kind of spirits? In folklore, there are plenty of examples of bottles that hold various spirits for a bevy of reasons. One of the best-known spirit-in-a-bottle stories involves a djinn (a powerful wild spirit in many cultures whose name is often westernized to "genie"). While plenty of people imagine a djinn tucked away in a little brass lamp a la Aladdin, in a lot of folk stories from collections like the *Alf Layla wa-Layla (The Thousand and One Nights)*, the djinn get trapped in bottles or jars. In the story of "The Fisherman and the Djinn," for example, the titular angler drags up a bottle with a lead seal bearing the mark of King Solomon on it. When he prises off the seal, a thick smoke emerges and takes the form of a vengeful djinn. Only through a bit of deft trickery can the fisherman coax the murderous creature back into the bottle, where he replaces Solomon's seal—the magical force that binds the djinn within the container.

A similar, slightly newer tale would be *"The Terrible Old Man"* by famed horror writer H.P. Lovecraft. In that narrative, we are introduced to a wretched old fellow who keeps a number of fishing lures dangling within bottles. As the tale progresses, we learn that each little lead weight or cork bobber is the spirit of a trapped mariner that the Old Man keeps on hand to do his bidding or answer his questions.[1]

More contemporary examples of folk magic also make use of the containment and binding power associated with jars, cans, and bottles. The famed "witch bottle" involves taking a number of broken pins and needles, glass, or other sharp objects and placing them in a jar with some urine from everyone in the house. This jar is then buried in the corner of the property or under the stairs as a way to capture any malevolent spirits or baneful witchcraft worked against those who dwell within, shredding them with the spiky bits inside.

Two other well-known examples are sweetening and souring jars, both of which are designed to contain someone and keep them in a snowglobe-like haze of good feelings (sweetening) or misfortune (souring). Fundamentally, these simply require you to have the name and/or some other representation of a person, like hair or fingernails, then place that in a jar of sugar/honey/molasses to sweeten them on you and make them think kindly of you or in a jar of vinegar or brine to cause them bad luck until you release them. The jars are often shaken and stirred periodically to amplify the effects, and other ingredients can be added, like vanilla or cinnamon in a sweetening jar (to cause feelings of romantic love or friendliness) and red pepper or poppy seeds in a souring jar (to cause "hot" suffering that works quickly or to create a confused mind in the target).

Another way spirits could be trapped in jars involved collecting feathers from the pillows of a potential target. Several stories from North American folklore discuss the appearance of feather "crowns" (a type of matted formation of feathers that occurs in down-stuffed pillows on occasion). These were thought to be caused by witches, who would steal feathers from the pillows and keep them in jars until crowns formed. In one account, this method was reversed, and the crowns were discovered by the victim before the witch could collect them, so instead the family put the crowns in their own jar after removing them from the pillow. They tightened the lid down slowly, day by day, which caused the cursing witch to experience feelings of breathlessness and suffocation, turning her curse back onto her.[2]

Another bit of folklore says to place an open jar next to your hens during a thunderstorm, which will "catch the lightning" and keep the coop safe, while also ensuring that the hens keep laying. This sort of spell can be deployed for home protection by placing open jars on windowsills during storms. As an added bonus, you wind up with fresh "bottled lighting," which you can use whenever you need a burst of energy or ideas by simply opening it up and setting it next to you (on a clear day only, as you don't want to suddenly rile up an existing storm).

There's also a long-standing Southern African American tradition of making "bottle trees" in one's yard. These can be decorative, as they are often very pretty, but there may be a bit of lore under them that speaks to capturing any wayward or unwanted spirits before they can get in the house. The basic idea is simply to place empty bottles over the limbs of trees, usually dead ones or ones that have not sprouted or bloomed. Usually these bottles are blue, although green and clear bottles show up sometimes. This may be related to some practices in the West Indian system of magic known as obeah, involving tying bottles in trees to prevent theft from one's garden.[3]

Some other bottle spells involve placing things in bottles to remove particular conditions. Two fairly widespread examples include nosebleeds and bedwetting. In both cases, some of the bodily fluid in question is collected in the jar. With nosebleeds, this is sometimes done by catching the blood on a handkerchief or a bit of wood, and then sealing it in the jar and hanging it in the rafters of the home. For bedwetting, the urine is collected by itself or the wet bedclothes or laundry can be placed in the jar instead, but a hole must be left for it to "drip" out. This is then placed in a grave or, if possible, a coffin with someone about to be buried, and the bedwetting will supposedly stop (although you might have some questions to answer from local authorities).

Urine is also collected in jars and kept under the bed to prevent errant partners from straying in a relationship, although that's presumably only if they don't find you've been surreptitiously bottling their pee and storing it in the bedroom. Another spell says to collect hair from each lover and tie them in a knot together, then cover them in alcohol (usually something like whiskey) or urine and keep the jar in a secret place. Some variants also say to add things like coins, silver, gold, or other valuable objects to the jar. This will make it impossible for them to leave you.[4]

A final use of formulas in jars isn't quite a containment spell. In fact, it's really designed to do the opposite: explode! The witch bottle mentioned above is also used to reverse bad magic, for example, by heating it in a fire when one suspects that a curse has been laid upon a person or household. The bottle will bubble and shatter, which should send the curse flying back at whoever sent it. There's also a specialty formula known as "War Water," or sometimes "Mars Water," which is a particularly nasty little mixture designed to put down a curse wherever it's thrown. Zora Neale Hurston gives the ingredients for this blend as "oil of tar in water," or alternatively creolin in water.[5] Other variations include mixing things like rusty nails into swamp water. An Irish variation involves mixing lead shot, whiskey, vinegar, and water, then placing it under the person's pillow or under their side of the bed to curse them and make them leave. The War Water is bottled, and the bottle is thrown at the feet or doorstep of the person who is to be cursed (often using small bottles, so this is where those baby food jars come in handy). This is often a very public declaration of cursing, as opposed to many more private methods.

If you were hoping for three wishes when opening these bottles, well, we do hate to disappoint you. But read on, as there will be some brighter uses for bottles, jars, and cans ahead!

Bottling Fortune and Putting a Stopper in Fate—Divination with Containers

While containment might be an obvious way to use bottles, cans, and jars in folk magic, there is a surprisingly large collection of lore related to telling the future or divining one's fate using these objects. This might not really surprise anyone who grew up in the tail end of the twentieth century playing with the ubiquitous Magic 8 Ball™. After all, what is a Magic 8 Ball if not a round black plastic jar full of liquid and a little fortune-telling die inside? You could easily make your own variation on this by putting distilled water in a jar with a bit of rubbing alcohol to keep it relatively sterile, then adding a die or dice of your choosing. Gaming dice like those used in tabletop role-playing games, such as D-20s or D-16s, work well for this. You could connect them to things like the I Ching, with its sixty-four hexagrams, and whichever numbers appear "up" after shaking could correspond to a particular passage (you'll want to invert the jar and use the bottom as the "peephole" for this, since the top is sealed with a lid). You could create your own set of meanings through trial and error, or use numerology to interpret what you get.

Beyond an improvised Magic 8 Ball approach, there are lots of other ways to use jars and bottles for divination:

- Take a jar of fresh spring water or dew outside on the morning of May 1, without speaking, and hold it up to the light. The image of your future lover or lovers should appear within.

- Take dried peas or beans, soak them briefly and dry them off, then place them in a jar while making a wish and seal them up. If they sprout, your wish will come true; if they rot, it won't.

- While opening a can or jar of fruit, if some of the juice splashes on your face it means good luck or money will come your way soon.

- It's considered a sign of good luck if you drop a jar or bottle and it doesn't break. However, if you drop a jar of vinegar or milk and it breaks, you should expect bad luck soon.

- If you keep a piece of camphor in a jar, you can predict the weather. When the jar gets cloudy, a storm is coming soon.

- One love divination involves putting a snail into a glass jar and leaving it overnight. In the morning, you can look at the trail where the snail climbed around the jar, and it should reveal the initial of a future lover or spouse.
- Another love divination says to write a love letter and put it in a bottle. Toss the bottle into running water, and whoever finds it will be your true love.[6]

There are a few great tales of using jars in divination. One story, from African American lore, speaks of a man learning whether he had the power to "conjure," or do magic, by carrying around a devil's shoestring root on his shoulder with a little jar held close underneath. He would then walk around someone's house and speak blessings or curses, and if the root slipped off his shoulder into the jar, it meant he was destined to be a conjure worker. This was especially true if the root changed color when it went into the jar.[7]

Another example is that of a Virginia witch named Rindy Sue Gose. She was known to carry around a little beetle in a small medicine bottle, which she would feed with blood from her shoulder. She would let the beetle out and then put on some "witch's grease" (a name for various magical salves, some of which reputedly give the witch the power to fly or change shape). This would make her shrink, and she could ride the beetle through people's keyholes and walls to get into their homes to work mischief. In this case, the beetle also seemed to go in and out of homes gathering information for Rindy Sue before she committed her magical breaking-and-entering crimes, meaning her little familiar was acting as a divinatory spirit of sorts for her.

Finally, British cunning person Bridget "Biddy" Early was known to keep a little blue bottle on hand full of some mysterious liquid. She would hold it up to a person and use it to diagnose any illnesses they might have, magical or otherwise, and then help to find a treatment for them if one could be had. This isn't all that far from the story of "Soldier Jack" found in various European fairy tales, in which Jack is given a similar bottle that lets him see if someone will live or die and then use a magical herb to treat them.[8]

Whether you're shaking up dice or tending to your magical pet insect, you hopefully have some brand new shiny magical ideas to try out!

I'd Rather Set a Light than Curse Your Darkness—Using Jar Candles and Lamps

We mentioned Aladdin and his lamp earlier in this chapter, and we can't end it without talking about the way that jars, bottles, and cans can be repurposed for making magical incendiary devices (we're thinking candles and lamps here, rather than Molotov cocktail versions of War Water).

At one time, tin cans were often used to hold old wax or tallow, which would then be melted to "dip" candles for household use. You can still do that if you like; it just requires time and patience to accomplish. If you're living at a slightly faster pace, you can just repurpose jars and cans into candles. A word of warning here: many jars are made from glass that is not designed to come into contact with high heat or open flame, and using tin cans can mean dealing with very hot metal. You should always be safe and wear heatproof gloves and eye protection when working with flames and other materials, and make sure to never leave a burning candle or lamp unattended.

In our modern age, it's fairly easy to make candles using a pourable kit or mixture available from craft stores. You can often get vegan soy-based waxes, natural beeswax, or even glycerin-based waxes. These are generally heated gently in a double boiler (or a metal bowl set over a pot of simmering water), then poured into a mold with a wick carefully positioned in the center using a pencil across the jar or tin rim. If you're looking to make an enchanted candle, adding a bit of essential oil or a small amount of powdered herbs or roots can be effective. Just be sure to err on the side of "less is more," because too much of anything can result in a dangerous accident waiting to happen. You can carve a seal into the top of the wax or, even better, use markers or paints to decorate the jar or give it specific magical intentions to guide the spell. Burn the candle safely on a heatproof surface in a well-ventilated space, and feel free to add in other spellwork.

Another fun option is to make an oil lamp using floating wicks. These are much more in line with the lamps from Aladdin and would have been fairly common throughout human history—even more so than wax candles. You can buy floating wicks at craft stores or online, and they are usually just wicks held in a slice of cork with a small heatproof disk on top of the round cork piece. The rest of the wick dangles below the cork in the oil of your choosing. Most oils will burn in some way—even things like olive oil or peanut oil from the kitchen work well. You can opt for lamp oils or do some research to find an oil you prefer. The nice thing here is that you can add just about anything to the oil beneath: herbs, seeds, papers with sigils on them. As long as you don't let the oil get low, they are not as likely to combust, and thus the flame can burn and carry your spell for a long time. When you're done, the cleanup is very easy, as you just empty the oil, dispose of the wick and other ingredients, and clean the jar out to ready it for its next use! Cory has used oil lamps like this with great effect. Here's one of his favorites:

For Job Success (Finding a job, getting recognition, or getting promoted)

You need:
- A glass jar, preferably a pint-sized Mason or Ball canning jar (or an empty tin can if you prefer)
- Some allspice berries
- Some dried cloves
- Some bayberry oil (if available)
- A bay leaf
- Some cinquefoil (five-finger grass) or a four-leaf clover
- A paper with your intended results written on them (or a sigil or other similar marking)
- Playing cards: the king of clubs, the eight of clubs, and the two of clubs[9]
- Some carrier oil (something sweet like peanut or almond oil works best, but use what you have)

- A floating wick
- A Sharpie™

Write your intended results on the paper. Include your name, and ask specifically for the raise, recognition, etc. that you want. Place the paper at the bottom of the jar. Take the jar and fill it with the allspice berries, cloves, a few drops of bayberry oil, a bay leaf, and the cinquefoil (or clover). Place the three cards under the glass jar on top of a heatproof surface like a plate. The king of clubs should be in the center of the three cards. Top the jar with oil to about three-quarters full. Unwind the floating wick and leave just a quarter inch of it above the cork disk. Let the rest coil at the bottom of the jar with the ingredients. Carefully set the wick on top of the oil and let it float. It should sit for at least an hour, preferably overnight, to saturate the wick with the oil.

When you're ready, place the jar between your two hands. Repeat your petition for whatever it is you want success with. Ask the king of clubs to help you achieve your goals, and offer him the light of the oil lamp in his name. Then light the wick and sit with it for a few minutes. It may take a few tries to get the wick to stay lit. Once it has burned for at least ten minutes, you can carefully blow or snuff out the flame. Pull the wick up a bit carefully when it cools, so about a quarter of an inch of the wick is always above the cork. Repeat this ritual for at least seven days, or up to forty days, to bring about your desired effect.

As you can see, there is so much you can do with a humble jar or tin can. So the next time you finish off that jar of peanut butter or jelly, you could recycle it (which we'd encourage). Or, you could turn it into a magical wishing lamp, Magic 8 Ball, or even a bit of bottled lightning!

NOTES:

1. For an excellent rendition of the *Alf Layla wa-Layla*, I'd recommend the edition entitled *The Annotated Arabian Nights*, edited by Paolo Lemos Horta and translated by Yasmine Seale (Liveright Publishing, 2021), which I was introduced to by the Carterhaugh School of Folklore and the Fantastic (https://carterhaughschool.com/). The Lovecraft story can be found in *The Dunwich Horror and Others*, edited by S. T. Joshi (Arkham House Press, 1984).
2. From Harry M. Hyatt's *Folk-Lore of Adams County, Illinois* (Alma Egan Hyatt Foundation, 1935), p. 38, 447.
3. See Zora Neale Hurston's "Hoodoo in America," in The Journal of American Folklore 44, no. 174 (1931): 324.
4. See Vance Randolph's *Ozark Magic and Folklore* (Columbia Univ. Press, 1947), p. 124; and Hyatt's Adams County, p. 422.
5. Hurston, "Hoodoo in America," p. 412. Creolin is essentially a distilled turpentine product, and is used in a number of industrial cleaning applications, but is not a common product to find on most shelves now. If you wanted to make this formula, a simple substitute would be turpentine blended into some "stump water," or rainwater that collects in the divot of a tree stump. The Irish variation on the War Water recipe is found in Hyatt, *Adams County*, p. 426.
6. These bits of lore are collected from Hyatt, Adams County, pp. 17, 194, 207, 274-79; Randolph, *Ozark Magic and Folklore*, pp. 68, 173-76
7. Hyatt, *Adams County*, p. 417.
8. See Hubert J. Davis, *The Silver Bullet: And Other American Witch Stories* (Jonathan David Publishing, 1975). For more on both Rindy Sue Gose and Biddy Early, also see Cory's article "The Beetle in a Bottle: A Forgotten Divinatory Charm," in T*he Witches' Almanac*, issue 41 (Witches Almanac LTD, 2022), pp. 95-97.
9. Not that we're trying to push Cory's books constantly, but if you're interested in why these cards are included here, he has another book on the folklore and practice of using playing cards in divination and magic. It's called *54 Devils: The Art and Folklore of Fortune-telling with Playing Cards* (2023 revised ed. [2013]). You can find it through most major booksellers or order it online.

9. In the Pantry

A Larder Full of Lore

When we were but wee witches, we spent a lot of time baking cookies during the holidays. Laine's mother still makes tons of desserts for the holidays, like Hello Dollies, Gooey Squares, and too many cookies to count. Cory's mother would build elaborate gingerbread houses and sleds filled with candy and icing that she'd give away as gifts. Of course, they'd always keep one to pick at and nibble, like fairy tale children getting into trouble, for the week or so before the big winter festivities. Gumdrops and candy canes and M&M's would mysteriously vanish every time Cory walked through the room where the house stood. Despite the sugar-fueled nature of the holidays, those became central memories, and ones that Cory has been passing down to his own children. Being the slight oddball he is, the focus is less on gingerbread men and houses now, and more on making and decorating the most unusual gingerbread monsters he can with his kids. There have been iced sasquatches, witches, and even something that came to be known as a "shark-to-pus" (a combination of a shark head and an octopus body) to savor (and fear) during the yuletide season.

Baking is sometimes thought to be a bit more rigid and rules-driven than the more freeform recipes of cooking. After all, you must get your ratios right if you want dough to rise or if you want flaky layers between your pastry bites. But there's still something wonderfully creative that happens when we dig out our cookie cutters, canisters of flour, shakers full of spices, and more. It's almost like…well, magic!

The pantry and the spice rack have always been places to turn to for enchantment. This chapter will look all the way to the back of the shelves to see what kinds of enchanted twists you might be able to find in your own dry goods.

Sugar and Spice and Everything Sorcerous—Mystical Dry Ingredients

When you open a pantry, you are already tapping into a little bit of magic that humans do: preserving food. We may use the fridge to keep food fresh and have it available a little longer than it normally would be, but the pantry is where we keep the food that we have ground, bottled, salted, sweetened, dried, smoked, or otherwise made into something we can enjoy for months to come. Cory often spends the end of summer taking any and all produce from his garden or the market and turning it into things like apple butter, berry jams, or even home-canned tomatoes and salsas. That has become a part of his yearly cycle, and it makes it a little more magical because he's doing that most fundamental form of sorcery: transformation.

The pantry, then, is stuffed full of dried herbs, sacks of flour and sugar, and bottles or cans of produce that are just waiting to be opened and revived. A little life in the form of yeast, hunger, and/or heat will transform them again. Each item has its own lore, a story or two tucked into the folds of the bags and under the rims of the bottles and knowing those tales can make the magic of transforming them all the more powerful.

Perhaps nothing in the pantry is quite so versatile in terms of its occult applications as the humble salt cellar. Salt is well-known enough that virtually everyone has heard that if you spill some, you must toss a bit over your shoulder to stave off bad luck. In Appalachian and English lore, this is often said to be a way of blinding the devil, who is looking over your shoulder at this opportunity to give you more misfortune. A few versions of this belief also say you should say a prayer, or toss the salt while saying "In the name of the Father, the Son, and the Holy Ghost." Laying down a line of salt across a doorway or windowsill prevents wicked witchery and evil spirits from entering, as they are supposed to have to count every grain before they can come in. In Naples, Italy, most shops would have a bowl of salt handy to sprinkle on the floor and counters. It would then be swept up and thrown away to remove any evil eye influences or bad luck at least once a day. In Midwestern American folklore, mothers put little bags of salt around their children's necks to stave off chills, although in other places sprinkling a bit of salt in one's shoes is said to have the same effect.

It's unlucky to give back or repay salt if you borrow some, but you can give back an equal measure of sugar instead if you don't want to ruin the relationship. One of Cory's favorite housewarming traditions is to give a little jar with salt, bread, and a penny to people when they move someplace new. The penny is so they'll never know poverty, the bread so they will never know hunger, and the salt so their lives will never lack flavor. This blessing is one he inherited from his family, which has roots in the Bialystok and Vilnius regions along the Polish/Lithuanian borderlands, but we've also found it referenced as a Jewish tradition and in a few other places. Similar traditions say that salt, pepper, and sugar should be the first things brought into a new home, or that salt and bread should get that honor.

Salt is also good while you're sleeping. It can be kept under the bed to ward off nightmares and provide a good night's sleep. There's also a folk belief that if you do have a nightmare, you can simply burn some salt on the stove when you awaken, and the bad dream will be dispelled. There's a ritual dating back to at least the Colonial Era in North America that deploys salt to give dreams. In that little spell, a person would hard-boil an egg, then hollow out the cavity where the yolk was and fill it with salt. The person would then eat the entire salt-filled egg and go to bed. In their dream, someone would offer them a glass of water, and the person who did so would be the form of their future spouse. Not exactly an ideal pre-bedtime snack, but sometimes you just need to know![1]

The pantry has more than salt to offer, of course. Some of these other larder staples have their own enchanted uses.

Beans or Peas (Dried) - These are often carried or worn for luck in specific numerical sets, with three or seven being most common. There are also ways to use beans for fortune-telling, a practice known as *favomancy*. This essentially means tossing beans onto a cloth that is divided into four quadrants, then interpreting the way the beans land (with a cleft facing up or down or left or right) to figure out specific fortunes. While a full system of favomancy is too much to get into here, you could try a simplified system by taking three beans and assigning them values, such as "with all clefts facing up/right, the answer is yes; with all facing down/left, the answer is no; any mixed combinations mean the answer is a maybe or unclear."

Dill - This ingredient has associations with beauty and money. Applying dill mixed into a face cream is thought to be able to remove "bad looks," and there are freckle potions that suggest using dill infusions to lighten or remove freckles. Dill can also be sprinkled around a cash register or near a business's entrance to invite money to come in.

Garlic - Keeping a braid of garlic is not just for warding off vampires. In Italian folk tradition, it's associated with St. Michael the Archangel, and keeping it in the kitchen or by the door is protective and wards off bad spirits and bad magic.

Horseradish - This pungent root has been used in folk medicine for rheumatism and headaches (Gainer, p. 106). It's also sometimes mixed with buttermilk and used as a lotion to improve complexion or rubbed over the body to remove headaches. One old belief notes that you should only eat horseradish in months that have the letter "R" in them.

Mustard Seed - The tiny seed that grows into a big bush is used for making plasters to heal congestion and chest colds, but it also is added to drinks sometimes to work as an aphrodisiac. Additionally, mustard seeds are sometimes used to curse people, especially by cooking them in an iron skillet until nearly black, then tossing them into a jar with some vinegar, chili, and garlic with the person's picture or name and shaking it up.

Nutmeg - This is one that has a surprisingly large amount of lore. Most beliefs about the nutmeg have to do with whole nutmegs, which are carried in the pocket or worn on a string around the neck to prevent everything from rheumatism to nosebleeds to headaches. One old gambling charm calls for drilling a hole in a nutmeg, filling it with liquid mercury, and sealing it up to carry for luck. Since mercury is dangerous, a better alternative would be to take an old "mercury dime" or any small silver coin and wrap it up with the nutmeg to carry with you for a little boost in luck. One belief says sprinkling sugar and nutmeg on onion peels and then burning them will draw money to you.

Red Peppers - Those long strings of dried red peppers don't just look good, they also are thought to bring good luck and provide protection from curses and the evil eye. You can also keep one tied up with string in your pocket to ward off bad luck.[2]

Sage - This herb's name associates it with wisdom and insight, but it's also got some remarkably eerie powers! For example, one bit of English lore says that a young woman can pluck leaves from a sage plant on a certain day (usually around Halloween or close to May Day) and they will reveal the image of a future spouse. One could likely do something similar either by burning the leaves or stirring them into a simmering pot of sauce or soup and seeing if they reveal an image in the smoke or bubbling liquid.

Sugar - Much like spilling salt, spilling sugar is bad business. One proverbial expression says, "If you spill sugar you spill joy." Sugar is often used in work to "sweeten" people, which can mean making them like you or even making them *like*-like you. "Love powders" are used to spark up a romantic flame or bring back a wandering lover. In North Carolina, these were described as powdered sugar that had been scented with perfumes and often dyed colors like pink or blue in a rather old-fashioned gendered approach to winning love. You could easily adapt this to your needs today by taking powdered sugar and putting it in a jar with things like vanilla pods (warm feelings), lavender flowers (flirtation), or even chili peppers (spicy and sexy) to make love powders. These powders can be added to food or sprinkled around one's home or even in one's shoes or clothes in small amounts to invite love and affection. It's not all sugary sweet romance, though. One bit of lore says not to keep sugar and salt on the same shelf, lest it lead to a quarrel in the household.[3]

There are a number of other herbs and spices you might find useful, such as bay leaves for success or cinnamon for both better business and friendship. There are many books out there that get into the magical associations with herbs and other botanicals, so we'd suggest going to something like Scott Cunningham's *Cunningham's Encyclopedia of Magical Herbs* (Llewellyn Publications, 1985) or Cat Yronwode's *Hoodoo Herb and Root Magic* (Lucky Mojo Co., 2002) to round out some of the other things hiding behind the seasoning salt and the ketchup bottle.

Rolling Pins vs. Magic Wands—A Bewitching Baker's Dilemma

We've all got that friend who can just…*bake* things. They seem to effortlessly produce a tray full of beautifully iced cookies, or a cake that seems ethereally light and moist and absolutely sings with flavor when you eat a bite. They wander into the kitchen while you're looking at the back of a book and jotting down a note to call the dentist later in the week, and when you look up they've somehow conjured a plate full of freshly baked scones and a little pot of homemade lemon curd. How do they do that?

It's probably magic.

Truly, there are just some very gifted bakers in the world, but the idea that there could be a spell or two woven into the baked goods produced from the pantry has plenty of precedent in folklore. All sorts of beliefs and traditions surround the household hearth and its crusty, flaky, and oh-so-delicious carbohydrate-filled treats. Bread alone has a nearly endless store of superstitions, customs, and beliefs:

- Bread that splits while baking is a sign of bad luck to follow, as is bread that burns. Often it indicates a quarrel between sweethearts or neighbors. Even worse, if you burn your bread on purpose or toss it into the fire when you have a bad loaf come out, then you'll be punished with bad luck (or even a visit from the devil in some stories).
- To avoid splitting and bad luck, you can mark the bread with a cross on the top (slashing two intersecting lines). This will allow the bread to rise more evenly by offering a space for moisture and heat to vent from within, and it supposedly blesses it.
- Once it's out of the oven, be careful with the bread. Turning it upside down is bad luck (unless you're doing the quick "tap test" to make sure it's fully baked). Dropping bread on the ground is thought to be bad luck, especially if it falls butter-side down once it's well-slathered.
- Taking the last piece of bread is bad etiquette, but it can also be bad luck—especially if you already have food on your plate. Offering to "kiss the cook" or baker will negate that misfortune, though.
- Perhaps one of the strangest, but very oft-repeated, bits of lore says that eating bread crusts will give you curly hair! This is often perpetuated by parents trying to get their children to eat their crusts and not waste food. In the Ozarks, at least one belief says eating the crusts makes you better at hunting and fishing.[4]

All of this is to say nothing of the specialty breads that get associated with various holidays, such as *pan muerto*, which is used in Mexican and Mexican American Day of the Dead rituals and festivities.

There's so much more than bread in the world of baking magic. Cakes also have a lot of occult secrets. In fact, one of the oldest and most widely used bits of folklore involving cakes sees people hiding various objects in the cakes to foretell the future. One of the early English diarists, Samuel Pepys, spoke of just such a ceremony being done during the traditional Twelfth Night festivities. These celebrations, which ran until the Feast of the Epiphany on January 6, included the baking of a cake with a token such as an uncooked bean, a ring, or a coin inside. The cake was then sliced, and whoever received a particular token became the "king" or "queen" for the festivities and would receive both good luck and the obligation to provide the cake for the following year. These "king cakes" are used today, especially in places like New Orleans, where they are a part of the pre-Lenten Mardi Gras celebrations, and a small plastic or metal baby has become the de facto token in the pastry.

Wedding cakes have a great deal of lore to offer. For example, the bride is not supposed to have anything to do with baking the cake, or else she invites bad luck to the wedding. Another belief says that the cutting of the cake must be done with the groom's hand on top of the bride's and not the other way around, or else the marriage may be fraught with arguments or infertility. Some wedding cakes have historically had tokens similar to those in king cakes baked into them shaped like horseshoes or cupids, providing little blessings and surprises (and possibly chipped teeth) to those attending the wedding. Many couples will save a slice of the cake and put it in the freezer until their first anniversary, when they'll eat it (or perhaps nibble a bit at it, given how stale and freezer-burned it is likely to be) to ensure continued blessings on the marriage. The couple can also toss a piece of wedding cake outside on their wedding night and tell by the number of birds eating it in the morning how many children they shall have. (This is not recommended, as the cake is not good for the birds.) If someone manages to sneak a slice of wedding cake home with them, they can wrap it well and hide it under their pillow, and they will dream of a future spouse or lover.

Birthday cakes have their own magic. Who doesn't remember your first magic spell of wishing on a birthday candle and blowing it out? Other holidays and celebrations can also occasion the use of enchanted baked goods. Chinese bakeries will often carry moon cakes—delicious stuffed pastries—to honor the full moon during celebrations like the Mid-Autumn Festival. Pennsylvania Germans bake *fastnachts*, a heavy fried donut, right before Lent to provide sustenance and blessings through the next forty days—a tradition mirrored in other places by the holiday known as Pancake Day. The Jewish holiday of Pesach frequently involves special cakes, known as paas, to be made without leavening. In New England, there was once even a tradition of baking a special spiced cake with raisins on Election Day!

In at least one account, there is also something called a "thundercake," which is to be made between the time the first loud peal of thunder is heard and the time the storm breaks. This would mean using a quickbread-type cake made with baking powder or soda, and the folklore is not terribly clear about just *why* someone would make this cake (although I'd speculate that, as with much baking, it was about bringing fortune or even fertility to the household).[5]

Cookies are also full of magical possibilities, especially since they can be shaped into just about anything. One excellent method for making simple magical charms involves making a "cinnamon dough," out of powdered cinnamon and a binding agent such as applesauce or glue (or both), then cutting it into the shapes desired and baking until firmly set. They can be painted to look like gingerbread cookies and a hole can be added to the top (preferably before baking) so they can be hung on holiday trees as ornaments. Another use of these, however, would be to choose shapes and decorations that have magical qualities. For example, one might use a Halloween cookie cutter to make a cinnamon dough cookie in the shape of a witch, and decorate her with a little charm written on the back saying something like, "little kitchen witch, guard my hearth and home." Then she could be hung in the kitchen near the stove to provide abundance and security throughout the year. You can play with the shapes and styles you wish to use, and even incorporate other magical elements, such as baking little tokens into the dough or even baking a piece of paper with someone's name on it so that you can use it like a little poppet or doll for magical purposes.

All magic takes is a little flour, sugar, spice, and imagination!

The Runic Rhenish and the Marvelous Merlot—Uncorking Enchantment

Okay, so the wine isn't always kept in the pantry, but it's definitely more of a pantry than fridge item, at least until it's opened (if you don't happen to finish the bottle with some friends right away). While wine has a little bit of lore of its own—think proverbs about new wine and old wineskins or vice versa—some interesting tidbits of lore pop up about wine corks, if you'll forgive the pun. Some mid-century English lore says that champagne corks are kept as good luck, especially if you slit it open and push a coin in it to make a lucky charm. You can either keep it until you open your next bottle of champagne or for the rest of your life if it's your first "official" bottle over drinking age. Supposedly, keeping a wine cork under one's pillow will keep away cramps or other pains while you try to sleep. Baseball players sometimes keep the cork of a whiskey bottle in their pockets for good luck.

An Italian folk spell involves taking red wine and water and placing them in a jar—about two thirds water to one third wine. Then slowly rub the jar over a person you think might be suffering from fatture (or a curse/bad luck condition). Put the jar in a dark place like the pantry and check it the next day. If it's still basically the same as it was, then there is no fatture. If it's gotten cloudy or any other strange effects have happened, the test is positive. and countermeasures should be taken.

A few final bits of lore say that spilling wine on your clothes, especially at a wedding, is considered bad luck. If you happen to make wine, you are supposed to do so under the light of a moon and when the weather is fair to avoid cloudy or off-tasting wine.[6]

Whatever you're digging out of your pantry, we hope that you find a little more magic in it after this chapter. At the very least, save us some of your most conjured cookies—and maybe a glass or two of your witchiest wine!

NOTES:

1. The lore here comes from a range of sources. Many of the folk beliefs about salt can be found in both *Folk-Lore of Adams County, Illinois,* by Harry M. Hyatt (Alma Egan Hyatt Foundation, 1935) and *The Frank C. Brown Collection of North Carolina Folklore,* Vol. VI (1961). Additional lore comes from Patrick W. Gainer's *Witches, Ghosts, & Signs* (West Virginia Univ. Press, 2008), p. 123, and the lore from Napoli is from Mary-Grace Fahrun's *Italian Folk Magic* (Weiser Books, 2018), p. 100.
2. The mustard lore is from Gainer, Signs, Cures, and Witchery, p. 107; The nutmeg lore is from Hyatt, *Adams County,* p. 282; and the red pepper lore is from Fahrun, *Italian Folk Magic,* p. 99. .
3. Sugar lore here comes from a few key sources, including the Brown Collection previously mentioned and *A Dictionary of Superstitions,* by Iona Opie and Moira Tatum (Oxford Univ. Press, 1989), p. 381. The garlic lore is from Fahrun, *Italian Folk Magic,* p. 96.
4. The above bits of bread lore are all found in Vance Randolph's *Ozark Magic and Folklore* (Columbia Univ. Press, 1947), pp. 56–60; *Folk-Lore From Adams County, Illinois,* by Harry M. Hyatt (Alma Egan Hyatt Foundation, 1935), pp. 17, 81–86; T**he Frank C. Brown Collection of North Carolina Folklore,** Vol. VI (1961), pp. 350–54, 460–63, 538-4; and Daniel and Lucy Thomas's *Kentucky Superstitions* (Franklin Classics, 2018 [1920]).
5. Many of the examples listed here for cake lore are found in *American Folklore: An Encyclopedia,* edited by Jan Brunvand (Garland Publishing, 1998); *A Dictionary of Superstitions,* by Iona Opie and Moira Tatem (Oxford Univ. Press, 1989); Hyatt's *Folklore of Adams County*; and *The Encyclopedia of American Folklore,* edited by Linda S. Watts (Facts on File, 2006). The example from Samuel Pepys is from his famous *Diary,* an excellent edition of which can be found from Penguin Publishing, 2003.
6. The wine-related lore here comes from Opie & Tatem, *Dictionary of Superstitions,* p. 69; Hyatt, *Adams County,* p. 310; and Fahrun, Italian Folk Magic, pp. 123–24.

10. Washing Up

Magic in Everything, Including the Kitchen Sink!

Until Laine was sixteen, her family didn't have a dishwasher. Well, they did have one, and her name was Laine. But an electric one didn't happen until circa the turn of the century. Okay, that was actually 2001 and only about twenty years ago, but that makes it sound so much more legitimate, doesn't it?!

It has to be done. There's just no way of getting around it. The floors must be kept clean, at least within reason, the spots need to be wiped from the mirrors, and there's a stain on the knees of someone's pants that needs to be pretreated before it gets thrown in the wash. But it doesn't have to be all mundane cleaning and pruney fingers, because we can find plenty of magic in cleaning up.

You use What?!—Magical Cleaning Supplies

Harshly scented cleaning solutions with abrasive chemicals and artificial odors may not seem like a particularly likely place to find folk magic, but it's there if you look for it. One of the most common household cleaning agents, ammonia, acts as a substitute for urine in some spells. Some practitioners say that ammonia can be used in spells focusing on protection and in spells designed to improve sales, either at a business or of a home. Others mention ammonia's great psychic cleansing powers and note that putting a little bit down the drain after a house blessing and cleansing will help finish the job.[1]

In a similar vein, we find plenty of uses for that old pantry/laundry/cleaning-closet standby, vinegar. All vinegars can be good for simple crossing (cursing) work, according to Southern folk magic, which includes the use of "souring" work that employs vinegar. One of the best-known versions of this sort of hexing involves putting a representation of someone into a jelly jar, covering it with vinegar, and closing it. Then you simply shake it daily to "sour" the person's life. Some people also add things like chili pepper flakes (to make them feel the heat for whatever transgression they've made) or mustard seeds cooked in a cast iron skillet until brown or black (or you can use black mustard seeds, but the cooking makes the seeds give off their harsh, cutting oil to boost the working). There are contemporary versions of these "souring jars" that add things like iron nails, and these seem to be rooted in earlier practices. I found an interesting hexing combination of vinegar and ammonia in Zora Neale Hurston's article on "Hoodoo in America":

> To Punish.
> When you want a person who is indicated punished, write the name of the person in jail on a slip of paper and put it in a sugar bowl, or some other receptacle of the kind. Put in red pepper, black pepper, one penny nail, fifteen cents of ammonia and two keys. Drop one key down in the bowl and lean the other against the side of the bowl. Go to the bowl every day at twelve and turn the key that is standing against the side of the bowl to keep the person locked in jail. Every time you turn the key, add a little vinegar[2]

We find it interesting that ammonia and vinegar seem to be able to perform cleansing functions in a household, but when applied to an individual, their corrosive nature seems to become destructive. We think this illustrates the principle of the two-sided coin of magic nicely, though, as the same ingredient that can save you from nasty spirits might also be turned around to damn an enemy. It is crucial to note that adding things like metal to ammonia or vinegar can cause some very powerful chemical reactions, and when sealed in a jar (a sugar bowl's lid doesn't completely seal) these can eventually explode! Practice safe hex, and don't get hit with cursed shrapnel, please!

The famous Pine-Sol cleaner has been found in grocery stores for almost 60 years. The product was born in Mississippi, and even today it contains pine oil (along with a hefty dose of chemical salts and alcohols) to give it cleaning power and its trademark scent. Pine oil is another spiritual cleanser and refresher, in addition to having some mundane cleaning properties as an antibacterial and antiseptic disinfectant. It works a lot like lemon does in spiritual cleansing—so much so that one of Pine-Sol's first offshoot scents was lemon, although now they have half a dozen aromas to choose from. While we'd never suggest using a commercial pine cleaner on the body (or in the body especially . . . that's a big no-no!), some folk magical traditions have used pine oil-based treatments for medical ailments (there's a fine example in Pennsylvania German folk medicine from John George Hohman's *Long Lost Friend*, for instance). So the presence of lemon and pine has the power to cut through spiritual ailments as well as the nasty germs lingering on your kitchen floor. You can make a variant of your own pine oil cleaner by adding pine oil to some salted water with some castile soap dissolved in it. It won't be as strong as Pine-Sol, but it also won't be quite as harsh. You could even add a bit of lemon juice or lemon oil to that for extra kick (spiritually and microbially speaking).

What about simple soap, though? Does that have any magical uses or applications? Well, soap is a common focus for superstitions regarding luck. For example, theater folk in touring shows sometimes adhere to a belief that leaving one's soap behind after a stay in one city means bad luck or a poor performance in the next. Nowadays, of course, most hotels provide fresh cakes of soap for each guest, but many people still carry their own soap bars or other hygiene products, and the belief once attached to soap now applies to shampoos, conditioners, deodorants, tampons, shaving cream, and more. Still other superstitions tell that dropping or breaking soap is a bad omen, usually tied to a loss or death. A story from the Scottish Highlands in the late nineteenth century tells of a woman who repeatedly lost a large cake of soap while doing the washing, with her local shopkeeper becoming increasingly concerned for her health. Eventually, the woman was found drowned in the place where she'd been washing.[3] A Welsh belief says that if someone borrows soap from you and thanks you for it, they are a witch, although it just seems polite to us (but then, we sympathize with witches an awful lot).

Soap is also a good magical tool because it has a number of practical applications. It's relatively easy to get soap-making kits using glycerin at craft stores now, or even to learn old-fashioned soap-making using lye and fat (although we advise you seek professional guidance when learning this, as lye is caustic). Once the soap begins to "trace," or turn into streaks of soap within the mixture, you can often add magical ingredients like crumbled flowers or herbs. Even without knowing how to make soap, it's easy to apply this method using hand-soap dispensers in the home. Simply add a few magical ingredients like dried cloves and allspice for friendliness or a bit of rose water for gentle love to the dispenser and top with the liquid hand soap. Delicately shake or swirl the contents to infuse the soap with your ingredients. To make it even more magical, you can include things like written charms on paper, small bones, or even little plastic figures representing your intention to the bottle. A short prayer over the bottle to activate it, and voila! You've got some magical soap that will give you a little enchanted boost every time you wash your hands (remember to sing the "Happy Birthday" song twice! For magical reasons, of course).

Don't Sweep After Dark—When and How to Clean

Well, whenever things get dirty, of course! Traditionally, though, there are a few rules about the timing of cleaning one's domicile. It's always nice to start the New Year off with a clean, well-appointed home, for example. In some traditions, this is not mere vanity or hygiene, but a spiritual necessity that must be done on New Year's Eve to ensure that the home is clear and ready for the coming year. Although some traditions warn you to not do any washing on New Year's Day lest you wash away all luck for the coming year.

Even beyond holidays, there are some beliefs about cleaning that shape how people do their magical work. A good example is the common English (and Southern) folk belief that one shouldn't sweep after dark. Doing so is thought to bring bad luck or offend particular spirits like house fairies, and so sweeping is best left to the daylight hours. That also makes sense, given that sweeping in the dark means you're likely to miss a few more crumbs than you might otherwise!

When you're mopping, you might want to just dump your water out when you're done, but if your cleaning involves doing magic then you should always save a cup or so of the dirty wash-water. Then, you can take it and throw it toward the setting sun in the west if you're banishing or removing something unwanted or pour it out in the east as the sun rises if your wash-water was to help bring in something like love or money.

You probably think you know how to clean just fine already, right? Funnily enough, in magical practices the method of cleaning that you use is often just as important as any ingredients or tools you employ. Workers in Southern Conjure and Hoodoo traditions tend to have specific techniques for sweeping, often going from the topmost floor of the house to the bottom and working from the back of each floor toward the front (though I've seen variations on that, often depending on specific needs—getting rid of a bad spirit might involve sweeping out the back door, for example).

Clearing the Air—The Power of Magical Smells

You don't do windows, you say? Well, you should at least open them! Whenever you do a good house-cleansing, throwing up the windows and letting some fresh air circulate is vital to getting everything "right." It helps balance out all the forces in the home, allows bad spirits to leave, and refreshes the air in the house. It's cold to do this in winter, of course, but turning the heat off for ten minutes and letting a little fresh air in can make all the difference in getting a home feeling good and happy again. Likewise, the doors should be opened for a bit to let the air circulate.

When it comes to washing doors and windows, you can really use any of the same washes you might use in floor washing, although they can leave streaks in many cases. You can also use a variety of other ingredients to get things right at all your entrances and exits. For example, many folks take a little olive oil (or holy oil, which is basically blessed and sometimes lightly scented olive oil) and make a little sigil in the corner of every window, to seal that entrance against evil intrusions. Some folks put blue bottles in the windows, or jars full of sand or marbles, in the hopes that any witches who might try to get in will be forced to count the contents of the container and be unable to do so before daybreak (when their power ends). You can make a wash water of red brick dust, urine, and salt in warm water and use it to scrub your door to add a powerful layer of protection. You can also sprinkle salt or brick dust lines down at the threshold and in the sills of every window to keep out unwanted spirits and spells.

Once the house has been aired out and all the windows and doors cleaned and opened for a while, some folks like to light some incense, use room sprays, or even just make a little something in the kitchen to add an element of magic to the home. We've already mentioned pine and citrus scents as powerful agents for spiritual and physical cleansing. Other odoriferous offerings to your home can include:

- **Fresh Bread** – One of the best symbols of abundance and prosperity. Bake a loaf in your oven and let the scent fill the home. Cookies are also good for this.

- **Floral Scents** – Like jasmine, rose, or lavender. All of these have specific uses and add specific magical "vibrations" to an area (rose fragrances inspire love to many, for example), so look into the flowers you like and figure out what note they will set in your newly cleaned domicile.

- **Sweeteners** – Sugar can be a bit strong when burned. If you are airing your house out, however, a little honey, brown sugar, molasses, or even table sugar might be a good thing to burn or warm on the stove, as it will provide a sublimely "sweet" feeling to the area.⁴

So That's Where the Missing Sock Went—Mudroom Magic

When someone shows off their living arrangements, they may sweep and mop and vacuum in places like the living room, kitchen, or even bedroom because they want to make a good impression on their guests. The mudroom—a space where we keep cleaning supplies, wash our unmentionables, and kick off a pair of dirty shoes after soccer practice—often winds up just getting hidden away behind closed doors. For many people, laundry is strangely private. We don't like the idea of someone seeing a pair of our panties or a loose bra flung over the back of a chair, and our soiled clothes stuffed into hampers are kept carefully out of view from those who do not already live in our households. For many folks, though, laundry can be a strangely public affair. Cory remembers making plenty of late-night trips to the laundromat during my young adult years, often with a friend or a good book. Laine went to a laundromat attached to a seedy bar in college, so there was no mystery for her when a sock went missing (…it was definitely the beer). Everyone is on equal footing in the local Duds 'n' Suds, with the spinning, whirling, whooshing clothes tumbling behind glass portals like a psychedelic television program.

Even beyond laundry's hypnotic qualities, there's magic to be found in the soapy water and the fresh-from-the-dryer joy of burying your face in a clean, warm set of sheets.

Some of the ingredients used in laundering have parallels in the cleaning supplies we've mentioned already. For example, using a room or linen spray that incorporates scents like lavender or jasmine can provide peaceful sleep or intimate connection to those sharing the bed. There's a special bit of color magic that appears in Southern folk magic including Hoodoo and conjure involving the use of something called "laundry bluing." Bluing often comes as a powder or in little hard pellets called "bluestones," the most famous of which would probably be the Reckitt's brand. The blue color once may have been derived from the indigo plant, but it is more commonly derived from iron now. (It also had a form that involved copper sulfate at one point that proved to be less than healthy over long periods of use.) The blue color gets added to laundry to enhance whites, as the faint tint of blue counteracts the natural yellowing that happens to white clothes over time, making them appear brighter and whiter. Why is this magical? Well, the bluing acts as a purifier, removing harmful influences and spirits, while also adding a layer of magical protection, especially when using the iron-based bluings. Some practitioners will even add a bluestone to their floor washes to use when dealing with nasty spirits they want to get rid of or to help settle a house after a period of unrest.

Sheets can also be "powdered" between washes. One Southern Conjure woman we know mentions that she remembers sheets being powdered with talcum or baby powder every night before bed to freshen them and provide special protection to those sleeping there.⁵ You can make a simple sheet powder by taking three parts cornstarch, one part baking soda, and a good-sized pinch of baby powder and mixing them well.

Then you simply give a very light sprinkle over your bottom sheet and top sheet before bed. The powder will help keep the sheets smelling and feeling fresh, and the salt-like baking soda will make a light protective barrier around you during the night.

Finally, the laundry basket can be a source of some good magic. The clothes we wear are very intimate to us, and so, magically, they are considered effective proxies for us in spell work. If you want to make a useful poppet of someone—including yourself—finding a worn and unwashed sock or T-shirt and transforming that into your doll figure is very effective and rooted in folklore. There are several stories that tell of old pairs of long underwear pillaged for spell ingredients to make things like poppets, charm bags, and packet spell.

That's a lot of cleaning! But it's always good to have a clean home, for practical and spiritual reasons. Give some of these a go and see how they work for you! And if you missed your New Year's cleaning deadline, well, you can always do these things during your spring cleaning.

NOTES:

1. See Catherine Yronwode's *Hoodoo Herb & Root Magic* (2002) in her entry on "Ammonia," and Draja Mickaharic's *Spiritual Cleansing* (1982 [2022 reprint]) for more on the way this ingredient is used in a variety of folk magical applications.
2. From Zora Neale Hurston's "Hoodoo in America," in *Journal of American Folklore 44*, no. 174 (1931): 382.
3. This story is found in an abridged form in Opie and Tatum's *A Dictionary of Superstitions* (Oxford Univ. Press, 1989).
4. Mickaharic, *Spiritual Cleansing*.
5. See Starr Casas, "The Making of a Starr: Working Old Style Conjure," in *Llewellyn's Complete Book of North American Folk Magic* (Llewellyn Publications, 2023).

11. Cobwebs, Dust, & Dirt

Or, Sorcerous Reasons to Neglect Your Chores

One of the inevitable facts about the junk drawer—and by extension our everyday lives—is that it can get very messy. Whether we keep a tidy home or we accept a bit of clutter and a more "lived in" look to our domiciles, no space we occupy is immune to a little dust and dirt gathering over time. Before you start twirling your feather dusters in the corners and wiping the tops of the shelves, you should know that even the messy parts of life have their magical history.

In the coming pages, let's make a little space for the cobwebs and the smudges and the grease, and have a little fun getting dirty with the spellbinding side of the untidy.

Magic Beneath Your Feet: A Field Guide to Various Magical Dirts

Dirt, soil, earth, dust—we call the stuff that makes up the very ground we walk on a lot of names. It can be composed of dozens of minerals and consist of clay, limestone, loess, peat, chalk, sand, and more. Trace amounts of metals and gases can be contained within it. Under every square foot, there can be hundreds of feet of mycelium—the thin threads of fungal life that connect one side of a forest to another in some cases. There can be creatures milling about, like earthworms, beetles, centipedes, and grubs. I know, I know, you're rethinking the choice to wear flip-flops now or go barefoot, but we are part of all this too. The dirt beneath us is what eventually reclaims our bodies in many cases, and the dust settling on your furniture is often mostly made up of the dead skin and hair cells your body sheds on a daily basis.   Side note: Over time, you could probably save up enough of it to make a sort of Frankenstein version of yourself, and with enough glue you've got a companion for the carpool lane!

Dirt is ubiquitous, but the dirt of any particular place is unique. It can be used in forensics to identify suspects in cases where a bit of garden soil stuck to a shoe tells the story of someone being somewhere they shouldn't have been. Sir Arthur Conan Doyle's famous detective, Sherlock Holmes, identified a number of soils on sight as part of his criminal investigations, for example, and that use of soil in criminology is hardly limited to fiction.

The uniqueness of soil particles in particular places is also what ties it to magic. Dirt gathered from particular locations can become a way to bring the enchanted properties of those locales into one's home or cauldron, so to speak. Here are just a few of the types of better-known magical dirts found in folk magic:

Crossroads Dirt - This is simply dirt collected from a crossroads—the intersection of two or more pathways. In some cases, the soil needs to be gathered from the "four corners" of the crossroads, meaning the V-shaped intersection points around the central crossing. Crossroads dirt is useful for interactions that require contact with a spirit realm since an intersection like this is considered a liminal space between worlds. It can also be used for opening up new opportunities (work that is traditionally called "Road Opening" work).

Graveyard Dirt - Dirt collected from the graves of particular individuals has a fairly long history in folk magic. There are a wide variety of graveyard dirts that can be collected, often depending on *from whom* they are being collected. Some accounts talk about getting dirt from over the "heart" of a soldier, for example (the area of the grave that would be closest to the mid-chest in the coffin below). That soldier's grave dust would then be used in protection charms, or even to attack someone magically for a transgression. Dirt taken from the "head" of a judge might be used to make the law work favorably in one's case, or to turn a legal case against someone else. There are several stories about nabbing dirt from children's graves and employing their aid in anything from love to cursing, although one would have to grapple fairly hard with the ethics of that, we think. Some stories say the dirt is taken from the top foot or so of soil at a gravesite, while others insist that a person must go up to an arm's-length deep into the soil to gather the dirt properly.[1] In almost all cases, though, graveyard dirt must be "bought," or paid for in some way. Some will bring pennies or dimes to place at the grave or in the dirt, and some will leave offerings of flowers, whiskey, or other earthly delights in return for the dirt and the spirit's aid. Since taking dirt from a grave is considered desecration in many places, it's advisable to check local laws before attempting this. If you decide, though, to donate your time cleaning local cemeteries, and you happen to clean a grave and keep a bit of the dirt you sweep off? Well, this would probably fit the bill magically, and your service cleaning up would be a good form of payment.

Brick Dust - This is not exactly a "dirt," but instead the powdered form of red clay bricks. Ones from old buildings are particularly good (as modern bricks are engineered with minerals to create a stronger, lighter structure). The red clay used in the bricks has associations with blood due to its high iron oxide content, which gives it a distinctive ruddy hue. Blood is also red due to oxidized iron, so this is a reasonable correlation. The bricks are powdered by smashing them thoroughly with hammers or other crushing forces, and the dirt can be sprinkled at thresholds and property boundaries as a form of protection. Bricks are a wall-building item, and their blood connection adds a bit of that "living" power to them.

Foot Track Dirt - One traditional dirt bewitchment comes from the African-derived practice of "foot-track magic." This works one of two ways: either a person can gather the dirt left from someone's footprint to work specific magic on them from a distance, or they can scatter dirts and other ingredients where someone will walk over them and absorb their occult powers through the feet. The dirt gathered from someone's footprints is particularly potent and is a powerful way to connect them to a magical working. If you intend to do long-term spellwork on someone, using dirt from their footprint—or even gathered from their shoes—would be a great way to maintain a bond with them during your witchery.[2]

Building Dirts - If you happen to live near a hospital or medical center, it might be worth picking up a little bottle of the dirt from the grounds (although if you're there as a patient, collecting dirt may be the furthest thing from your mind). Hospital dirt is used in healing spells or spells in which warding off sickness is required. Similarly, dust collected from a bank can be used in money-based spells, or even spells designed to help acquire property or business loans. A good version of this spell would be to take a bit of bank dirt and the business card of a loan officer at the bank and put them both into a little bottle of honey or syrup to make them view you more favorably. Finally, dirt taken from the land around or under a courthouse is excellent for dealing with legal issues, according to folklore. Typical uses include adding it to a spell designed to help avoid (or encourage) a verdict or using it in a working to gain favorable outcomes from a judge.

Each of these can be used as a material for crafting little packet charms or talismans—writing a wish on a piece of paper and adding a bit of the dirt and a few other ingredients, then folding and wrapping it in red thread to carry in one's pocket or purse. They can also be sprinkled around a space to imbue it with the power of the dirt's source, used to stuff dolls, or mingled with wax to make figures.

Some people will also add dirts to things like incenses, bathwaters, or even oils to use in spellcraft. It's useful to remember, though, that in some cases dirt collected from near old buildings may contain things like lead from deteriorating paint. Crossroads dirt may have pollutants from passing cars and runoff from paving and road treatments. While a pinch of dirt in an oil used to dress a candle or tossed onto a bonfire under an open sky likely won't have any ill effects, always exercise caution about the things that come into contact with your body.

Tangled Up in Witchery! Spiders, Webs, and Buggy Magic

In Cory's house, he's the one you call if there's something creepy-crawly on the bathroom wall. He'll bring a glass and a bit of paper to cover it, catch the little houseguest, and safely remove it to another location (outside of the house). Only then can everyone else go back to showering and brushing teeth as normal.

Squashing spiders is just one of those things that we try to avoid on principle: the spider's just living its life, after all. Beyond that, there are folkloric reasons for treating them well. In folklore throughout English-speaking countries, for example, there is a rhyme that goes, "If you wish to live and thrive, let a spider run alive." Another rhyme says, "Who kills a spider, Bad Luck betides her."[3] Killing spiders is considered bad luck, and so letting them live is thought to protect a house and give it good luck. There's some good reasoning here, as the spiders—especially if they are not particularly venomous species like black widows or brown recluses—are often able to catch and kill more threatening insects, such as mosquitos or flies, that might spread diseases.

The spider's home is also of folkloric value. In the world of theater, for example, it is considered bad luck to remove cobwebs found backstage or in dressing rooms before or during the run of a show. Webs found in barns or on boats are also lucky, and if they are removed there is some ill streak of luck coming, such as a horse going lame or a boat capsizing or being lost at sea. Spiders are thought to be beneficent protectors of these spaces. Remember crying at the end of *Charlotte's Web*, for example? There are even tales that say that a similar spider wove a web above the cradle of baby Jesus in the manger to protect him, thus earning a blessing.[4] If you happen to have a spider that builds a web near your doorway, watch to see if your initials appear in it. If so, that's thought to be a sign of good luck to follow soon. One bit of lore I have heard from a Southern person from the Appalachian area, handed down from their grandmother, said that the exception to this rule was if you had "showed your teeth" to a spider and then found your name or initials in the web, which could be a sign of death to come. In New England, spiderwebs found on the ground in the morning are a sign of good weather for the rest of the day, and if someone sees spiderwebs in the air or attached to trees or sail riggings in autumn, it indicates more fine weather for the rest of the season.

Cobwebs have a very long history of being deployed in medicine. Roman historian Pliny the Elder recorded that fractures of the head were treated with a mixture of cobwebs, oil, and vinegar, and that cobwebs were used to patch cuts made while shaving.[5] This application of webs to cuts and scrapes was so common that even Shakespeare references it in his play *A Midsummer Night's Dream* (III i.) when one of the fairies named Cobweb is told that they should be applied to a cut finger. The cobweb lore spread into North America, and several sources in Appalachia and the Ozarks mention using cobwebs to treat small cuts or wounds. This led to many people collecting them over time to use as a sort of gauze or bandage.[6]

There are some slightly more gruesome applications of spiders in folk magic. For example, there's a well-known curse used in Hoodoo called a "Live Things in You" working. In this spell, a dried spider and its eggs are ground into a powder and added to the food of a target. The person thus cursed will have the sensation of crawling and itching on their body and even see things moving under their skin until the curse is removed. Other insects, such as wasps or centipedes, can be used for this, but spider eggs are a fairly common ingredient. One other bit of lore says that if you have pertussis, also known as "whooping cough," you can treat it by catching a spider in a bit of cloth or a pair of walnut shells, then tying this up to be worn around the neck. It is said that when the spider expires, the cough will go away.[7]

Considering how many wonderful things spiders can do, though, why kill them? I'd much rather have a spider write my initials and tell me I'm "SOME PIG," like Charlotte did for Wilbur.

We can't cover every bit of insect-related enchantment here, but we thought we'd leave you with a few more bits of folklore about the magic of our six-plus-legged neighbors:

- Wasp nests are often used in folk magic. In some cases, they are powdered and added to cursing mixtures, but one of the most interesting uses for them involves adding a bit of the powdered nest of a dirt dauber wasp to charms—or even food— to maintain a happy home and a healthy domestic partnership.
- An empty hornet's nest is often hung in the attic of homes. This deters any new wasps from building there and is thought to add protection and domestic blessings to the house. It especially is thought to keep passion in a marriage or partnership.
- Some people in the South will watch to see how high up the wasps build their nests each year. If they build fairly close to the ground, the coming winter is thought to be mild with little snow, but if they build high, expectations are set for a very white winter.
- Wooly worms are also sometimes used to predict weather. These are little tiger moth caterpillars with brown and black bands of "wool" (actually a form of hair). If the bands of black are thick, a cold and snowy winter is thought to be coming (although a few people say the thickness of the brown bands is the better indicator).
- Earthworms are sometimes used to make treatments for a variety of illnesses. In some accounts they're fried in a fat of some kind, like lard, and then the resulting goop is rolled and dried into pills that are used to treat jaundice. Another application says to collect earthworms in a glass jar and leave it in a sunny window until it's turned to oil. This is used as a topical treatment for pain (think Ben-Gay, but worm-based). Worm oil was a common treatment in the Renaissance, and worm oil jars can be found in a number of museum collections.[8]

Don't Throw It Away! I'm Enchanting with That!

As a final note, we wanted to touch a bit on what our friend and author of *Southern Cunning* (Moon Books, 2019), Aaron Oberon, has called "trash magic." This stems from an understanding that most folk magic comes from people who don't often have a lot, and so if something is going into the trash pile it's something of a loss. That also means that trash is a powerful thing, because it's the last banishment, and something going into a plastic bag to be buried in a landfill can make us feel very removed from our own impact on the world around us.

Trash, though, can be a source of magic. For one thing, you can use the banishing power of trash to dispose of some spell ingredients if you're trying to permanently get rid of someone from your life. Think of the "breakup spell" so many people do after a relationship ends. This is the sort of spell that gets done by people who don't even realize just how close to a magical working it is. They might throw photos, letters, mementos, or more into a small trash can and light it on fire (not in a bedroom please, but somewhere with fire safety gear nearby and outside with adequate ventilation. Practice safe hex!). The ashes can be buried or added to other garbage, mingled with rotting food, or even flushed down a toilet to really eliminate that person's presence. Writing someone's name on a banana peel and watching it brown, then decay, can be a powerfully cathartic experience too.

Used lunch bags—the brown paper ones especially—are often used to write petition papers. These are basically small written spell charms with a request for a specific outcome—a new job, a returning lover, or a little windfall of cash—that are frequently combined with candle-burning or charm bag spells.

The creatures associated with trash—flies, rats, and even raccoons—all have their own lore worth digging into. Flies are one of the creatures sometimes used in the "Live Things in You" spell mentioned earlier, for example. Rats are actually notoriously clean creatures, but when in close proximity to humans they can wind up living in squalid conditions and even carrying diseases, making them a perfect "messenger" creature to work with going between "upper" and "lower" worlds (like streets versus sewers).

When it comes to creatures like spiders and rats, or things like cobwebs and dirt, our first impulse is often to reject them or ignore them. With just a little bit of knowledge, though, even that dust bunny under the couch might be holding onto a bit of extra enchantment. So go ahead and grab a little bit of dirt in a jar, collect your cobwebs, and be nice to your house spider. If anyone asks, just say you're not ignoring the housework, you're gathering spell ingredients.

NOTES:

1. Much of this lore can be found in the work of pioneering folklorist Zora Neale Hurston. In her article, "Hoodoo in America," she outlines the process for buying graveyard dirt by bringing seven pennies to a grave and collecting the dirt in a jar from various points on the grave (*Journal of American Folklore*, vol. 34, no. 174, 1931, pp. 317–417). Then, in her survey of folk magic and religion in Haiti and Jamaica, *Tell My Horse*, she examines the claim that the dirt taken from deep in the grave was imbued with the germs that had killed the coffin's occupant during outbreaks of scarlet fever, yellow fever, and typhoid, even pointing to previous medical literature that indicated the germs for these ailments lingered in the soil years after death (Harper Collins, 1938 [2008], pp. 237–8). This dirt was then used to "curse" by attempting to spread disease to a target, but this is obviously a little shaky in terms of medical fact and ethical implications.
2. An example, from Hurston's "Hoodoo in America" article: "Take the right foot track of the enemy and parch it. (Use dark bottle.) Take nine dirt dauber nests and parch and powder them, some ground red pepper, get a soiled sock or new piece of cotton goods, and tie all this up in it. Turn it from you as you work. Carry to river at twelve noon. When you get about forty feet from river, run fast and wheel suddenly at brink and hurl dirt over left shoulder and don't look back. Say, 'Go and go quick, in the name of the Lord.'" Similar lore citing the use of footprints and tracks in folk magic indicate it could be used for love or banishment, as well as cursing (Frank C. Brown, v.6, p. 570). *Lore from North Carolina* notes that even stepping in someone else's footprints can be used to give that person headaches (Frank C. Brown, v.6, p. 206).
3. Found in *A Dictionary of Superstitions*, by Iona Opie and Moira Tatem (Oxford Univ. Press, 1989), p. 371) and cited to 1863 and 1909 editions of the publication *Notes & Queries*.
4. For more lore on spiderwebs in weather prediction, and the story about the spider in the manger, see *Household Tales: With Other Traditional Remains, Collected in the Counties of York, Lincoln, Derby, & Nottingham*, by Sidney Oldall Addy (1895), p. 66. The lore about webs on the ground or in the air comes from *A Treasury of New England Folklore*, by Benjamin A. Botkin, ed. (Bonanza Books, 1947 [1965]), pp. 347–50.
5. Pliny the Elder. *The Natural History of Pliny*, J. Bostock and H. T. Riley, trans. (1855-7), vol. V, p. 410.
6. These bits of cobweb-treatment lore are found in *The Foxfire Book*, Eliot Wigginton, ed. (Anchor Books, 1972), p. 231; *Witches, Ghosts, and Signs*, by Patrick W. Gainer (West Virginia Univ. Press, 2008), pp. 109–11; and *Ozark Magic and Folklore*, by Vance Randolph (Columbia Univ. Press, 1947), p. 101.
7. Opie & Tatum, *Dictionary*, p. 370-71.
8. See "Syrup Jars for Earthworm Oil," on *Ridiculously Interesting*, 15 July 2019 (https://ridiculouslyinteresting.com/2019/07/15/earthworm-oil/).

12. Brooms

A Sweeping Survey of Spells

Why do witches ride brooms? Simply put, they don't. Not really in the way we think of, anyway. In fact, we've yet to see any of them actually fly in the physical sense (although there are suggestions that entheogens—divine intoxicants—can be applied). Yet few tools or symbols are as quickly associated with a witch as the household broom. This domestic keystone of American folk magical practices appears in numerous cultures and settings. Sometimes it retains its associations with witchcraft, but very often it is simply a reflection—and manifestation—of the relatively mundane nature of magic in the lives of historical folk.

Not Just for Flying Anymore: Brooms beyond Flight

Cory was once asked to help on a project for a local folklorist looking for information on broom lore, and he wound up with easily twenty pages of notes on the topic from a wide variety of sources. To say that brooms are magical is a vast understatement. When we think of brooms and magic, however, we often first conjure up the image of a witch sailing across a full moon in flight astride her broomstick. There are good reasons we make those associations, but flight is likely the least magical thing a broom can accomplish.

Still, brooms are the ubiquitous witch-in-transit mode of choice in the popular imagination, despite not having the singular association with witches they currently do until the nineteenth and twentieth centuries. To be sure, brooms were sometimes thought to be used in witchcraft, but riding them at night was more of an invention of popular children's stories than of folk belief among European or American groups. A fairly common but not entirely well-documented reason for this association may come from medieval witchcraft trial records in places like Italy and Germany. In those locations, some accused witches, or those who claimed to witness witches doing their wicked work, indicated that the broom was used to apply a thick magical unguent to the witch's body (especially in particularly sensitive areas of her anatomy), which would then cause her to go into a trance and experience a form of psychic "flight" out of her body. While these accounts do pop up, the broom is hardly the only tool indicated, and the above-mentioned farm implements like the pitchfork would be just as likely to get a nod during an interrogation.[1]

A number of the ideas we have about witches and brooms really only appear once printing becomes popular, as early woodblock print books and broadsides were where the first widely disseminated pictures of witches riding brooms appeared. The conventional thought was that witches were using these brooms as a means of flying away to their diabolical meetings (called Sabbats because there was a lot of anti-Semitic sentiment mixed into early Modern witch portrayals). In folklore, brooms were only one of the preferred methods for nocturnal transportation to Sabbat rites. Other mounts included pitchforks, stangs, goats, and eggshells (and even the occasional human being fitted with a magical bridle, in the cases of alleged "hag-riding").[2]

Head to your cleaning closet, pick up your broom, and hold it in your hand. Even if it is a cheap assembly of plastic and aluminum, you are holding quite possibly the most quintessentially "witchy" tool available. Look at Halloween decorations, television shows like Bewitched, or even the covers of books marketed to magical practitioners, and you will see brooms everywhere. People, by and large, believe that witches spend their time flying around at night on broomsticks, but only because the type of magic we see depicted in popular culture insists on instant results. Even a brief glance at true broom lore will tell you that the power in a broom is the slow-brewing, long-simmering kind.

Sweeping Clean vs. Knowing the Corners: Brooms in Domestic Folk Magic

Where brooms really get magical is not in the night sky, but in the home itself. Dating back to the Roman period, brooms have been used for magical rites to protect and purify the domestic space as a way of counteracting spiritual forces that sought to do harm to those who dwelled there. Brooms, with their numerous bristles and built-in associations with removing debris and dirt, could disrupt harmful spirits and force them to leave a home (or at least delay them from taking any hostile actions). Eli Edward Burriss notes in his Taboo, Magic, Spirits that the Romans believed a new baby and its mother were in danger of being tormented by woodland spirits—particularly one called Silvanus—and goes on to quote St. Augustine about a three-part, three-tool ritual in which several spirits were invoked to provide protection.

> '. . . After the birth of the child, three protecting divinities are summoned lest the god Silvanus enter during the night and harass mother and child; and to give tokens of those guardian divinities three men by night surround the threshold of the house and first strike it with an ax and a pestle; then they sweep it off with a broom, that, by giving these signs of worship, the god Silvanus may be kept from entering.'-St. Augustine

Burriss goes on to note that the iron in several of the implements provide the expected protection from evil, but the ceremonial sweeping is what actually drives away the wicked spirit. The axe, composed of iron, would have been threatening to a forest divinity, and a pestle would assert domestic control while also symbolically "pulverizing" any rogue harmful spirits lingering in the doorway. The broom, though, cast out the spirits and denied them reentry.[3] Other groups, including the Roma in Europe, deployed a mixture of broom straws and iron under the pillows of birthing women to protect them in a similar way. Later Christian traditions picked up the sweeping spell, including a rite recorded in the nineteenth century that involved sweeping salt out of a household to confuse and deter the spirits of the dead. The salt was then gathered and deposited in the churchyard, returning the dead to their rightful place.

The broom's many bristles also make it a helpful tool for preventing harm. Leaving a broom across a threshold was believed to prevent a witch from entering a house, as she would have to stop and count the bristles on her way in. In North American folklore, brooms retain much of their purifying and protective power, but we also see signs of new adaptations. African American folk practices show a strong connection between brooms and domestic bonds. For example, one well-known African American cultural tradition involves a wedding practice of "jumping the broom" to seal the ceremony. Rooted in the deeply oppressive and controlling plantation slave system of a pre-Emancipation United States, jumping the broom became a form of de facto marriage among African American enslaved people, since formal marriage among them was legally forbidden in many places.[4] The practice is common enough that in 2011 a romantic comedy film about an African American wedding was titled Jumping the Broom.

The broom's connection to marriage and the household appears in a number of superstitions and folk spells addressing weddings and love:

- Sweeping under someone's feet was almost always a bad sign. In most cases, it meant the person who had been "swept" would not marry (either soon or ever, depending on who described the belief).

- Sweeping under someone's feet could, on the other hand, result in marriage. If you swept under the feet of someone sitting on a table, they were to be married before the year ended. Sweeping under a person's chair means that the person will marry more than once.

- One belief says that you should not let anyone sweep entirely around the chair on which you are sitting, or else you will remain single seven years longer.

- If you break a broom handle you will soon break someone's heart.

- Sweeping the house after dark was thought to bring sorrow in love and romance. In some cases, though, if you did find yourself sweeping at night, you could expect a "gentleman caller."

- Some believed that a broom could bring good luck in love. Young unmarried women could wet the bristles of a broom and sprinkle the water around their houses to invite love into their lives.

- If an engaged girl dropped a broom, she could divine her romantic future by the way it fell: if the handle pointed north, she or her fiancée will break their engagement, but a south-pointing broom meant she would marry him and live a happy life.

- It was considered very unlucky for a bride to see a broom on her wedding day before she went to church.
- And, of course, there's the proverb that "a new broom sweeps clean, but the old one knows the corners," which was a reminder not to give up what was good in pursuit of something shiny and novel (which translates to keeping one's marital vows).

The broom's protective power and its association with witches become increasingly complex in the New World. In addition to the broom's use as a powerful protective charm when put across your doorway, you can also reverse a jinx or witchcraft by stepping backwards over a broom. Brooms can also be a component of spells to reverse the evil eye, according to *curandero* (Mexican folk healing) lore. One account of a curandero treatment of *mal de ojo* (the evil eye) describes an intricate ritual involving an egg, some water, and a broom straw. In this particular treatment the broom straw was used as a sort of stylus to inscribe crosses onto an egg, which was then placed under the crib of an afflicted infant. To the surprise of everyone, the next day the egg was completely cooked through! The child, thankfully, was cured of his disorder.[5]

The broom has also been shown to be a protective object in popular culture. Who could forget the movie Practical Magic when Sally assembles a coven and asks each person to bring their own broomstick? Later, the brooms laid around end to end act as a protective circle.

We've also noticed an interesting modernization of broom lore and a tendency to conflate brooms with vacuums. Again we can turn to Practical Magic, where one of the ladies comes to the coven with her dustbuster® in hand. And *Hocus Pocus* gives us Mary Sanderson, who rides her upright vacuum like her two sisters ride brooms. In the 2022 sequel. she even "hoverboards" with the help of an enchanted pair of robot vacs. Many modern witches use their vacuums in similar ways to brooms. We've heard of putting a few drops of diluted essential oil (perhaps spearmint or frankincense) on a cotton ball in the bag of a vacuum to help spiritually cleanse the space. Not only does it help spread the oil and its scent throughout the room, the vacuum sucks up the negative energy much the same way a broom would sweep the energy away.[6]

Brooms also play a part in the magical lore of moving house, too. You are not supposed to take an old broom with you, but instead break it or burn it before leaving the house, and a new broom should be one of the very first objects you bring into a new home, too. Many people also believe one of the first things you should do in a new home is sweep it completely, from top to bottom and back to front. This provides a blessing on the house and clears away unwanted lingering spirits or energy that might cause problems for the new resident. Some traditions indicate that you should go to the fireplace as soon as you move into a new home, sweep it with a broom, then throw the ashes out the door to ensure that all bad luck is swept clean of the house before anyone sleeps there. Likewise, a new home can be blessed with good luck by throwing a broom over it.

Before we leave the topic of brooms completely, here are a few little spells, rituals, or traditions that might help make your broom seem more magical.

- If a bunch of straw comes out of a broom when sweeping, name it and place it over the door, and the person named will come to call.
- Sweep on New Year's Day, and your house will be dirty all year; but if you leave the dirt in a pile on the floor until the next day, your home will instead be clean all year.
- Sweeping on Monday causes bad luck (all week some say). But bad luck that comes from sweeping on Monday can be warded off by keeping the dirt in the house until the following day, or by sprinkling the dirt with salt and burning it.
- If you sweep on Monday, you are sweeping away all of your company that week.
- Folklorist and writer Zora Neale Hurston once recounted a spell she'd found among her informants. To draw your enemies to you (so that you may know who they are), clean out your stove, all the time keeping your wish in your mind, but don't speak it. Then break a stick into four pieces, all of them the same length, and pin them together in the middle . . . and set them afire . . . Then go to the four corners of the room, with your wish in your heart and mind, (but don't say it), and sprinkle salt. Then, when you see your enemies coming, go outside your door and throw your broom down careless and step over it into the house and talk to them across it . . . They can't come in, but they can't help from coming to your gate.
- To make an unwanted guest leave, place a broom upside down behind the door.
- If a very young child, without being told, picks up a broom and starts sweeping the house, you might as well prepare for a visitor, the idea apparently being that an innocent child can see things in the future that grown-ups cannot and knows that the house must be tidied up for the company.[7]

And just for fun, you should listen to blues legend Robert Johnson singing "I Believe I'll Dust My Broom." Sometimes a broom can be a metaphor for more than just magic.

NOTES

1. Those interrogations were notoriously biased. When not conducted under the threat or act of physical torture, psychological intimidation was often used to coax confessions or accusations out of people by the interrogators. Historian Ronald Hutton has done an excellent job surveying some of those accounts, including a review of some of the most famous trance-flight stories collected by historians like Carlo Ginzburg in Italy, and determined that while some stories may have a root in truth, they were often embellished by questioners. Hutton also notes that the typical narrative of church interrogations seeking heretics were far less common than local political authorities seeking to out subversive groups that threatened political harmony, and psychotropic-using witches entering trances would have been seen as very subversive. See Ronald Hutton, *The Witch: A History of Fear, from Ancient Times to the Present* (2017).
2. One bit of folklore recommends that householders thoroughly crush up their eggshells before depositing them on the family waste pile lest over-eager witches begin stealing the shells from the family for their night transits. In many tales, even if you helped a witch inadvertently, you gained her notice, and that could lead to trouble down the line. See *Historical Dictionary of Witchcraft*, by Jonathan Durrant and Michael D. Bailey (Scarecrow Press, 2012), pp. 23–24.
3. See Eli Edward Burriss, *Taboo, Magic, Spirits* (Macmillan Co., 1931), p. 35.
4. If you know much about the historical practices at the governmental and local levels that hedged and hemmed the legal options African Americans had in terms of marriage partners, home ownership, and other civil rights, this practice makes a tremendous amount of sense. African American magic, including Hoodoo, often reflected the need for domestic stability because of the bevy of threats most African Americans faced on a regular basis, so using a domestic tool in a marriage ritual was (and is) a way of protecting that union.
5. See Keith A. Neighbors, "Mexican-American Folk Diseases," *Western Folklore*, vol. 28, no. 4 (Oct. 1969), pp. 249-59.
6. Another fascinating trope in popular culture is to make the broom a sort of "living servant" of the witch. Think of Disney's *Fantasia* (1940), with its "Sorcerer's Apprentice" segment, in which an ambitious wizard's apprentice (played by Mickey Mouse) uses his magic hat to enchant a broom to haul water for him. Things soon get out of hand, with one broom becoming many and a veritable flood ensuing. Similar depictions of conscious brooms responding to their cartoon owners appear in *Looney Tunes*, where Witch Hazel's black broom seems to listen to (or flee from) her commands.
7. See Zora Neale Hurston's *Mules and Men* (1935) and her extended essay "Hoodoo in America" from the *Journal of American Folklore* (1931) for a plethora of great African American folk magical lore, much of it focused on domestic items like brooms.

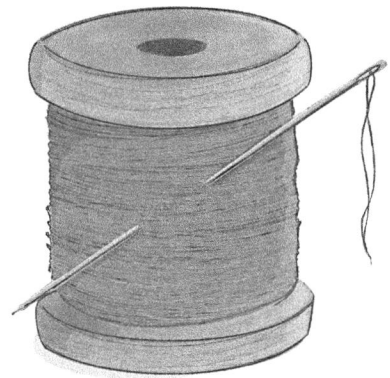

13. Ribbons, Strings, & Cords

Winding Magic 'Round Your Fingers

Strings and magic have long been bound up together. From the Greek Fates or Scandinavian Norns who would spin, measure, and cut the string of human life, the spider god Anansi from the Akan people in West Africa, to Frigg who was said to spin the clouds at her spinning wheel. Spinning a common string is so often compared to the act of creation itself, representing life, fate, and motherhood.

Common Thread—Folk Magic with Knots and String

While spinning string can be seen as an act of the gods, we want to focus on the folk magic that grew up around cord and knot magic. When you think about it, many of us have experience with knot and cord magic already! If you ever made a friendship bracelet, you know it is a system of well-placed knots that creates the amazing designs. Or maybe you played cat's cradle, finding symbols in the way a piece of string flows between your fingers.

Knotting thread, especially red thread, around someone's wrist with a certain number of knots—usually seven—was used as a magical ward against headaches and other ills. Cunning folk traditions from England suggest that using bits of rope from a hangman's noose can alleviate these sorts of aches and pains. We see the use of knots and threads in the form of a "witch's measure," a concept adopted in a number of occult systems like Wicca (where it is often called a cingulum and can be used to "bind" an initiate to their coven). In Hoodoo, a similar use of a measure involves taking red thread or yarn and measuring a partner's genitals, then wetting them with sexual fluids and knotting them to prevent a partner from straying. A similar principle was used when taking two pieces of clothing, one from each partner (preferably worn and unwashed), then knotting them together to ensure fidelity.[1]

Cory always has a red thread charm on him—a little gift made by his daughter when she was young, made of a bit of scrap yarn and tied with a few imperfect knots. He's also got a more intricate red-thread woven bracelet made from the strings from a gift given to him by a dear friend. Cory views the threads as a little bit of protection carrying the strength of one more person with him when he needs it. He remembers his daughter and his friend and has a bit of their fierceness and energy by his side, as well as a perpetual link to them.

The untying of knots also has occult power in folklore. For example, in the Appalachians and Ozarks, women were sometimes advised to unbind their hair during birth to ease birthing pains. Sailors heading out to sea might acquire a cord made by a local witch with a series of knots in it. If their ship were becalmed and unable to move, they could untie each knot to raise a different degree of wind. One knot could bring about a light breeze, while all the knots might summon a hurricane.

And how could we talk about threads, strings, and witchcraft without mentioning the popular (and often nefarious) witch's ladder? This is a magical talisman made by braiding three cords and knotting them nine times while placing an object into each knot. Usually, these objects were bones or feathers from birds, often geese, which may connect the charm mythologically to figures like Frau Holle.[2] While each knot was tied, the witch would curse the intended target, then hang the ladder secretly in the home of their victim with the intent of causing them to suffer and eventually die unless the knots are unbound or the ladder is destroyed somehow. Late twentieth-century Wiccan author Scott Cunningham revised the witch's ladder a bit for more positive purposes, turning it into the "wishing ladder," which uses similar magical structures to create charms that get a witch what she wants out of life.[3]

There are many other magical crafts and lore associated with things like strings, yarn, and ribbons. Crafts like the *ojo de dios* or the oft-appropriated Ojibwe dreamcatcher use the concepts of threads and knots to create talismanic effects. We've also been delighted to see the enthusiasm for needlecraft among contemporary feminist witchcraft practitioners, who cross-stitch their intentions into spell-like wall hangings with phrases like "hex the patriarchy" on them.

By Knot of One, the Spell's Begun

Cord magic is one of the earliest types of magic that Laine can remember doing. It was easy and quick, and she could keep any evidence of a spell out of sight. But with the physical act of tying knots and reciting a charm, it felt powerful and like she had really accomplished something. Laine first remembers reading about it in *Teen Witch*, a common "Wicca 101" type of book by Silver Ravenwolf for people around her age.

Teen Witch is where she first read the ubiquitous rhyme from whence comes this section's title. Here it is in its entirety—

> By knot of one, this spell's begun
> By knot of two, my words are true
> By knot of three, it comes to be
> By knot of four, power in store
> By knot of five, this spell's alive
> By knot of six, this spell is fixed
> By knot of seven, the answer's given
> By knot of eight, I meld with fate
> By knot of nine, the thing is mine![4]

There are variations for almost every line—particularly, "By knot of three, so mote it be," among others. Ravenwolf also instructs where on the string to tie the sequence of knots, but this can change from witch to witch. Imagining the line below is a string and the numbers are knots in the order they were made, we personally prefer this order of knot tying—

3—7—5—9—1—8—4—6—2

You can keep it that simple just by using some twine, string, or even unwaxed dental floss. But there are other factors to consider if you'd like to go more in depth, such as:

- What color is the cord? Think of color correspondences. While red, white, and black are traditional, any color can be used. You could try knotting together a few threads of different colors to make a more specific correspondence.
- What material is the cord made from? Is it from natural plant fibers, like cotton or bamboo? Or animals, like sheep, alpacas, silk worms, or rabbits? Or is it synthetic, such as acrylic or rayon?
- How many plies does the cord have? Knotting a protection-based string for your family might benefit from having the same number of plies as the number of people in your family, for example.

Author and crafter Brandy Williams dedicates a whole book full of these questions (and how to answer them) in her book *Cord Magic: Tapping into the Power of String, Yarn, Twists & Knots*, which we recommend if you'd like much more information on this topic.[5]

Spinning, Knitting, and Crochet: Definitely Cord Magic!

With all this talk of cord magic, we have to talk about knitting. Laine has knitted for about twenty years, spun for about ten, and crocheted for just a few years now. She has miles and miles of yarn, hundreds of finished garments, and an undisclosed amount of unfinished projects, thank you very much. And while Cory doesn't knit, he has a lot of friends who are prolific knitters. He holds his own, though, with his hand-sewing and mending skills. We've long said that fiber arts are magical. After all, what are they but really fancy cord magics?

Have you heard of the sweater curse? The curse is often mentioned as The Boyfriend Sweater Curse, but as knitting has modernized, we like to think the curse has too. The story goes that if you start to knit a sweater for your significant other (that you aren't married to), the relationship will be broken up before the sweater is finished. This is a bit of superstition that serves to warn new knitters of people who might not appreciate your handmade efforts, but many will warn unmarried knitters away from this, fully believing in the curse!

A more positive spin on knitting is the idea of knitting with intention. Holding the recipient in your mind and knitting your love (and any other objective you might have) into each stitch is an easy way to infuse your stitches with magic. Some do shadow knitting (also known as illusion knitting), which appears as simple stripes from one angle, but viewed from another shows an image as intricate as you want to make it. Or, who could forget Madame Defarge, Charles Dickens' famous *tricoteuse* from *A Tale of Two Cities* who would knit the names of those to be guillotined into her scarf? With a delightful mix of history and modernity, knits and purls could be translated to ones and zeros, and with a binary translator you could knit whatever words you wanted into your garment.

Let's not bypass embroidery. If you're intimidated by this craft, don't be! It's easier than it looks, and the results can be really satisfying. We've personally used embroidery to embellish mojo bags as well as mundane things like tea towels. Some ideas are perhaps to embroider a sun, a plant of your choosing, a good luck symbol, or your initials for an extra magical boost.

One of our favorite things about cord magic is that it can be as simple or as complicated as you want. Whether you want to use some old twine that was tying up a package you got in the mail last week, or if you want to spin your own Blue Faced Leicester wool into an S 3-ply yarn (yes, sometimes we get a bit nerdy about our hobbies) that you dyed with berries you picked yourself, we hope we've given you a few new ideas for cord magic.

NOTES:

1. These bits of lore sourced from several collections, including: *Folk-Lore From Adams County, Illinois*, by Harry M. Hyatt (Alma Egan Hyatt Foundation, 1935); *The Frank C. Brown Collection of North Carolina Folklore*, Vol. VI (1961); *Ozark Magic and Folklore* by Vance Randolph (Columbia Univ. Press, 1947); *The Cunning Man's Handbook: The Practice of English Folk Magic 1550-1900* by Jim Baker (Avalonia, 2014); and Zora Neale Hurston's "Hoodoo in America," in *Journal of American Folklore 44*, no. 174 (1931).
2. These bits of lore sourced from several collections, including: Folk-Lore From Adams County, Illinois, by Harry M. Hyatt (Alma Egan Hyatt Foundation, 1935); The Frank C. Brown Collection of North Carolina Folklore, Vol. VI (1961); Ozark Magic and Folklore by Vance Randolph (Columbia Univ. Press, 1947); The Cunning Man's Handbook: The Practice of English Folk Magic 1550-1900 by Jim Baker (Avalonia, 2014); and Zora Neale Hurston's "Hoodoo in America," in Journal of American Folklore 44, no. 174 (1931).
3. See Scott Cunningham, *Earth Power: Techniques of Natural Magic* (Llewellyn Publications, 1983 [2006]. The Wishing Ladder specifically appears in "Chapter 12 - Knot Magic."
4. Silver Ravenwolf, *Teen Witch: Wicca for a New Generation* (Llewellyn Publications, 1998 [2005]).
5. Brandy Williams, *Cord Magic: Tapping into the Power of String, Yarn, Twists & Knots* (Llewellyn Publications, 2021).

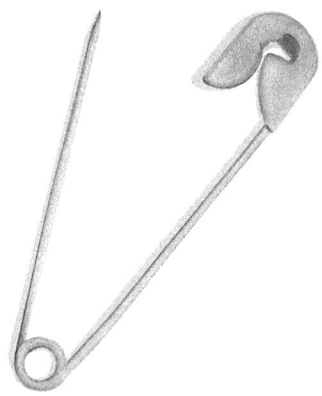

14. Needles & Pins

Magic that Will Have you in Stitches

When it comes to folk magic, less is often more. Few folk magical objects embody that quite so well as the humble sewing needle and its close cousin the pin. Whether you're trying to find one in a haystack or counting the dancing angels atop the other, needles and pins are synonymous with teensy-ness. Yet they are absolutely loaded with folk customs, beliefs, and magic! Perhaps this has something to do with the transformational quality of needles: when it comes to sewing, the ability to use thin threads to turn bits of old cloth into something new like a coat or dress or Halloween costume really does seem like witchcraft. There are even internet memes that joke about knitting needles being witchcraft wands that can be waved around until a sweater magically appears.

Needles appear in blessings, curses, divinations, and luck charms throughout a number of cultures. Let's look through the little hollow eye of the needle—or go waltzing atop a pinhead—to see what kinds of magic we can find!

Stick a Pin in Me; I'm Done!—The Problem with "Voodoo" Dolls

Probably one of the first things to come to mind when looking at sharp and pointy things is the popular "voodoo doll," which is essentially a European-style poppet. These poppets are stuffed with botanicals, curios, dirt, rags, and/or personal items from the intended target and then manipulated to control him or her. Films and television frequently portray only harmful magic being done through these dolls, but a witch or conjurer can also use them to cast love spells, healing spells, or even health and wellness spells. They appear in a variety of forms dating back to European roots, frequently crafted from materials like wax or clay, although their composition greatly depended on local resources. We touch a bit more on dolls in the chapter on Toys, Games, and Cards, but because of the deep connection often made between the "voodoo" doll and the use of pins, it's worth separating fact from fiction here.

There are some African roots to the voodoo doll phenomenon, including the *minkisi minkondi*, which were little wooden dolls from Kongo where spirits were thought to live. The doll's owner would drive a spike into it to "provoke the forces within them" and then the owners would be able to command the spirit to perform certain tasks.[1]

Other cultures have certainly used small effigies of human beings to cause hurt or help, including corn dollies, clay or wooden fetishes, Greek *kolossoi*, and other similar magical poppets.

Pins and other sharp objects can be used to cause magical harm even without the use of a doll (which makes sense according to the folk belief in the Doctrine of Signatures, which states that like things affect like things, so a pin poking anything might poke *something*, magically speaking). Zora Neale Hurston recorded a sinister curse that involved taking nine new pins and nine new needles and boiling them in a nefarious formula called "Damnation Water" in order to cross one's enemy.[2] An Old World carryover (likely from England, but found in Southern communities where conjure is common) says that burying a pin taken from the clothes of a living person with a dead person will cause the target to die within a year.[3] Conversely, boiling nine unused pins in a pot of water with a few drops of urine from someone suffering from bewitchment was thought to break the spell in Nova Scotian lore.

Probably the most gruesome application of pin-and-needle magic had little to do with the magical effects of these tools and all too much to do with their physical dangers: "One instance is given [in an account from 1895] of 'toad heads, scorpion heads, hair, nine pins and needles baked in a cake and given to a child who became deathly sick.'" Curing magical maladies often involved finding pins used in spellwork and disposing of them in a ritual way: "He went at once to the hearth, took up a brick, and found sticking in a cloth six pins and needles. He took them up, put salt on them, and threw them in the river. The needles and pins were said to be the cause of so many pains." Not all piercing spells used metal points. An account of Clara Walker, a former enslaved person from Arkansas, describes her getting help from a rootworker who made a mud effigy of her master and ran a thorn through the back of it, causing severe back pain in him (see Chireau, *Black Magic...* in the chapter notes).[4]

A number of 'Shut-up' spells—tricks that involve tying the tongue of a gossip or potential witness against you in court—involve taking a slit tongue from an animal like a cow or sheep, packing it with hot peppers, vinegar, and/or salt, along with the name paper of the target, and pinning it up with a number of pins and needles (usually nine, but often more). We've got a bit more on tongue spells back in our chapter on the Icebox, but using pins to secure a tongue was just as popular as the freezer for a long time.

The use of needles in wicked works is not the purview of "voodoo dolls," which are largely a scapegoat for a variety of folk magical practices and frequently used to depict African-derived peoples as "primitive." Instead, the use of pins in folk practices is widespread, and the dolls and poppets they are sometimes used on are part of numerous cultures with magical beliefs.

Witch Bottles and Gallows' Nails: Protective Pin Magics

Pins and needles needn't be used in solely malicious work. Healing spells from England resemble wart charms found in Appalachia and also mirror some of the rootworker cures found in the U.S. Southeast. These cures require pins that have been used to poke or pierce a wart to be sealed in a bottle and buried in a newly dug grave (see note 3 for this chapter). An account of a mojo bag from the days of African American enslavement tells of "a leather bag containing 'roots, nuts, pins and some other things,' which was given to [the slave] by an old man."[5] The purpose of this bag was to prevent whippings on the plantation where the slave toiled, which could be quite severe.

Another Hoodoo-sourced application involves the use of a series of nails of increasing size, starting with little "brad" nails and getting progressively bigger until you use railroad spikes at the end. The spell is often referred to as "nailing down the house" and requires a practitioner to start by putting the small brads into the corner of each room, and nailing them down, while speaking magic words about protection, prosperity, and stability. Then the conjurer takes bigger nails and nails down the four corners of the house, again praying the magic words. This pattern continues until the conjurer reaches the four corners of the property and nails iron railroad spikes into the dirt, thus sealing the home from harm and ensuring that the owner will remain in the home and not be evicted. I've heard one rootworker say that adding a little urine to each of the nails helps with this work, as a way of "marking one's territory." Another bit of lore from North Carolina mentions that a person can stick a pin in the ground under a witch (presumably her house) and it will cause her power to be broken.

Pins (and urine) are also frequently used in witch-bottle spells, which cover a number of magical traditions, including this version from Hoodoo: "Bottles of pungent liquids, pins, and needles were interred by practitioners or strung on trees as a snare for invisible forces" (Chireau, *Black Magic...*). Witch bottles have been found in homes dating back to the 1600s and are usually filled with pins or nails—usually bent or broken—and urine. They sometimes also have other objects in them, as in one English witch bottle (sometimes called a "bellarmine") that contained a small cloth heart pierced by the nails.[6]

How exactly do you make a witch bottle? We're glad you asked!

A Simple Witch Bottle for Home Protection
You will need:
- Nine pins, needles, nails, or other sharp pointy metal bits (preferably bent through the process of regular use)
- A small bottle (think baby-food jar size)
- Some wax or a candle (in a color you associate with protection)
- Urine

Yes, urine. Urine has a deep, powerful history in folk magic, and it is used in a wide variety of spells involving things like protection, although it can be used for cursing too. In theory, you should use the first morning's urine from each person in the household (thought to be the strongest and most closely tied to the person who made it). Urine is not dangerous or hazardous if it comes from a healthy person, and you can wear gloves while collecting it. If you have trouble getting it from people, and in our modern society people do seem to be reticent about having anything to do with natural bodily functions, you can use a substitute. Some folks use vinegar with a bit of hair from each household member added. Another idea is to make "feet water," which is simply water used to wash the feet of each person.[7]

To make the bottle, add the bent pins and nails to the jar, then cover it most of the way with the liquid of your choice. The jar is then sealed with a lid, and a candle can be burned on top of it or wax melted to keep it closed—you can draw or imprint a seal of protection like a pentagram or a solar cross on the top of the wax to add another layer of anti-evil power to it.

The witch bottle should be buried near your home, in a corner of the garden, for example. It can be put into the wall of your house—a common practice with some European witch bottles—or even buried in a potted plant near your doorway or window.

There is some concern about the use of metal and corrosive substances in a contained space, which over time can lead to a gaseous buildup and even cause a small explosion (more like a "pop" than something a 1980s action star would be jumping away from). That is partly why it's good to bury these. If you notice that the bottle has broken at any point, that's thought to be a sign that it's taken a "hit" for you, magically speaking, and a new bottle may need to be made.

Pin Him to Your Side!—Some Love Divinations and Charms using Pins and Needles

Given that sewing needles are used to literally connect things, it only makes sense that there are plenty of love spells involving notions from the sewing drawer. In some cases, these are "binding" spells, designed to link people together, but just as often they seem to be connected to divinations of love or even love drawing spells for someone on the lookout for a new companion. Here are some prime examples from North American folklore:

- Finding a pin on the floor or in the street will bring you a date within a week if you stick it into your coat or garments. Pay attention to which way the pin is pointing, as that indicates the direction from whence one's date will come.
- A person can open a package of new pins and take a row of them (or a number significant to them such as seven, nine, or thirteen) and stick them into the sleeve of their pajamas. While doing so, the person should ask for a vision of their future lover, who should then appear in a dream.
- Bent and broken needles can be divinatory. A bent needle indicates a hug coming one's way, while someone who is being fitted for a dress or other clothing can count the times pins catch on their undergarments, which will indicate the number of kisses they can expect before day's end.
- A person can secretly put a hairpin into a significant other's left hip pocket, which will make them think of their lover and keep them faithful.
- While walking, if a person finds a large safety pin, they can name it for a man they wish to see, while a small safety pin can be named for a girl they wish to see. Supposedly this helps one's paths to cross with the intended other person

(and it should be noted this seems more to do with the size of the person—so a large person could be indicated by a large pin and a small person by a small pin, regardless of gender).
- Sewing on Sunday is considered bad luck, and in some cases people believe that every stitch sewn on a Sunday will lead to the Devil (or some other evil force) making you take them out later.[8]

The binding power of pins in love spells makes a good bit of sense and seems deeply entrenched in popular culture; think of high-schoolers being "pinned" in a state of semi-betrothal (an antiquated notion, I know) or of the description of Cupid shooting arrows or darts to cause romantic feelings in his victims... er, targets. Amorous magic incorporating prickly things is not all letterman's jackets and floating naked babies, however. A somewhat heavier love spell from Zora Neale Hurston summons back an errant lover:

> Use six red candles. Stick sixty pins in each candle – thirty on each side. Write the name of the person to be brought back three times on a small square of paper and stick it underneath the candle. Burn one of these prepared candles each night for six nights. Make six slips of paper and write the name of the wanderer once on each slip. Then put a pin in the paper on all four sides of the name. Each morning take the sixty pins left from the burning of the candle. Then smoke the slip of paper with the four pins in it in incense smoke and bury it with the pins under your door step. The piece of paper with the name written on it three times (upon which each candle stands while burning) must be kept each day until the last candle is burned. Then bury it in the same hole with the rest. When you are sticking the pins in the candles, keep repeating:
>
> 'Tumba Walla, Bumba Walla, bring (name of person desired) back to me.'[9]

Hurston's spell is one of the more formal and active ways of incorporating pins into magic, and there's a bit of dubiousness to her rhyme's significance, so feel free to change that specific aspect.

As a decades-long knitter, Laine also wants to mention knitting needles. They come in sizes ranging from 1.25mm to ones the size of broomsticks, and they are made from many materials. You can easily find knitting needles made from wood, bamboo, plastic, and various metals—nickel, brass, and aluminum. Knitting already seems a bit magical to us—waving around a couple of sticks and string that produces something warm and useful is definitely magic. So why not use a knitting needle as a makeshift magic wand? Use bamboo for spells for growth, nickel for money and prosperity, or any needle for spells for creativity.

Finally, we wanted to share an adorably sweet childhood rhyme that does not use actual pins, but merely the words as part of a wishing spell performed when two people accidentally speak the same words at the same time. From Hyatt's *Folk-Lore From Adams County, Illinois*:

After two persons speak the same thing at the same time, the little finger of the one is held crooked about the little finger of the other and these words spoken alternately:

'Needles, Pins,
Triplets, Twins,
When a man marries,
His troubles begin,
What goes up the chimney,
Smoke, Knives,
Forks, Longfellow,
Shortfellow.'

They then make a wish and together say Thumbs.[10]

There are dozens more applications of pins-and-pokey-bits magic we could explore, but hopefully this gives you some idea of what you can do with a simple sewing needle or a little pack of pins. Even the littlest objects can be powerful magical tools if you know what you're looking for and how to use them. But for now, we've waxed on long enough about this topic, so let's stick a pin in it and call it done.

NOTES

1. For a good deal more on African American folk religious practices and magic, I highly recommend Yvonne Chireau's *Black Magic: Religion and the African American Conjuring Tradition* (Univ. of California Press, 2006). Other excellent texts include *Slave Religion*, by Albert Raboteau (Oxford Univ. Press, 2004) and *Mojo Workin'*, by Katrina Hazzard-Donald (Univ. of Illinois Press, 2012).
2. Zora Neale Hurston, "Hoodoo in America," in *Journal of American Folklore*, vol. 44, no. 174 (1931), p. 334.
3. See William G. Black, *Folk Medicine*. Publications of the Folk-lore Society, 1883.
4. See "Folk-Lore Scrap Book: Conjuring and Conjure Doctors in the United States," in *Journal of American Folklore*. Vol. 9, No. 33 (Apr.–Jun., 1896), pp. 143–147.
5. Chireau, *Black Magic*.
6. Historian Brian Hoggard has done a number of examinations of witch bottles in the U.K. and has pointed out their apotropaic (protective magical) nature based on the places in which they are buried and their contents. If you want to know more about witch bottles, I highly recommend his book *Magical House Protection: The Archaeology of Counter-Witchcraft* (Berghan Books, 2019), as well as his articles "Witch-Bottles: Their Contents, Contexts and Uses," in *Physical Evidence for Ritual Acts, Sorcery and Witchcraft in Christian Britain*, Ronald Hutton, ed. (Palgrave, 2015) and "The Archaeology of Counter-Witchcraft and Popular Magic," in *Beyond the Witch-Trials*, Owen Davies & Willem de Blecourt, eds. (Manchester Univ. Press, 2004).
7. A good example of feet water in folklore can be found in the Irish story of "The Horned Women," collected by Lady Augusta Gregory and reprinted in *Celtic Fairy Tales* by Joseph Jacobs in 1892 (https://www.sacred-texts.com/neu/celt/cft/cft07.htm).
8. These examples are found in *Folk-Lore From Adams County, Illinois*, by Harry M. Hyatt (Alma Egan Hyatt Foundation, 1935). The final example is from "Belief Tales & Superstitions," student project coll. by Linda Lingle (PSU-Harrisburg, 1978) in the archives of the Pennsylvania Center for Folklore.
9. See Zora Neale Hurston, "Hoodoo in America," in *Journal of American Folklore* 44, No. 174 (Oct.–Dec. 1931), pp. 317–417.
10. Hyatt, *Folk-Lore From Adams County, Illinois*, Entry No. 8643.

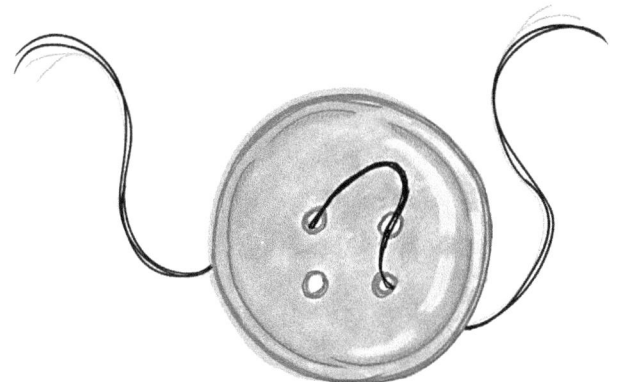

15. Buttons

Opening Grandma's Enchanted Cookie Tin

There's something so deeply charming about a big bowl or jar full of buttons. It can be deeply satisfying to just dig your fingers into the cascade of wood, bone, or plastic rounds and feel them slip around your hands (as long as you haven't accidentally dropped any sewing needles in there). Buttons also have wonderful folk magic applications. This chapter will look at the easily overlooked button and its compatriots in the sewing kit (other than the pins and needles mentioned in the previous chapter). Let's take the lid off grandma's butter cookie tin and see what sorts of lore and spells we find!

The Lucky Button

There is a great deal of luck folklore associated with buttons. Widespread folk belief says that finding a button brings good luck, somewhat similar to finding a lucky penny or other coin. In fact, one variant of this belief from North Carolina indicates that any button found and carried for luck should be smaller than a penny (or other lucky coin). The kind of button found can also have magical significance. A button with two eyes is good luck, while a button with five eyes is bad. A button from a coat might indicate that a letter is coming soon, while a white button foretells a lawsuit (so maybe leave those where they are). In the Ozarks, finding a black button indicates misfortune.[1]

Buttons are the focus of a number of folk spells and rituals, such as these found in Henry M. Hyatt's collection *Folk-Lore From Adams County, Illinois*:

> Buttons strung on a thread can be put around a baby's neck to aid in teething. Some say the buttons should be cut from a man's shirt for this purpose. (**NOTE: DO NOT PUT ANYTHING LIKE THIS AROUND A BABY'S NECK!**).

You can "sell" your wart to someone for a button, and as long as you keep the button the wart will go away (see also the chapter on Coins for similar spells).

Picking up a button you find as you leave your home allows you to make a wish. Other sources indicate that you can do this ritual with any button you find, so long as you pick up the button and place it in your shoe (which would be most comfortable if you were wearing penny loafers). One variation from North Carolina says that throwing a found button over your left shoulder will offer you a wish.[2]

One particularly neat divination found in Hyatt's collection is similar to the "calling circle" sometimes performed to discern a baby's future on its first birthday. This time, however, the button is one of a set of objects that can be used to determine your future at any age:

> "Into a pan of water on the table drop a button, coin, nut, ring and stone; then blindfold yourself and with a spoon attempt to scoop out one of the articles from the pan — three trials being allowed: if you lift out the button, you will live in single blessedness; if the coin, you will acquire wealth; if the nut, you will toil for a living; if the ring, you will marry; and if the stone, you will travel a rocky road. Halloween is the usual time for this divination."[3]

This sort of divination game is similar to other party games, and the Halloween setting ties it to similar occult play, such as the use of "nutcrack night" fire rituals or even the slightly more spin-the-bottle-esque game of snap apple (or, in a similar vein, bobbing for apples).

There's something about the ways we store buttons that can be a little magical. We tend to pile them into containers like old Mason or Ball jars, cardboard cigar boxes, or even those butter cookie tins we mentioned at the beginning of the chapter. What's remarkable is that buttons seem to multiply in those circumstances, and they frequently attract all sorts of other objects to them: needles, coins, rubber bands, dice from forgotten board games, and maybe even stranger things like a baby tooth from a child or an old piece of jewelry (because we somehow instinctively know that we're never going to throw anything from our button-box away, so it seems a spot for safekeeping). In fact, in one of Robert Frost's witchiest poems, "The Witch of Coos," an old witch-woman begins her tale with a snippet of the children's game rhyme, saying that summoning spirits is more complicated than playing "Button, button, who's got the button."[4] Later, she's confronted by a rambling, shambling skeleton and needs to find a missing finger-bone to put him to rest, and where do you think she turns?

> "The finger-pieces slid in all directions.
> (Where did I see one of those pieces lately?
> Hand me my button-box—it must be there.)"

Later, it says she never did find the finger-bone she wanted "Among the buttons poured out in her lap."[5]

That image makes for good inspiration if you're interested in creating a sort of household divination kit, too.

The Button-Box Oracle

This is a simple oracle-style reading, using the principle of geomancy (or reading the positions of objects in a particular place). There are a lot of great geomantic methods, including some traditional ones in African Yoruba religions that require extensive training and initiation. But for as long as there have been people seeking answers, there have been people practicing forms of *sortilege*, or the "casting of lots" to divine the future.[6]

In this method, you will need your standard button box (or button jar, or whatever else you keep your buttons in) and a casting cloth or apron of some kind you can spread on your lap—a handkerchief would work nicely. Your button box could contain buttons that you collect specifically for this oracle, or it could literally be your everyday button box with a wide assortment of things in it. To use the oracle, spread your lap with your apron or casting cloth, then shake up your button box. Tip out a handful of objects and watch where they land.

- Near the left leg - Something coming to you or something you'll receive.
- Near the right leg - Something you will do or that you need to take action on.
- Near your nether regions - Something personal to you, something important. Might indicate sex, but just as easily can represent family, home, your inner life and psychology, etc.
- Out Towards your Knees - Something happening outside of your control

These are just suggested placements, and you could easily design a casting cloth that gives you more precise information by dividing it up into a circle with quarters or astrological divisions, or a compass with cardinal and ordinal directions that you associate with particular meanings.

Look at the particular objects and see what meaning you can make of them. You may have buttons with specific patterns or images on them that might be significant to you, or you might count the holes in each button or whether it lands "up" (with the indentation visible) or "down" smooth side facing up). Some sample meanings based on folklore might include:

- Black button - bad luck; misfortune
- White button - legal matters
- Button with two eyes - good luck
- Button with five eyes - bad luck
- Small button - good luck, money, and fortune
- Coat button - travel or a letter from someone
- Button with a thread still in it - work left undone; a process
- Penny - small good fortune
- Dime - protection
- Quarter - duty, soldiering, war (see the chapter on Coins)
- Tooth - maturity, growth, change, childhood (and depending on if it's an animal tooth, it could have additional meanings)
- Finger Bone - What are you doing in your spare time???[7]

The combinations in this oracle are going to depend entirely on you and what you wind up collecting in your box. If you have an extremely full box, you might just reach in and grab a small handful of objects to cast them instead of spilling the whole container.

An oracle like this is built upon your own associations with the objects and what they mean to you. However, the use of this form of lot-casting divination is rooted in folklore. As we're seeing in this chapter, buttons are also very tied up with folkloric meaning (forgive the pun).

A Thimbleful of Well-Measured Magic

Before we leave the butter cookie tin completely, it's worth looking at other little objects we often find in our button boxes: the thimble and the measuring tape. These probably are more associated with the needles and pins in the previous chapter, but we felt like that was where the "sharp" objects should be, and this chapter fits these "softer" or "duller" items quite nicely.

Thimbles were used in a game much like the "Button, Button" game in which participants took turns denying they had the thimble in their hands until everyone guessed at who the real thimble-thief was. That association could make thimbles a good oracular symbol of truth and lies, in addition to the potential symbolism of being tiny finger armor for the swift-handed tailor. There are a few other associations with thimbles in folklore:

- A new mother would carry or drink water from a thimble the first time she drank after the birth of a child, or else the wee one would grow to slobber a great deal.
- Teething children's gums could be rubbed with a silver thimble to ease their pain (which actually would feel good on gums, as the cool metal would provide temporary relief). Given how small a thimble is and the choking hazard it presents, we do NOT recommend this.
- Silver thimbles were used to ward off ringworm by rubbing the infected area nine times in a circle. (This is a folk charm and NOT medically sound.)
- A divination ritual for young unmarried folks involved eating a thimbleful of salt right before bed (no water allowed!). You would then dream of someone offering you a drink, and they would be your future lover or spouse.
- Another divination involved baking several objects into a cake, including a thimble. The person who got the thimble in their slice would be doomed to be unmarried. A Midwestern variant on this practice involves baking objects into a wedding cake to predict the fortune of guests: a ring for marriage, a penny for wealth, a thimble for labor. If you wish to avoid a broken tooth, you can attach the charms to ribbons and put them under the cake so they line up with individual slices, too.
- Dreaming of losing a thimble meant that you would be slandered or the subject of gossip[8]

One of the best-known associations with the thimble is the famous Parker Bros. Monopoly game, where it's one of the "poverty" pieces, along with the iron and shoe.

Turning to measuring tape, the tape is not often mentioned as magical in and of itself, but the act of measuring something or someone has a folkloric history of exercising control over others. In some Hoodoo practices, a person could use a red thread or piece of yarn to measure their partner's sex (usually a penis), then mark it with sexual fluids. The partner who controlled the string could then tie knots in it to prevent their lover from being able to stray with anyone else.

Other acts of measuring included marking off a person's height when they were sick onto a tree or a broomstick. The tree would then have a hole drilled in it and be "plugged" with a rag used to rub the ill person (often a child). As the rag rotted in the tree the disease would leave the victim (or in the case of a child, as they grew past that height, the illness would diminish). The broomstick method involved similarly standing the person against the broomstick and cutting a notch to measure them, then hiding the broom in the attic and never using it again, thus transferring the disease away (again, often this was used for children, since they were the ones most likely to be shorter than a broom).

A wart removal cure involved a slightly different sort of measuring: counting the number of warts and tying knots into a string to match them, then burying the string under the eaves or gutter spout of the house so that it would rot away and take the warts with it.

A final form of measure could be used as a protective device for women. A two-meter-long ribbon would be marked with the woman's height, then a prayer known as the "Beatitudes of the Virgin (Mary)" would be written on the ribbon and it would be worn around the body, either draped over the neck under the clothes or tied like a girdle around the waist. These Beatitudes seem to be the ones found in the Bible in Matthew 5, usually nine in number, plus an additional Beatitude taken from the "Ave Maria/Hail Mary" prayer: "Blessed are you amongst women and blessed is the fruit of thy womb, Jesus." When worn, this measure was thought to prevent any harm to the wearer.[9]

As we leave the sewing kit and button box behind, we should note that there are so many other notions that you can investigate for folklore: lace and tatting, shirt collar tabs, and cuff links all have folklore associated with them, and a resourceful house-witch could easily find a measure of magic in all of them. Yes, we know, we can hear you groaning at that. Perhaps you'd like to write us a scathing letter about our puns, which is just as well, as we're moving on to the magic of pen, paper, and other desk-drawer items!

NOTES

1. From *The Frank C. Brown Collection of North Carolina Folklore*, Vol. VI, pp. 390, 430–33.
2. From *Folk-Lore From Adams County, Illinois*, by Harry M. Hyatt (Alma Egan Hyatt Foundation, 1935), p. 206; *Ozark Tales and Superstitions*, by Phillip W. Steele (Pelican Publishing, 1983); and *Encyclopaedia of Superstitions, Folklore, and the Occult Sciences of the World*, by Cora Linn Daniels and Charles M. Stevens (J.H. Yewdale & Sons, 1903).
3. Hyatt, *Adams County*, p. 206.
4. The game of "Button, Button" is a sort of combination between "Duck, Duck, Goose" and Shirley Jackson's "The Lottery." Children in a circle hold out their hands as another child takes a button and touches it between their palms. Then, everyone tries to guess who has the button. If they cannot guess, everyone stays in the game, but if they pick the correct button-holder, that person is out (and thankfully not stoned to death as in Jackson's story).
5. Frost has a number of witchy poems worth looking into. "The Witch of Coos" is one of his longer and more intriguing ones, especially given the narrative of the woman/witch chatting with her son and an unnamed traveler (and eventually almost confessing to covering up a murder of one of her lovers by her deceased husband). Others with a hint of witchery in them include "A Star in a Stone-Boat" and "Ghost House." If you enjoy witchy poetry, we'd also highly recommend looking at work by Anne Sexton, who wrote extensively about witches and fairy tales in her witty, haunting works.
6. The casting of lots is an ancient practice and is even mentioned several times in the Bible (including Hebrew priests using a form of divination involving sacred stones taken from their breastplates and a New Testament mention of people casting lots for the clothes of Jesus after his death). The term *sortilege* connects to the word "sort," with some fairly obvious meanings, but it is also the root of the word "sorcery," from the French translation of "the casting of lots," *sortilegerie*. That makes this a particularly witchy way of doing some divination!
7. It's worth noting that bones are more common in a button-box than you might think. Many buttons used to be made from carved bone or animal horns, so if you have a button like that it could be a good way to incorporate their symbolism into the oracle!
8. These examples from Brown, *Folklore of NC*, pp. 15, 579, 660; Hyatt, *Adams County*, 7366; Daniel and Lucy Thomas's *Kentucky Superstitions* (Franklin Classics, 2018 [1920]) no. 1330; and *Aunt Sally's Policy Players' Dream Book* (reprint) (Lama Temple, 1984), p. 112.
9. Brown, *Folklore of NC*, xxix, p. 12.

16. Desk Set

Spilling the Magical Ink

Is there anything *more* magical than a blank piece of paper, waiting to be filled with doodles, notes, thoughts, ideas, sketches, and more? We are perhaps a bit biased in that we have degrees related to writing and a love of the printed page. Even a person casually watching a young child, however, cannot miss how readily our imaginations engage and we begin creating images, worlds, and wonders when someone hands us a few sheets of paper and a box of crayons or a pencil. That sense of endless possibility and wonder fuels our relationship with our creative side, and the fact that some of our greatest achievements begin with a doodle on a cocktail napkin or a couple of words jotted on the back of an old envelope only goes to show how important ink, graphite, and paper can be.

This chapter will pull open the drawers of your desk and show you some of the folklore and magic hiding in those incredibly simple objects. We'll see how we can turn a sticky note into a spell or write a letter that charms its reader with more than our thoughtfulness. If you're the sort of person who gets giddy when you unwrap a new notebook, box of pens, or pencil sharpener, then read on!

A Blotter of Bewitchment—Paper Packets, Petitions, and Talismans

Even if you're not a great artist or writer, there's something about the siren song of paper that invites us to create and make. While paper as we think of it has not always been available everywhere, we seem to have been compelled to fill any number of blank spaces with images or writing for nearly as long as we've been able to band together in groups. The cave paintings of Lascaux, France, the cuneiform inscriptions on Mesopotamian clay tablets, and the hieroglyphics of Egypt all document aspects of our existence as human beings and help us to tell a more complete story of ourselves. Unsurprisingly, even some of our oldest writings and images are thought to have been connected to the supernatural, bringing luck to hunts among our neolithic ancestors or guiding the souls of the dead into the afterlife in the cradles of early civilization.

Our own interactions with paper and folk magic have been massively changed by just how ubiquitous it is. Since the advent of printing presses in China and Europe, paper's availability has skyrocketed, and so have its applications for making charms and talismans. Writing has a long history of magical power, for example. In Jewish lore and tradition, paper or parchment scrolls with inscribed passages of the Torah can be worn or carried (a charm known as *tefillin*) or placed in a small box to be affixed to a doorway (in which case it is called *mezuzah*). These written talismans can be protective, with at least one scholar positing that the name for the *mezuzah* comes from a pun in Hebrew meaning "death departs." They can also be used to calm colic or other disorders in children and are sometimes placed near the door of a delivery room during childbirth.[1] In China, a whole range of spellcrafting practices evolved around the creation of *fu* talismans, made by inscribing specific calligraphic symbols onto strips of paper and carrying or posting them around a home. These papers are thought to essentially command spiritual forces such as demons or lower deities or to petition the aid of higher gods and spirits, and the origin stories of the talismans are connected directly to the creation of writing, said to have been discovered by the legendary Cangjie when he noticed symbols in the patterns of bird tracks. Similar talismanic scrolls and papers are found throughout Japanese Shinto practices, including both the *ofuda* (a type of stiff paper marked with characters) or *omamori* (scrolls carried in small wood or bamboo tubes).[2]

While symbols and sigils are a wonderful way to deploy paper in folk magic, one of the most common methods is simply to use paper to make petitions, sometimes also called by other names such as "tickets." These are essentially written requests for luck, love, money, or any other boon. Crucially, they often involve putting down the name of a person to receive the request (often the spellcaster or their client), and then writing the request around the name. One method is to begin above the name and begin writing the request in a circle, using cursive and connecting all the letters, completely encircling the name without raising the pen off the paper. After the request is made, the spell writer can then go back to dot the i's and cross the t's as needed. So, for example, if Cory wants to write a really good book that is useful to people, he might create a petition paper that looks something like this:

Another method involves writing the request at the paper's edges, thus "capturing" the request and creating a barrier so that the luck or fortune cannot get away from the named individual. Still one more approach, known as *zauberzettel*, involves doing a petition using a biblical verse connected to the request, but abbreviating each word of the verse to its first letter or two. Thus a fragment of Psalm 23—the famous "The Lord is my Shepherd" one—might be rendered: t.l.i.m.sh.i.sh.n.w.h.m.m.t.l.d.i.gr.p.a.l.m.b.t.st.w (for "The Lord is my Shepherd, I shall not want. He maketh me to lie down in green pastures, and leadeth me beside the still waters"). This might be carried in a pocket or purse, or folded and wedged into a doorframe or windowsill to create a protective charm for a person or home.[3] These petition papers can also be incorporated in other spells and placed under a fireproof item like a plate while a candle is burned over them to add to the mystical influence.

Some insist that paper used for spells must be "virgin," or essentially unused paper, often of high quality. Some of the most formal ceremonial magicks are quite particular about using virgin parchment made from highly treated animal skins. Most accounts seem to say that a good blank piece of paper is all you need, however, and some forms of Hoodoo and Southern Conjure will even make use of old scraps of brown wrapping paper, like that used in grocery bags or lunch sacks.

In addition to petitions, name papers are also a powerful bit of folk magic. These are simply pieces of paper on which the spell crafter has written a person's full name. In sorcerous lore, possessing a person's name is equivalent to having power over them, and so name papers can do some powerful magic—for better or worse! One spell involving a name paper helps to get rid of someone that is bothering you by simply blotting out a new letter of their name every day, covering it completely in black ink until the entire name has been redacted, which should drive the person out of your life completely. Other spells involve taking the person's name paper and putting it into a jar or box with particular ingredients like honey to make them "sweet" toward you or vinegar to "sour" their life if they've been causing you trouble. An extension of this sort of working can use their business card, which might be more closely linked to them as they will likely have touched and handled it at some point.

Still another application of written charms is the packet spell. These are spells that are bundled in cloth or paper and carried to bring their influence and magic along. Placing a few key ingredients, like a bay leaf, a bit of allspice, and some cinnamon in a petition paper with your name and a phrase like "my business shall prosper," is the first step. Then, you would fold the bundle carefully so the ingredients and the words of the petition are on the inside of the paper packet. Then wrap the whole thing in a few turns of red thread or string and tie it tightly when you finish. Some folk magicians will use printed pages from books like the Bible or other holy texts, or even folded currency to make these spells.

Making Grandma Proud of You: The Uncanny Power of Sending a Letter

Getting mail feels exciting. You open your mailbox and find an envelope from someone you love or a postcard from far away detailing a friend's adventure. Many of us grew up with parents or grandparents who insisted that birthday or holiday gifts merited a brief "thank you" note dropped in the mailbox soon after we received them. Junk mail doesn't pack the same oomph as a birthday card, but sometimes we get excited over catalogs for favorite shops or even newsletters from our groups. One form of mail, however, seldom elicits any sort of positive response: the chain letter.

Chain letters are copied letters sent from the receiver to the next senders, usually with brief stories in them about the benefits of keeping the letter going—riches or luck in most cases—and the consequences of breaking the "chain," which can involve deeply tragic misfortunes. For example, if Jimothy Realhuman receives a chain letter, they might be asked to make seven copies of the letter and send them to seven friends or family members. The letters will often contain a list of recent recipients and any blessings they've received, and poor Jimothy will be warned that a curse of bad luck awaits them if they don't put those letters in the mail in the next seven days! Folklore collector Harry M. Hyatt noted that he received such a letter in 1933, and shortly thereafter saw a tremendous burst in chain-letter sending, going so far as to call it a "mass hysteria" that swept across the United States. He provided an example of the written content of a chain letter in his *Folk-Lore from Adams County, Illinois* (Alma Egan Hyatt Foundation, 1935):

> "We trust in God. He supplies our needs.
> Mrs. F. Streuzel .... Mich.
> Mrs. A. Ford .... Chicago, Ill.
> Mrs. K. Adkins .... Chicago, Ill.
> Mrs. R. Arlington .... Ill.
> Mrs. .... Quincy, Ill.
> Mrs. .... Quincy, Ill.
> Copy the above names, omitting the first. Add your name last. Mail it to five persons who you wish prosperity to.
> The chain was started by an American Colonel and must be mailed 24 hours after receiving it. This will bring prosperity within 9 days after mailing it.
> Mrs. Sanford won $3,000.
> Mrs. Andres won $1,000.
> Mrs. Howe who broke the chain lost everything she possessed.
> The chain grows a definite power over the expected word.
> DO NOT BREAK THE CHAIN.
> See what happens on the 9th day.
> Hoping it brings you luck."[4]

Some people may consider these letters a nuisance and ignore them (at their peril!), but these letters do have a good bit of history behind them. The tradition of copying these letters goes back at least into the eighteenth century, with reproductions of magical letters that were supposedly "dropped" from heaven in places like Koenigsberg, Prussia, in 1714–15 and told stories of magical acts that stopped spreading fires and thus offered protection from fire and other natural disasters to those who bore a copy of the letter with them. Copied letters like this date back into antiquity, even being mentioned by early Roman Church philosopher Hippolytus in the sixth century C.E. The Pennsylvania German community in the United States has a long-standing tradition of circulating and copying these letters, which are called *himmelsbriefen* or "heaven letters."[5] While chain letters have diminished significantly in the twenty-first century, they were replaced by similar phenomena like chain emails—so the basic idea remains in circulation. If you want to try to revive it and start sending out a few magically charged missives to friends and family who might not mind, you'd be participating in a long and storied history!

Mail has a lot of folklore around it, as well. Much of it dates from when letters were the primary way of corresponding with distant relations and connections, but there's no reason that some of it can't be relevant today. A number of signs herald your imminent receipt of a letter, including:

- If your right eye itches
- If your left palm itches
- If your nose itches
- If you find a hole in your clothes
- If you find a button or pin on the ground
- If you find a feather in your hair

You can also encourage a letter to come with a few small folk charms. If you find your dress hem turned up and kiss it, you'll soon get a letter. If a ladybug lands on your hand and you say, "Ladybug, ladybug fly away home, and bring me a letter whenever you come," then let it go, you will get a letter shortly after. Similarly, if you happen to find a hairpin and make a wish to receive a letter, you can hang the pin in a pine tree to draw the correspondence your way.

There are some rules about letter-writing linked to folklore and magic. For example, if you receive a letter from a friend, you should not burn it or tear it up, or else you will damage the friendship and invite bad luck on you both. Certain days were thought to be lucky and unlucky for writing or receiving letters. Writing a letter on a Thursday is supposed to bring you whatever you ask for in the epistle, while getting a letter on a Monday means more letters will be coming within the week. Letters received on Tuesdays or Saturdays are thought to portend ill news or luck. Similarly, a letter with insufficient postage or a stamp placed upside down foretells bad fortune.

Finally, before you write a letter, you should always say "I hope I am lucky," which will bring good luck to both you and the recipient. And don't forget to SWAK—seal with a kiss.[6]

The Real Ghost-Writers: Automatic Writing for Fun and Profit!

In his collection of Ozark lore, folklorist Vance Randolph tells the story of Josie Forbes of Wayne County, Missouri, who was locally dubbed "The Witch of Taskee," and her method of telling the fortunes of her neighbors:

> "[She] used to sit at a table with the client and make four dots with a pencil on a piece of paper. She marked one N, one E, one S and one W. 'Them's the four directions,'

she said solemnly. Around these four characters he traced random curving lines, until the whole thing looked like a conventionalized Arabic inscription. Then she began to talk, glancing carelessly down at the paper from time to time as if for confirmation."

Josie's approach seems to essentially be a unique form of "automatic writing." This practice, while quite old, had its heyday with the rise of the Spiritualist movement of the nineteenth and early twentieth centuries. Spiritualism depended on the belief that human spirits wished to communicate with the living and would do so using a variety of tools, including "talking boards" like the famous Ouija, pendulums, mediums who would act as vessels for the dead during seances, and through practices like automatic writing. Automatic writing was so popular at one point that authors like Sir Arthur Conan Doyle (of Sherlock Holmes fame) and Irish poet William Butler Yeats used it in their writing process. Entire books were written with the aid of spirits, including *Oscar Wilde from Purgatory: Psychic Messages* (penned by Hester Travers Smith) and *Jap Herron: A Novel Written from the Ouija Board* (by Emily Hutchings said to be channeling Mark Twain/Samuel Clemens).[7]

In the most widely known forms of automatic writing, the idea is for the person acting as a medium for the otherworld to begin writing without looking at the symbols or letters they're marking on a piece of paper, continuing while in a trance and responding to questions from those around them. Another form involves putting a pencil or pen into a *planchette*—the little pointing device used in a Ouija board but with a hole near the tip to allow the writing device to be inserted so it can just barely rest on the paper beneath it. The members of the seance or table reading would ask questions, and like with a talking board, place their hands on the planchette until it moved. When the session was done, the paper would be removed and any letters, markings, or words would be interpreted.

Both of these are perfectly useful methods, and if you are already fairly good at getting yourself into a trance they might be a great way to see what great-grandmother Hester would like you to do with her costume jewelry. For those who find the trance component more challenging, you can still use a variation of automatic writing. You simply set a timer and begin transcribing a page of work, preferably one you associate with the spirit you're attempting to contact, such as a diary or favorite book. When the timer ends, you go back through your transcription and look for errors—spelling, grammar, anything—and highlight or circle those words. Then you take those words and interpret them as the message. They may take some rearranging, and you can experiment with reworking letters and other symbols you find in this process.

This can be a fun way to practice light trancework and mediumship for those interested in exploring their own inner Spiritualist.

A Smudge of Sorcery: Lore and Practice with Pens, Ink, and Pencils

What of the writing utensils, then? If the writing we do has magical lore associated with it, surely the pens and pencils we use to shape that writing must have similar superstitions and stories attached? The answer is "yes"!

A great deal of the lore around pens involves the ink that fills them. For example, it's considered bad luck to spill ink, and it can even be a sign that whatever one is writing will lead to bad ends. Even worse is to spill ink on a wedding dress, which is thought to be a blight on the marriage it represents and probably will lead to a very unhappy bride no matter what. However, if your ink blots on the paper while you're writing, not from spilling but by dripping from your pen accidentally, then the person to whom you are writing is thinking of you.

Trying to rush ink drying is considered unlucky, because it is supposed to dry in its own natural time. Those who hold wet ink before a fire or otherwise rush the process are particularly inviting bad luck.

When it comes to pencils, the best thing to do is avoid a broken tip, which can variously mean that someone is spreading gossip about you, that bad news is coming your way, or that you can expect to be disappointed soon. One belief says that for every time your pencil tip breaks, someone will tell a lie about you. If your tip does break, though, you must make sure not to sharpen it on a Sunday, which will bring you bad luck all week.

Pencils aren't all doom and gloom: Finding a pencil is thought to be good luck, and the larger or longer the pencil is, the greater your luck will be. One delightful bit of folklore says that you can wear a pencil in your hair, and it will keep away any bill collectors or others to whom you owe money.[8]

Pencils can also be used in a strange little folk fortune-telling game. It's called "Charlie Charlie," and it was something of an internet sensation for a minute, with many people getting very freaked out by the idea that a ghost or demon was communicating with them through their No. 2 Ticonderogas. It's important to remember that games like Charlie Charlie have been played for a very long time, often by young people, and much like the Spiritualism stalwart Ouija board mentioned above, these folk divinatory games seldom elicited much concern before the mid-twentieth century. To play, you draw four quadrants on a piece of paper and label them "Yes/No/No/Yes." Then you put one pencil in the center of the paper, flat along one of the quadrant dividing lines. The other pencil gets balanced on the first one crosswise, and those playing the game begin. They must ask, "Charlie Charlie, can we play your game?" and wait until the top pencil rotates on its own to indicate "Yes" or "No." If it's a no, the players can ask again up to three times. Once they get a yes, they can ask any yes/no questions of the Charlie Charlie spirit. To finish the game, they must ask, "Charlie Charlie, can we leave your game?" and continue doing so until they get a yes for that answer as well.

A final magical practice of lore directly from Cory: If you want to add a bit of extra magic to your writing work or ink-based charms, take apart your pens and slip a little scroll of paper with magical writing or sigils on it into the barrel around the ink cartridge. Cory has a pen that he specifically uses when writing major projects or spell charms that has just such a scroll inside it, and it's been wonderfully useful to him. (You are reading a book he helped to write, after all!).

Sticky Note Sigils: Doing Magic at the Office

We know that not all your ink, paper, and office supplies are at home. If you happen to work in an office or other workplace where you think you don't have much in the way of magical tools available . . . well, yes, you do! That pad of sticky notes and your push pins for the bulletin board are just waiting to do some spellwork with you!

We thought we'd end this chapter with a few ideas about things that use more contemporary office supplies. These are not based on particular folklore, but are our own improvisations and ones we've had a bit of luck with:

- If you need to add a little pop of magic out of sight, consider drawing a sigil or other magical marking on a sticky note. You can stick it under your chair, under your desk, or even behind your computer monitor or beneath your keyboard very easily where it can work its magic unseen.
- Don't have much in the way of sewing skills but need to make a magical poppet or doll? Take some paper and fold it in half, then cut out the rough shape of a person. Use a stapler to stitch together the "seams" around the edge of the doll, leaving one space where you can stuff some herbs or other ingredients inside to stuff it (crumpled paper works, too, if you just need a quick stuffed doll). Staple it shut, draw a face on it and write the name over the chest (in symbols if you need to make sure no one knows who it is if it gets found). Voila! Quick paper doll for magic!
- Push pins come in a variety of colors, and it's easy to use those associations to have particular effects. For example, if you want your boss to be thinking about giving you a raise, you can write that on a piece of paper with their name on it and poke the name with a green-headed pushpin (since green is the color of money). You could do similar things with the paper doll mentioned above.
- Paper clips can be wonderful for making little charms. You can fairly easily fold them into shapes, like stars or circles or spirals, and hang them around your desk or carry them with you for magical boosts based on what those symbols mean to you.
- Sticky notes are frequently in square shapes, and the sticky part is usually somewhat easy to rub off, meaning if you have any origami skills you've got a nice little supply of origami paper available! You can make shapes of animals or other folded paper creations to work with those animals even when you can't be near the real ones.
- Finally, you can do a bit of devious work that can be very useful in folk magic. Many folk spells require "curios" or "taglocks" from a person if you want to work magic on them, but getting snips of hair or clothing is probably hard to do while you're in the office with gossipy Marge from HR. Instead, you can use clear tape like 3M Scotch™ brand tape and "capture" things like their fingerprints or a bit of stray hair on their desk when they aren't looking. The tape will fold over and keep your captured impression of them safe as you tuck it in your pocket and take it home to continue working with it later.

Who doesn't love the smell of paper with fresh ink? The sound of a graphite pencil scratching away? Or even finding a little origami crane waiting on their desk from a thoughtful co-worker (who may be leaving a little spell of blessing in disguise if she's a bit of a witch)? Let your inner child loose to play in the world of imagination with pen and paper and ink and pencils, and see what sorts of wonders you devise!

NOTES

1. See Joshua Trachtenberg, *Jewish Magic and Superstition: A Study in Folk Religion* (Meridian Books, 1961 [1939]), pp. 145–59
2. For an excellent overview of the fu sigils, including history and practice, as well as a bit on some of the similar practices found in places like Japan, we highly recommend Benebell Wen's *The Tao of Craft: Fu Talismans and Casting Sigils in the Eastern Esoteric Tradition* (North Atlantic Books, 2016). The information cited in this chapter comes from that book, pp. 50–53.
3. An extensive treatment of *zauberzettel* can be found in *The Red Church or The Art of Pennsylvania German Braucherei* (Pendraig Publishing, 2009).
4. Hyatt, *Adams County*, p. 303.
5. A wonderful history of these letters can be found both in *The Red Church* (Pendraig Publishing, 2009) and in *The Pennsylvania German Broadside: A History and Guide*, by Don Yoder (Penn State Univ. Press, 2005). The fantastic translation of the Pennsylvania German folk magic classic text *The Long Lost Friend* done by Daniel Harms (Llewellyn Publications, 2012) also offers some background on these charms, and the book itself essentially begins with a form of *himmelsbrief* by its original author, John George Hohman, regarding the book itself as a sort of talisman.
6. These bits of lore all derive from Harry M. Hyatt, *Folk-Lore From Adams County, Illinois* (Alma Egan Hyatt Foundation, 1935), pp. 302–3 and *The Frank C. Brown Collection of North Carolina Folklore*, Vol. VI, pp. 547–50.
7. A truly excellent history of Spiritualism and its role in U.S. history and culture can be found in the books *Occult America: The Secret History of How Mysticism Shaped Our Nation* (Bantam Press, 2010) and *A Republic of Mind and Spirit: A Cultural History of American Metaphysical Religion*, by Catherine Albanese (Yale Univ. Press, 2008). If you're interested in spirit boards, Cory also writes about them in his book *New World Witchery: A Trove of North American Folk Magic* (Llewellyn Publications, 2021).
8. The lore in the preceding paragraphs comes from Harry M. Hyatt, Folk-Lore From Adams County, Illinois (Alma Egan Hyatt Foundation, 1935), pp. 302–3 and *A Dictionary of Superstitions*, by Iona Opie and Moira Tatem (Oxford Univ. Press, 1989), pp. 208–9.

17. Cards, Toys, & Games

Playing with Magic

One of the most common uses of magic in Ancient Rome was not a love potion, a spell for political power, or even protection from the perceived anger of a pantheon of fickle gods. No, it was cursing the opposing team in the local sporting event. A number of *defixiones*, or cursing tablets made of thin lead sheets inscribed with hexes to bring about the downfall of the person or persons you felt needed a bit of magical subjugation. These sheets would be rolled up and often deposited near the grounds of the event, and while common, could also get a person in trouble. Charioteers who engaged in defixion curses could be arrested or even executed if caught. All sorts of sports engaged in active hexing: chariot racing, wrestling, running. These tablets frequently included colorful imagery and flowery language that make the curse sound like a divine invocation against someone who had burned your house to the ground, rather than just the star charioteer or wrestler your underdog would be going up against. Take this example from a defixion made against a wrestler named Eutycian, likely sometime around the third century C.E.:

> *I hand over to you Eutycian, whom Eutyicia bore, that you may chill him in his purposes, and in your dark air also those with him. Bind in the unilluminated [eternity] of oblivion and chill and destroy also the wrestling that he is going to do ...this coming Friday.*[1]

Now *that's* taking your games seriously! Of course, plenty of people used *defixiones* to punish politicians and errant lovers (or even potential lovers whose affections were of the unrequited variety), but more than a thousand tablets focused on sporting events and games have been found, indicating that games are serious business when it comes to magic. Likely this owes to the fortunes won or lost through gambling on these events. But in the history and folklore of everyday popular magic, the connection to games, toys, and playthings has always been strong. After all, some of the greatest magicians I know are kids, whose imaginations allow them to push the possibilities of the "real" world and imbue it with wonder. Dolls are alive with personalities, and counting games or imagined worlds become nearly life-or-death scenarios where one wrong move drops the player into a pool of fantasy lava (only to be resurrected again as if by some expedient necromancy).

What has all this to do with what's in your junk drawer? If you're anything like us, you may well have an old stack of Uno™ cards, playing cards, poker chips, or even a doll's arm or plastic kid's meal–type toy floating around in there. All of these little tokens of games and fun can have some wonderfully magical applications. Let's rifle through a few common objects, games, and toys to see what enchantment we can find.

She Wets, She Cries, She Shoots Hexes from her Eyes: Dolls and Toys in Magical Lore

Likely you've heard of Annabelle. She is supposedly a very, *very* possessed Raggedy Ann–type doll in the collection of paranormal investigators Ed and Lorraine Warren, and the subject of a number of movies in the greater *Conjuring* film franchise. You may also have heard the term "voodoo doll" thrown around casually, although that's inaccurate and often pejorative when applied to the little rag-and-stick dolls used for magical purposes (which may include cursing but can also involve healing, protection, blessing, and more). And the less said about Chucky, the better.

Dolls are an uncanny sort of object. They are like humans in their design, and children often play with them as though they were babies or little companions, imbuing them with imagined life. Yet we also tend to let our fantasies run wild, imagining them doing all sorts of nefarious things when we're not looking. Annabelle and similar "haunted dolls" like Robert (found in Key West, Florida) are an extension of that fear that the little bit of life we ascribe to them will become more than we can handle.

Dollies and poppets (a sort of old-fashioned term for human figures made from wax, clay, or cloth, especially for magical uses) are a very useful part of folk magic. Their humanoid nature and the sense that they have life within them intrigues us and makes us sense the sympathetic connection between a doll and the person it's supposed to represent.[2] Take, for example, a woman in Monongah, West Virginia, who was known as The Hungarian Witch. She was known to have a whole "passel" of rag dolls in her home. Once, when a young girl who thought she might also have some witchy powers went to go visit the old woman, she saw all the dolls and asked the purpose behind them. The woman said that "each one represented a certain person, and if she injured one of them, that person would be injured." The woman then told the girl to come back in two days and she'd reveal if she was a witch. When she returned, she found The Hungarian Witch dead, and lying beside her was a rag doll with a pin pushed through its heart.[3]

Similarly, in the story of "Vasilisa the Beautiful," a Slavic folktale, the title character loses her mother early in the story. Before she dies, though, the mother gives Vasilisa a little doll and tells her to "feed it" and let it know any problems or troubles she has. The doll then helps Vasilisa with her chores and even gets her out of trouble with the local cannibalistic witch, Baba Yaga, who determines that the doll carries the mother's blessing within it.

Beyond the realm of story, dolls are frequently turned into proxies for those who will be the subject of magical work. This is what armchair anthropologist James George overwhelmed. A Skip might indicate that you need to lay low, or that you are being told to avoid a particular person or choice.

Plenty of other card games hold this kind of possibility. We've known folk magicians and chaos mages who love to pull out their favorite deck-build for Magic: The Gathering™, for example, and look to the archetypes or characters represented there to get insights into their own enchanted world. Other games like Pokemon™ or Yu-Gi-Oh!™ can be turned into divinatory or magical aids with a bit of imaginative exploration. Imagine getting a bug-type Pokemon card in response to a question about changing jobs and thinking about that as an indication that you'll have a new "hive" soon. Game cards pulled from old board games like Pictionary™ or Trivial Pursuit™ might also be great ways to get hints about potential futures and available options. And if you don't mind a hefty heaping of sarcasm (and, frankly, a lot of swearing and offensive humor), something like Cards Against Humanity™ is open-source and has a massive number of cards you could turn into a workable deck for divination (and occasionally playing).

Cards aren't the only common magical game out there. Dominoes and dice have a strong presence in a number of divinatory folk magics. Both were once frequently made from bone, and the spots on their surfaces can be read *geomantically*, following a system like Yoruban *ifa* divination or Chinese I Ching hexagrams. Some bone reading sets include dice as part of their typical arrangements, too, so they can be added into folk workings and magic that way.

You could also easily appropriate game pieces from board games to incorporate into either divinatory sets or magical charm-and-talisman creation. A little silver shoe stolen from a Monopoly board might be useful to indicate upcoming travel in a *sortilege* set, or it might be a charm you carry in your pocket, wrapped in a bit of cloth or paper inscribed with a Mercurial talisman to help you safely get to your destination. Chess pieces can become powerful tokens, with knights and queens representing a particularly strong ability to move and accomplish things. Wearing one as a necklace or keeping one in your purse or pocket might help to give you advantages in situations like job interviews.

The most famous board game associated with magic, however, doesn't involve tokens or game pieces. The Ouija board has long been a staple of sleepovers and seances. Since the mid-twentieth century, it has also been at the center of all sorts of beliefs about demonic possession and evil spirits. It's important to remember, however, that the game did not start off that way. It was a part of a wider movement called Spiritualism, which took hold in countries like England, the United States, Mexico, and Puerto Rico during the nineteenth and early twentieth centuries. One footnote on a folklore entry about the Ouija board notes "[t]wenty-five or more years ago the manipulating of a ouija board was a parlor pastime in many parts of America."[5] Using Ouija or "talking" boards was a way to ask questions and get answers from the spiritual world, and it often required working with a medium to really accomplish much. It was only with the advent of books and films like *Rosemary's Baby* (1968) and *The Exorcist* (1973) that Spiritualist practices were given widespread associations with demons and diabolism. (It's worth noting that there were conservative religious groups who made those associations in smaller ways well before Linda Blair began vomiting pea soup.)[6] A number of people still have Ouija boards, and they're easy to find second-hand. If you are nervous about using one, work with it in a trusted group of friends, follow the opening and closing procedures (usually just circling the board with the planchette piece in a clockwise motion to open, and counterclockwise to close ending on "Goodbye"), and wear a protective charm if that offers you some peace of mind.

Another movie franchise that we'd like to look to is *Paranormal Activity,* because these movies use toys or electronics to communicate with the ghost (spoiler alert, definitely not a ghost) haunting them. In Paranormal Activity 4, they use the Xbox Kinect's tracking abilities to "see" the demon. The lights cast a grid of green dots, picking up the demon standing right next to them. In *Paranormal Activity: The Marked Ones,* the family is playing the game Simon. While it seems like the game isn't working at first, they ask a silly question, and the green button lights up for "yes." They later determine that red stands for "no," and they use it to communicate and try to figure out what the demon wants. While we don't recommend invoking a homicidal demon into your family game night, there's no reason you couldn't use games like Simon as divinatory tools with just a little tweaking.

Magic in the Mailbox

Who remembers getting a catalog in the mail? For Laine, Pleasant Company (now known as American Girl) was the only one that mattered. Cory loved to grab the SpyTech catalog and dream about espionage gadgets. For others, maybe it was the Sears catalog, or if you're of the younger generation, perhaps the Target holiday catalog or the Amazon Toy Book. Regardless of which catalog had you waiting by the mailbox, most of us can relate to poring over the pages, imagining the fun we'd have, and hoping for that perfect toy. How many of us would grab a pen and circle the ones most important to us? Or, with the Amazon Toy Book, it even comes with stickers that say things like This One!

That feeling was magical, right? So how do we recapture that feeling of enchantment, that excitement that came in the mailbox with the glossy pages and corners just waiting to be dog-eared? One method I've used recently to incorporate toys into my practice is dedicating an altar to my childhood self. I put on it things from my childhood that I used to own, plus a few things that I never got the chance to own. The idea is to take you back to that time in your childhood where suspension of disbelief was incredibly easy. It wasn't even a suspension of disbelief, but a continuation of your actual beliefs. We hadn't learned yet that most people don't believe in magic.

Be your own magic—the magic your 10-year-old self would have loved. If you can't afford the toy you always wanted, or perhaps they don't make it anymore and eBay prices are exorbitant, grab a toy catalog and circle the things you would have loved as a child. Grab a magazine that speaks to you now, whether it's *Southern Living, Parents, GQ, National Geographic,* etc. I like to view this as a childlike approach to a vision board. Circle the things you want boldly to help bring them into your life. Perhaps you want a better organized home, for your toddler to sleep through the night, a more active lifestyle, or to travel more. Find what represents those things to you, circle them with a big Sharpie™ like it were a squeaky ink-smearing magic wand, and know that your wants and needs are valid and worthwhile.

We know a few men who weren't allowed to play with dolls when they were small, or who were only allowed to explore baking with a "Queasy Bake Oven," which involved baking "boy" foods in the shapes of bugs and monsters. And I know a few women who weren't allowed to have G.I. Joes or to paint their room blue. We personally see this as a form of self care—a way of celebrating your childhood wants and desires and telling yourself, "Your wants are valid, and you deserve them." This can be a powerful thing to accept about yourself, especially if you were not allowed to play with certain toys because of rigid parental views on gender.

This is your encouragement to buy that Lego set that was so expensive you never dared ask for it. Sit down with it, take your time putting it together. Buy that doll, with as many dresses as you want. Change their clothes, style their hair, maybe even give them a hug. Buy that science kit and do the simple experiments that you already know the outcome of. Magic is beautiful and wondrous and imaginative and, frankly, messy. Make a mess!

NOTES:

1. D.R. Jordan, "Defixiones from a Well Near the Southwest Corner of the Athenian Agora," in *Hesperia: The Journal of the American School of Classical Studies at Athens*, Vol. 54, No. 3 (Jul. - Sep., 1985), pp. 205–255.
2. One thing Cory learned in his time living and working in the Pennsylvania "Dutch" region was that many of the Mennonite and Amish people in the area were known for making very lovely cloth dolls that were never, ever given facial features. To do so, it was explained to him, would be to be overtaking the godly act of creation, making a sort of "graven image" in the shape of the Creator's own doll-like work: human beings.
3. From "Witchcraft and the Devil in West Virginia," by Ruth Ann Musick, *Appalachian Journal*, Spring 1974, vol. 1 no. 4, pp. 271–76.
4. See Cory Thomas Hutcheson, *Fifty-four Devils: The Art and Folklore of Fortune-telling with Playing Cards* (2013 [2022 Revised ed.]). There is also a "lite" version of the book's methods available free on the New World Witchery website: https://newworldwitchery.com/2010/09/10/blog-post-89-%E2%80%93-the-new-world-witchery-guide-to-cartomancy/
5. From *The Frank C. Brown Collection of North Carolina Folklore*, vol. 7: 5847. A ouija board is one of the best ways of divining things. The board can be purchased at any ten-cent store for a small sum. It has the letters of the alphabet on it, and a little carriage, which, when two persons' hands are placed on it, will spell out answers to any question one can ask it. It foretells deaths, accidents, marriages, and the like. [Jessie Hauser, Pfafftown, Forsyth County. Twenty-five or more years ago the manipulating of a ouija board was a parlor pastime in many parts of America. In its general character it has something in common with table tapping and levitation, although the successful use of the ouija board can be attained without the help of spiritualist practitioners.]
6. For an in-depth and academic breakdown of the role that talking boards and Spiritualist practices played in North American history, I recommend reading Catherine Albanese's *A Republic of Mind and Spirit* (Yale Univ. Press, 2007). If you want more depth on the way that Ouija boards became associated with evil spirits, you could also read *Lucifer Ascending: The Occult in Folklore and Popular Culture*, by Bill Ellis (Univ. of Kentucky Press, 2004).

18. Sticks and Stones

Going out on a Limb with Magic

When Cory was but a wee lad of 10 or so, he was absolutely convinced he was a powerful nature wizard. While this probably surprises no one, most of the neighbors probably wondered at the lanky kid wandering through the neighborhood on his bike with a long oak stick carefully balanced beside him as he made his way to the "dirt hill," a pile of soil leftover from a construction project nearby that served as a sort of de facto playground, mountain, and in Cory's case, wizard's tower. He'd go to the top of it and spend minutes raising his arms with the staff, trying to coax the winds to rise, then die down, then change the shape of clouds, and more.

You'd still have a hard time convincing him it didn't work.

Was it his inherent talent? His wizard's nature? Or was it all, in fact, the stick? Cory kept this staff, a long piece carved by his older brother for a summer camp and inscribed with a few notches and shapes of nonsensical value, for a long time. He was pretty sure that even if it didn't command the winds, it sure made him *feel* like he could. While eventually that staff wound up disappearing into the mists of time and history after a very long tour of duty with Cory, he still keeps an odd staff around his house. This one is a poplar branch that he's fashioned with a large wire hook and some twine wrapping, designed to hold a lantern with a flame in it. He's used this when participating in an annual event known as "The Parade of Spirits" in Philadelphia, which involves dressing as various winter holiday folk figures and wandering the streets. It also seems to be a nice protective little branch, and it stays in the corner to ward off any spiritual baddies that might wander by.

As we've emphasized a lot in this book, folk magic rarely comes from a store, but is instead built from the everyday objects around you. What could be more everyday than wandering outside and finding a nice big stick to use as a staff? Or a twisty little bit of ash or maple wood, just perfect for a wand? Or even a pretty stone just sitting there in the ground, waiting to become your partner in enchanted crime? This chapter, we'll be looking at some of these everyday outdoor treasures—and hopefully offering you some good lore and ideas to use in your own backyard.

The Root of Magic—Or, Getting to Know Your Local Tree Wizards

If you grew up reading J.R.R. Tolkien's *Lord of the Rings*, you're probably familiar with the Ents, a race of ancient tree-beings with deep knowledge who move very slooooooowly, but who also have tremendous power. This connection of trees, wisdom, magic, and time was hardly Tolkien's invention; it likely derives from much older lore about people like the Druids. These religious and magical figures were central to many pre-Christian regions in England, Scotland, Ireland, and Wales, among other places. We mostly have scattered archaeological evidence and a few Roman accounts of them, so piecing together their role in history is a dodgy affair, but we often find information about them gathering in groves of trees and using a variety of woods and forest products in their spiritual practices. They were known to use a formalized ritual to remove mistletoe from oak boughs during the new moon, and they seem to have regarded the yew tree as connected to the realm of the dead.[1]

There are a lot of trees in the mythology of the world. In Norse tales, there's the famed Yggdrasil, which connects the realms of the Norse pantheon and Earth. In Turkish stories, there's a poplar tree known as Baiterek, which houses branches upon which rest the realms of reality. Some Hindu legends also have a similar tree, a fig, that holds up part of the cosmos. Then there are the famed biblical trees of Genesis: the tree of knowledge and the tree of life. The former makes humans as wise as the gods (or spiritual beings, referenced with the plural *elohim* in Hebrew texts), while the latter keeps them immortal. In the Quran, only the tree of life is acknowledged, but it still possesses the power to stave off death and make the eater into an angelic being.

Beyond the mythology, particular trees have become associated with particular qualities over time, with many believed to have unique magical properties. A (very nonexhaustive) list of trees with a few of their folkloric traits follows:

Apple - Apple tree bark was once used to make a tea to help with fevers, and using a splinter from an apple tree was thought to help ease toothache. Apple trees are a common tree to use when "plugging" an illness, which means boring a hole in a tree the same height as a person with an illness and filling it with a bit of their hair and sealing it back up, transferring the illness to the apple tree (See our chapter on Weeds for a bit more on this practice). A bit of farm lore says burying the placenta from the most recent calf birth will ensure the next calf is female. A number of people will also bury bits of umbilical cord or placenta at the roots of a newly planted apple tree to ensure a long and prosperous life for the baby.

Ash - If ash trees begin budding before the oak trees, you can expect a hot, dry summer. If they bud after the oaks, the summer will be wet. Crosses made of ash and hung in the home protect against fire, and carrying keys carved from ash wood is thought to protect against witchcraft. An old divination game in England says that finding an even-leafed ash branch allowed the one who found it to call out "The even ash-leaf in my glove, the first I meet shall be my love," and discover the identity of a future romantic partner. Ash is also one of the traditional woods used to make witch broom handles.

Birch - The birch is deeply associated with a Germanic figure variously known as Perchta or Berchta, and it may very well be associated with other Germanic goddesses like Holle. Birch twigs are used to cleanse a person or place of evil spirits, often by making switches out of them and lightly beating that person or place with them. Birch bristles frequently make up the bristles of a witch's broom.

Beech - The beech tree's name derives from the same root word as "book," and beech wood was used for writing and recording purposes in Northern Europe before the spread of paper. To that end, written charms using beech wood are particularly effective. Keeping a beechnut in one's pocket or on one's desk can be a good way of staying motivated to write or do similar work. Rubbing warts with a twig of beech and then nailing it into the tree is thought to help cure them.

Cedar - A cedar tree is thought to be lucky when planted in the yard, but there are also places like Kentucky where the belief goes that once the tree is tall enough to shade a grave, someone in the household will die. It's also bad luck if a cedar tree on your property dies, and you should avoid burning it, to stave off bad luck. Medicine made from cedar was once thought effective against poisoning. A love spell says to take two branches of cedar and name them for two people, then knot them together. If the branches live, the two will fall in love.

Dogwood - One bit of Appalachian lore says that if a dogwood blooms heavily, it is a sign of a good harvest season. In Kentucky, a dogwood switch breaking after you've cut it is a sign of bad luck to follow. Additionally, you should not use a dogwood switch to drive a horse, or else you're inviting trouble.

Hawthorn - Washing your face in the dew from a hawthorn tree is thought to make you more beautiful. Tying strips of cloth to a hawthorn tree is reported as a love charm in the Ozarks (most likely by naming the cloth for someone you wish to woo or have woo you). Conversely, you are not supposed to get married while the hawthorn is blooming, or it can bring bad luck to the marriage. The blooms are generally considered bad luck to touch, which may be where the wedding taboo comes from.

Holly - Holly is said to be protective when planted around a home, to the point that some insurance companies recommend its sharp leaves as a burglar deterrent. Holly was also believed to protect against wild animal attacks in medieval Europe. And it's a key symbol of the winter holiday season in the Northern Hemisphere. Picking nine holly leaves at midnight, wrapping them in white cloth, and putting them under your pillow on a Friday will grant you a dream of a future lover.

Juniper - Juniper is supposedly good at dispelling ghosts, especially when burned (in either berry or wood form). It also has hex-removing properties when used to sweep down the body or make a wash water to cleanse someone.

Locust - Some superstitions say that the locust is the most likely of any tree to be struck by lightning. The locust is also used much like the apple tree for plugging cures. In this case, the cures are more targeted at childhood ailments, with the expectation that once the child has grown past the height of the plug the ailment will fade. Locust trees blooming heavily usually indicate a good year for crops.

Maple - The maple is another common tree to use for plugging magic, although in this case the targets are longer-term diseases like rheumatism and tuberculosis. One delightful bit of lore says that if you pluck a maple leaf during a new moon and keep it in a book, you can make a wish and have it come true. If the leaves of a maple tree turn "silver" or flip over during a wind, it means a storm is coming. A love divination ritual says to take two maple leaves, one named for each partner (you can use more than two if you have multiple partners), and drop them in a stream. If they stay together as they float away the relationship will last, but if they drift apart so, too, will the affections of those involved.

Oak - Oaks are used to make strong, durable objects, and that sense of strength is a big part of their magical lore. They can be used to make protective charms, especially if you happen to have a bit of lightning-struck oak to hang in your home as a deterrent to fire and storm damage. Oak, like the apple, maple, and locust, is also used for plugging-based cures.

Peach - Peach tree leaves are sometimes used as a dressing for wounds. There's a great story about soldiers during the American Civil War recovering in a peach grove whose wounds glowed with "angel fire" and healed more quickly. This turned out to be caused by a particular bioluminescent nematode in the peach trees that also had antibacterial properties. One sad bit of lore says that if a peach tree blooms early, a death is coming soon.

Pine - Pine needles are infused to make a drink a bit like an herbal lemonade, based on Indigenous lore from peoples like the Cherokee/Tsaligi. They have a lot of magical purification and cleansing associations (see our notes on the famous Pine-Sol cleaner in our chapter on Washing Up). Similar to the cedar lore, if you have pine trees large enough to shade a grave, you can expect a death to follow, according to Kentucky lore.

Poplar - Poplar trees sometimes "silver" like maples or turn their leaves over before a storm, so you can watch them for signs of wet weather. Poplar leaves are placed under the beds of those who are sick to help dispel any lingering illness. Growing poplar trees in your yard can mean having bad luck at love, or bad luck in general. Given that they were often used as lynching trees, that association makes sense, although we generally try not blame the tree for something terrible humans did with it. The buds of a poplar are sometimes called "Balm of Gilead" and distilled and mixed into a salve for healing. They can be placed around the home to ensure domestic tranquility and prevent harm from the Evil Eye.

Rowan - Rowan trees are protective. One of Cory's favorite charms is a set of rowan twigs bound by red thread into a cross shape. It hangs in his home or sits on his bookshelves, and it was made for him by a dear friend. This tradition of using rowan crosses may predate Christianity, with the crosses being equal-armed and acting as a barrier against evil. Some rowan trees are used like hawthorns to tie cloth to in a wishing or love ritual.

Sassafras - Sassafras should never be burned, or it will bring bad luck and financial ruin. Conversely, hanging sassafras roots over the door of a business or keeping a bit in a cash register brings good luck and prosperity. Carrying the root in your pocket is said to prevent disease from reaching you. Old country wisdom says to only stir soap with a sassafras stick, because it will make the soap a good protection from evil witchcraft.

Walnut - Like sassafras, walnut wood shouldn't be burned lest it bring misfortune. Juice from walnut rinds is thought to help cure warts, and soaking walnut husks in water and then using it to wash oneself is a good way to remove any curses or bad luck. Next to the locust, folk wisdom says walnuts are the next most-often struck by lightning. If the first three walnuts you crack in a given year are all excellent, you can expect to be married within the coming year, but if the first three are all rotten, then a death is expected.

Willow - This is famously a medicinal tree, from whence we derive aspirin, so it can be carried, worn, or placed nearby to ward off other "headaches" such as unwelcome guests or gossipy people. One bit of Kentucky lore says that planting a weeping willow will predestine you to the single life, but we prefer to think of this as claiming your independence. Like the ash, willow twigs can be rubbed over a wart, then buried to encourage it to go away. If you're the scholarly sort, put a willow leaf in the book you're studying, and it will help you pass any tests or exams related to the subject. Willow is used to bind up the bristles on the handle of a witch's broom.

Yew - Some yews are very ancient, with the oldest ones in England found in Surrey, Wiltshire, and Herefordshire dating back some four thousand years. The association with yew and the dead also led to a long-standing tradition of planting yew trees in English cemeteries, and it may also be connected with the practice of fashioning longbows from yew wood.[2]

Aside from the basic magical lore of the trees, there are plenty of things you can do with those sticks you find. There's the much-loved magic wand, which can be an incredibly complex construction of woods, metals, gemstones, and more. A simple, well-loved piece of wood, however, can just as easily serve as a wand. The best way to make a wand is to find a piece of wood that feels comfortable in your hand. Most are around eight to sixteen inches long, but you can work with what you like best. Then use a small craft knife or pocketknife to carve in meaningful symbols. If you don't feel up to carving, you can paint the wand with symbols. We recommend putting a bit of red coloring at the base of the wand, symbolizing its ties to you through blood, and many people will also finish the tip of the wand with white as a sort of "radiant" color to disperse energies. Wands are usually consecrated using incense smoke, the light of the moon, or blessed liquids like holy water or wine, and they are kept wrapped up when not in use.

A longer form of the wand would be the staff, like the one Cory used to carry to command the winds. In this case, you would do much the same as the wand in carving or painting meaningful symbols on it. In addition, you may wish to wrap part of it in twine or leather where your hand will most likely rest. In British Traditional Witchcraft, a brass nail is driven into the "foot" of the staff to ground it. A staff with a forked top is called a "stang" and resembles old-fashioned hay forks (which were once just as associated with flying witches as the now better-known brooms are). The fork can be used to hold things like a candle or even a skull (or skull representation), and it becomes a sort of portable altar space for some witches when they are working with Otherworldly entities.

Finally, you can easily craft little figures out of sticks. If you've ever seen the film *The Blair Witch Project*, you might remember all the little semi-human shaped figures hung in trees around the forest. In that movie, they become a sign that the "witch" is nearby and mark her territory. You can also craft a figure with the sticks from your yard, name it, and "feed" it with offerings of water, wine, coffee, or whatever you like. In Pennsylvania German traditions, this figure is called the *butzemann,* and it functions as a sort of magical scarecrow that will guard the property and magically help with household work. It is supposed to be burned every year, but a bit of the old year's butzemann is retained to be added to the next year's. You might also make figures like this that you name and bond with as a way to have a magical companion for your work (and if you make a few dozen of them and hang them around your house, you'll probably keep any uncool people far away by freaking them out just the right amount).[3]

All of which is to say, take the time to get to know your local trees! They may have a lot to tell you!

Witchcraft Rocks!—Or, Getting Stoned with Sorcery

If you have spent much time around witchy folk, you know that there are people who go absolutely *mad* for crystals and gemstones. People swear by their cleansing amethysts, love-drawing rose quartzes, or protective tiger's eyes. We don't have anything against those sorts of gems and stones, so long as they are mined ethically. In the spirit of the junk drawer and everyday branches of folk magic, though, what can you do with the rocks and stones in your own backyard?

A good friend of Laine's loves to have a vegetable garden every year, and last year she was really fighting to stave off squirrels, rabbits, birds, and squash bugs. One trick she had that makes a fun craft with the kids is to find smooth pebbles around the size of a strawberry and paint them to look as much like the fruit as you can. Garden pests may come by and think it's a delicious snack, but they get a surprise when they instead bite into a hard rock. Animals soon learn there's no point in eating the strawberries and leave your fruit alone.

Cory remembers being young and finding little stones on the playground with ridges all over them in nearly cylindrical shapes. These had a derogatory name (one not worthy of repeating now), but they were thought to be special and lucky at the time. Little did he know he had found something wonderful: a fossilized crinoid! These are a type of echinoderm related to creatures like starfish that lived long ago, but have since become stone. These little rocks have often been associated with money, having once been called "St. Boniface's pennies" in parts of Germany. They can be used to make necklaces, bracelets, or rosaries with a bit of careful hole-drilling, and they are a wonderful bit of our ancient world to carry with you. They aren't the only fossils one can find. Picking up a good field guide, such as the *National Audubon Society Field Guide to Fossils* (Alfred A. Knopf, 1994), will help you find all sorts of fossils in your world that you didn't know existed. Many of these have long been associated with protective powers, and their roots in our ancient world are a good way to connect with deep time and the Earth as a living being. Cory once spent part of a family vacation by the roadside in Utah and Colorado finding little fish fossils in shale deposits, which were incredibly thrilling discoveries for him. If you're near an ocean, you can find fossils that wash up from time to time—like sharks' teeth, which have long been worn for protection.

Stones known as "fairy crosses" can be found in the mountains of the Eastern United States. These are natural formations of the mineral staurolite, which forms in hexagonal crystallizations that sometimes intersect to create cross-like shapes. There's even a state park in Virginia named Fairy Stone State Park that allows you to go digging for these! They are associated with fairies mostly through colloquial legends about the Unseen Folk who wandered these mountains in Cherokee/Tsalagi lore, but the crosses are carried by people for good luck and blessings.

Finally, perhaps the most powerful "average" magical stone is the holed stone, sometimes called the "holey stone" or "hagstone." These are rocks that have a natural hole in them, usually found in or near riverbeds or the sea because the water erodes the gaps into the stone. Lore about the stones is found in various parts of western Europe and North America. In parts of Britain, very large stones with holes in them are treated as magical portals that have fairy magic in them that is capable of healing those who pass through the holes. In Cornwall, for example, a large stone in the Parish of Madron was used by parents to pass young children through to cure them of rickets (which was actually caused by calcium deficiency).

Smaller holey stones were often strung and hung up over beds to stave off nightmares and other evil spirits during the vulnerable sleeping hours. Red thread or ribbon was preferred for this, and the stones could also be worn around the neck for such protections. One account notes they were tied to the keys of one's house, which would bar any evil sorcery from being worked against the household—sort of like an anti-hex keyring! They can be placed along a windowsill as a barrier against bad magic. Holey stones are thought to be very lucky, even if not kept. An account from 1889 says that children would find them, spit on them, and toss them over their shoulders saying "Lucky stone! Lucky stone! Go over my head, and bring me some good luck before I go to bed!"[4] There seems to be some belief that one can peer through the hole as well, and see the unseen world of spirits and fairies. This bit of lore was taken up in the popular children's book series *The Spiderwick Chronicles* by Tony DiTerlizzi and Holly Black (Simon & Schuster, 2003–04).

Seeds of Spellwork—Or, Going Nuts with Enchantment

When you're wandering your yard or local park, you're sure to find leaves, twigs, and rocks everywhere. You're also likely to be stepping on or over (sometimes with a grumbling curse under your breath) all the seeds, acorns, nuts, and other "mast" dropped by our bark-covered and leafy elder citizens.

To finish up this chapter, here are a few bits of lore about all those little gifts you might find falling on the ground (or your head, if a particularly obnoxious squirrel targets you):

- Naming peach seeds after women who have had children will make the seeds more likely to grow.
- Finding dry beechnuts on or after November 1 indicates a rough winter to come.
- An apple can be named after a crush or love interest, and all the seeds over thirteen in number indicate how many children you would have with them. Additionally, a similar divination allows that odd numbers of seeds indicate a successful courtship, while even seeds are a sign of one to miss.
- An apple's pips (seeds) can be tossed into the fire and named for various lovers. The ones that pop loudly are the best matches, while those that fizzle are romantic dead-ends. This is especially done on Halloween Eve.
- Carrying a black walnut in your pocket can keep headaches away.
- Buckeye nuts are often carried to ward off everything from rheumatism to fevers to cramps.
- If you catch one of the maple "whirlybirds" (the little fluttering seed pods of a maple that spiral down like tiny helicopters), then you're supposed to make a wish before letting it fall the rest of the way to the ground.
- Walnuts or hickory nuts with thin hulls mean a light winter, but thick hulls mean a heavy one.
- Acorns, beechnuts, or walnuts in abundance on the ground means that Nature (or in some lore God) is providing for the animals before a particularly harsh winter.
- Eating walnuts is supposed to be good for your brain (based largely on the resemblance to a human skull and brain).
- Finding a worm in an acorn is a sign of poverty to follow, and if an insect flies out of it when the cap is removed it can mean war or conflict coming.
- Finding any two nuts growing together in one husk or hull is extremely lucky and is thought to protect against witchcraft and malefic magic. These are sometimes called "St. John's nuts."
- If you go collecting nuts on Holy-Rood Day (September 14), you can meet the devil. In some cases, you can ask him for a favor if you are fearless and brave. In some cases this also stands true if you go nut-collecting on any Sunday.[5]

This is but a small sampling—a snack mix, if you will—of the many bits of nut, tree, and stone lore that exist. We've tried to focus primarily on the lore associated with the sorts of things you might find just wandering outside. Hopefully the next time you're standing under an apple or walnut tree and get bonked on the noggin, it will jog your memory a little about all the wonderful enchantment around you. That, or you'll be plotting vengeance on that squirrel above you.

NOTES:

1. A nice, brief history of the Druids can be found in the wonderful *The Book of English Magic*, written by Philip Carr-Gomm and Richard Heygate (Overlook Press, 2009).

2. The tree lore here comes from a variety of sources: Iona Opie and Moira Tatem's *A Dictionary of Superstitions* (Oxford Univ. Press, 1989); *The Frank C. Brown Collection of North Carolina Folklore*, vol. 6 and vol. 7 (Duke Univ. Press, 1961); Patrick W. Gainer's *Witches, Ghosts, and Signs* (West Virginia Univ. Press, 1975 [2008 reprint]); Judika Illes's *Encyclopedia of 5,000 Spells* (Harper Collins, 2009); *The Book of English Magic*, written by Philip Carr-Gomm and Richard Heygate (Overlook Press, 2009); Daniel and Lucy Thomas's *Kentucky Superstitions* (Franklin Classics, 2018 [1920]); Harry M. Hyatt's *Folk-Lore From Adams County, Illinois* (Alma Egan Hyatt Foundation, 1935); and Vance Randolph's *Ozark Magic and Folklore* (Columbia Univ. Press, 1947). A note: there are some practices here, like tying cloth to trees, that can be detrimental to the tree or environment.

3. For more on the *butzemann* tradition, see *The First Book of Urglaawe Myths*, by Robert L. Schreiwer (Independently Published, 2014).

4. From Opie & Tatem's *A Dictionary of Superstitions*, p. 199.

5. These bits of lore taken from: Opie & Tatem's *A Dictionary of Superstitions*, pp. 3–4, 290–91; Randolph's *Ozark Magic and Folklore*, pp. 114, 153; Hyatt's *Folk-Lore From Adams County, Illinois*, pp. 9–10; and Gainer's *Witches, Ghosts, and Signs*, p. 118.

19. In the Weeds

Spell Stuff Between the Sidewalk Cracks

Who doesn't love a good weed? Okay, well, plenty of gardeners will scowl when errant bits of crabgrass, wood sorrel, or dandelion find their way into a well-maintained flowerbed, but if we really stop and think about it, weeds are just plants growing in places we think they shouldn't. In the end, that means what a "weed" is comes down to perspective.

Weeds are hearty little creatures. They grow from the thinnest of cracks in a cement sidewalk, take over the waste spaces around an abandoned industrial space, or turn an unused lot into a little meadow (or a tiny jungle in some cases). They share their habitat, too, providing food for pollinators like bees and butterflies—and even for us, if we know what we're looking for. If you've ever enjoyed a dandelion spring green salad, you know that the young greens of this common weed can be quite tasty and add a bittersweet crunch to a light lunch. They make homes for wildlife like mice, snakes, rabbits, and more, and they track the seasons almost as well as any almanac or clock.

You may have already guessed this, but we think weeds are also a source of magic. The plants that grow around us, unasked for, often have a lot to say about the interwoven power of the natural world, and they are usually more than ready to knit themselves into our enchanted narratives.

In this chapter, we'll look at some of the commonplace plants that you might find growing in a backyard, along a ditch, by a bit of scrubland, or an overgrown field. Importantly, we won't be focusing much on the herbal side of this—meaning we won't be talking about brewing up teas or tinctures out of these plants. Why? Well, for one, we are not botanists, even though we have a deep love for wild plants. It would be irresponsible of us to tell you to go nibbling weeds that you may well have a bad allergic reaction to, and even more irresponsible to tell you to heal your wounds using those plants when we are not trained in any form of medicine. There are literally dozens of other great books on the edible properties of wild plants and their applications in folk healing.[1]

While we may mention folklore involving eating, touching, or smelling plants, this is never intended as medical advice. You should always listen to physicians' advice about medical applications of any kind. Also, never ingest anything you've foraged without being completely certain of its identification and safety. Always check with experts first.

We will instead focus on the way that plants, shrubs, trees, leaves, and other green-and-growing things can be used more generally within folk magic more generally. There are lots of great folk uses for our botanical companions!

Blowing Wishes and Counting Kids: Divination and Wish Magic with Weeds

Plenty of people have seen or heard someone—in person or in a television show, film, or book—slowly plucking petals from the head of a flower and repeating the phrase, "he loves me, he loves me not." These sorts of counting and divination games using wildflowers have been a part of youthful puppy love for centuries. Sometimes it works with the simple yes/no dynamic, but there are more complex variations on the practice. Daisies, in particular, seem to have a good bit of folklore around plucking their petals, as they have enough of them to be too difficult to count at a glance, but not so many they can't be plucked in a brief sitting. One version of the charm from Dorset, England, in 1831 notes that the petals can be pulled off to help divine the occupation of a future lover:

> "I recollect some of my female friends, while gathering flowers in a meadow, would stop, and , plucking a large daisy, pull off the petals one by one, repeating… 'Rich man, poor man, farmer, ploughman, thief,' fancying that the one which came to be named at plucking the last petal would be her husband."[2]

Dandelions also have fortune-telling powers. Their puffy seed heads can hold the answers to several questions. Some children will ask the dandelion what time it is, then blow on the seeds and deduce from how many remain whether the time has come to hurry home for supper. Another variation says that however many puffs it takes to clear the head of seeds entirely represents the hours remaining before the child needs to get back home. The dandelion can also be asked whether or not someone is thinking of you, in a sort of "remember-me" type of gentle love spell:

> "Are you separated from…your love? [C]arefully pluck one of the feather heads, charge each of the little feathers with a tender thought; turn towards the spot where the loved one dwells; blow, and the seed-ball will convey your message… Blow again; and if there be left upon the stalk a single aigrette, it is proof you are not forgotten."[3]

Other questions that can be posed to the dandelion head include: "How many years before I am married (or find love)?" and "How many children will I have?" The number of seeds remaining after a puff on the "little feathers" will provide the answer, at least according to English-speaking folklore. How many puffs you use is slightly contentious, with some lore saying you only puff for as long as a single breath and some versions saying you should puff three times. We recommend experimenting to find out which works best for you, especially since it means spreading more delightful—and delicious—dandelions around!

Holly leaves can be used in a counting divination to ask when something longed for or expected shall come to pass. According to a bit of North Carolinian folklore, you should ask the holly leaf your question as you pluck it, then count the spiny points on the leaf, saying "this year, next year, now, never" as you go around. Whichever you end on will be your answer. Another variation allows you to do the same counting, but to name each point with a letter as you try to divine the first initial of a future romantic prospect. Additionally, some people will put a nine-pointed holly leaf under their pillow to lead to dreams of a future partner.[4]

Some flowers have less pleasant divinatory capabilities. Daffodils can foretell misfortune in some places, and a superstition persists that when one sees the first daffodil of the year its head should be hanging away from you, or else you can expect downcast fortunes all through the remaining year.

Wishes are also a part of the folklore of wild plants, and while they may not be the most rigorous sort of spellwork, they can be a quick bit of wild magic that anyone can do without raising many eyebrows. Dandelion seeds are a prime example, as many people believe that wishing on a dandelion head and then managing to blow all the little fluffy parasols off of it in a single gust means the wish will come true. Similarly, the "whirlygig" or "whirlybird" seeds of maple trees can be an opportunity for wishing. If you happen to catch one as it's falling from the tree, you can make a wish and then toss it back into the air to bring your wish to fruition. While it's incredibly fun to watch the little seed pods twirl their way to the earth, you should avoid that when making the wish, as you don't want to see it land.

Catching a falling leaf from most trees in autumn is also thought to be a sign of good luck coming your way, or an opportunity to make a wish. Maple leaves can be used to divine a relationship's future, if you have a stream nearby. The couple each takes a leaf (or you could name the leaves for each of the members of the romantic grouping, which makes this easily adaptable for polyamorous relationships). After the naming, the leaves are placed in a stream touching one another and left to float. If they manage to stay together for at least twenty feet—or ideally until out of sight—then the relationship is in solid standing and likely to last. Should they drift apart early, however, then it may be time to revisit those concert tickets you bought together for next year.[5]

Pricks, Scratches, & Pokes: The Sharper Side of Plant Magic

Not everything along the pathway or in the hedgerow is wishes and love predictions. There are a number of plants with less friendly components that have found their way into magical practices. As the 80s band Poison once sang, "Every rose has its thorn," right?

If you have a backyard full of roses, then you've got one of the best-known love charms. For example, a trail of rose petals left from the front door to the bedroom is a relatively clear indication that you want to do more than change the sheets when your beloved arrives. Similarly, you can incorporate roses into love potions and even foods to give a little romantic boost to your magic.

Rose Syrup
For this recipe you will need:
2-3 cups of clean rose petals (make sure not to use any treated with insecticides)
1 cup of sugar
Water

Begin by lightly sweating the roses in a small saucepan with a lid over low heat. You'll begin seeing condensation forming on the lid eventually, which is the rose essence you're trying to extract. Before the petals can burn, stir them and add the water, about one cup or a bit more if necessary. Bring to a bare simmer and let the rose petals infuse for at least 30 minutes, until the flowers are wilted and translucent. Strain off the liquid and discard the solids, then return the liquid to the pan and add the sugar. Bring to a boil and let boil until the sugar completely dissolves and the mixture reduces a bit. Bottle the rose syrup and keep in the fridge for up to a week.

What do you do with rose syrup? Well, it's used in lots of Middle Eastern pastries, so it's a great way to add sweetness and a floral note to something like pound cake. Serve that to a potential lover with a few rose petals around the plate (not the cooked ones, save a couple fresh ones for this). You can even draw sigils and signs into the cake with the syrup, then brush a layer of syrup over them to hide them if you wish.

You can try making your own rose water, which is a similar process to the syrup, but with a few extra steps and minus the sugar. You'd still add the petals to the water and simmer, but you'll also place a heatproof bowl in the pan (one that will fit when the pan is covered; ceramic cereal bowls are often great for this). Make sure no water can get into your bowl and that the petal/water mix only comes up about halfway around the bowl. Then turn the lid upside down, so the handle of the lid points down into your bowl. Get ice and pile it into the inverted lid (or use a metal bowl that you've had in the freezer and put the ice into that, then put that bowl on top of the inverted lid). This will cause the rose essence to distill, basically, and after thirty to forty-five minutes you'll have a healthy little bit of rose water ready to use. You can sprinkle it in places where you need love and kindness, or even add things like ginger to help spice things up in someone's love life.

Don't count out those thorns, though! They also can be functional, magically speaking. Many insurance agents and home security experts will point out how valuable it is to have thorny or prickly bushes like roses or holly near windows to deter thieves from entering. Thorns are also useful in curses, as they are frequently used in poppets or bottle spells as a way of inflicting painful-and-baneful magics. Blackthorn and hawthorn spines are particularly common in these workings, especially in English folk magic. In the United States, black locust spines would be an effective alternative.

But the thorny side of magic can have a positive side. For example, in parts of Appalachia the custom of finding and using "bramble arches" for their curative powers is part of the regional lore. These arches are natural curves of things like blackberries or other thorny plants that have grown into a hoop or arch. Some Southerners will even find a new-sprouted bramble bush and train it to grow in such an arch—perhaps defying the "natural" occurrence side of things, but still providing the arch for magical use. These arches are thought to have the power to pull off or shear away harmful conditions, and there are sources that discuss passing infants with conditions like whooping cough through such an arch to get rid of the ailment.[6]

One final prickly bit of plant magic involves not the spines on the plants, but the use of nails, pegs, or spikes driven into trees. This practice, called "plugging" in parts of the South, involved taking someone's measurement against a tree and marking it. Whatever condition afflicted them—usually something long-term like spinal curvature, asthma, a stutter, or a limp—would then be "nailed" into the tree with a railroad spike, knife, or iron nail. Sometimes a rag that had been used to wipe the person might be driven in with the spike, or a lock of their hair, a scrap of their clothing, or even a puff of their breath (especially in the case of asthma). The idea was that as the person grew past the plugged mark, their condition would lessen. If the tree died from the spike, it would also kill the condition—although some lore also indicated that if a person tied themselves to a tree this way the tree should be cared for instead, because its wasting and dying would bring a similar outcome to the person "plugged" into it.

One version of plugging was also used to defeat witchcraft done against a person: "To kill a witch, draw a heart on a holly tree, and drive a spike into her heart for nine mornings, driving it up at the last morning. Then she'll die."[7]

Sub-Rosa: Under the Power of Plants

Before we depart the garden, yard, sidewalk, or local park, I thought I should share two bits of lore with a bit less sharpness.

One is the term "sub-rosa." If you're someone working in the legal field, you may have bumped into this term a time or two, and you likely know that it means something done secretly or behind closed doors. It literally means "under the rose," though, so why are roses associated with secrecy? There are many potential origins of the phrase, including some tied to the Roman myths of Venus and Cupid, but one of the strongest contenders as to why the phrase stuck around is that many Catholic confessional booths had carved decorations of roses over them. Roses are frequently associated with the Virgin Mary, as well as with Jesus, and so someone passing beneath the rose was to receive grace and forgiveness for whatever they confessed, so long as they were sincere and willing to do penance. The confidentiality of confession then tied the rose to the act of secrecy. Later groups like the initiatory-and-somewhat-secretive Rosecrucians (whose name indicates a rose and a cross) also adopted the symbol of the rose within their architecture.

Finally, rather than being under the rose, what about being under the moss? A Caldwell County, North Carolina, love charm states that: "planting the entwined names of two persons under the moss on the east side of certain trees will bring them together."[8] Even humble moss has magical uses! There truly is much magic growing right beneath our feet.

NOTES

1. Some particularly useful books we'd recommend if you are interested in pursuing herbal remedy-oriented types of plant applications include: *Jude's Herbal Home Remedies*, by Jude Todd (Llewellyn Publications); the Peterson Field Guide Series including *Medicinal Plants and Herbs of Eastern and Central North America and Western Medicinal Plants and Herbs* (Mariner Books); *Edible and Useful Wild Plants of the United States and Canada*, by Charles Francis Saunders (Dover Books); and a pair of books that add in foraging, herbalism, and witchcraft from very knowledgeable and experienced practitioners' perspectives, *Wild Witchcraft: Folk Herbalism, Garden Magic, and Foraging for Spells, Rituals, and Remedies*, by Rebecca Beyer (Simon Element) and *A Witch's Guide to Wildcraft: Using Common Plants to Create Uncommon Magick*, by J.D. Walker (Llewellyn Publications).
2. From *A Dictionary of Superstitions*, by Iona Opie and Moira Tatem (Oxford Univ. Press, 1989), p. 115.
3. Ibid.
4. From *The Frank C. Brown Collection of North Carolina Folklore*, vol. 6 and vol. 7 (Duke Univ. Press, 1961).
5. Ibid.
6. One version of this is found Patrick W. Gainer's West Virginia folklore collection, *Witches, Ghosts, & Signs* (West Virginia Univ. Press, 1975 [2008 reprint]), p. 111. Crucially, this sort of treatment was used in times and places where "professional" doctors were hard to find, expensive, mistrusted, or any combination of those conditions. This is certainly NOT medical advice that should in any way take the place of professional treatment.
7. Brown Collection, v.7 p.132 - no. 569.
8. Ibid., no. 4273.

20. Fido and Fluffy

Adding Bark and Bite to Your Magic

When one thinks of animals and witchcraft, familiars come to mind. You might think of a black cat sitting by an altar, candlelight reflected in their eyes, or perhaps a raven perched on a desk, an old grimoire open next to them. Other common familiars closely associated with witches are dogs, toads, hares, rats, and even ferrets.

Familiars are animals that a witch can employ to help them with their magic. And there have been whole books written about familiars. But we'd like to explore the ways that our pets can be incorporated into our magic without them necessarily needing to be a familiar.

Laine once had a dual-coated husky mix that didn't leave dust bunnies—he left dust buffalo roaming the plains of her kitchen. She moved houses after he died and still found his fur in the new house. Many people keep mementos of their pets, especially after they've died. A lock of their fur, a collar, or an impression of their paw are all popular as ways to hold onto their memory. Collecting a pet's fur is one of the easiest things you can do to incorporate your pet's particular qualities (both for their personality or for their species as a whole) into your spellwork.

Magic that Gives You... Paws?—Dogs in Spellcraft

Dogs are eager, loyal, fun, sociable, and ready to learn—all of which are pretty great qualities to strive for and would be of great use in spells. Take a little of your dog's fur and create a packet spell for your job interview. A lot of those amazing doggy qualities are great to present to a potential employer! Or perhaps you're diving into a new hobby and want to make some friends. Just bringing a dog could inspire new friendships, since nothing breaks the ice like having a dog to bond over! But dogs can't be brought into every new situation—some people are afraid of them, or allergic—so carrying a lock of your dog's fur with you could inspire those same friendly, tail-wagging feelings in potential new friends.

Dogs also have jobs! Herding, search and rescue, and medical service dogs all work to make our lives better every day. These dogs are great at remaining calm under pressure and take instruction well. Carry the fur of a service dog with you while studying or while you take a test—or perhaps that of a breed that is known for its intelligence, like a border collie. Or its boundless energy and enthusiasm, like a Jack Russell terrier. Some dogs are considered particularly lucky. One bit of Somerset, England, lore notes that dalmatians—charmingly known as "plum-pudding dogs" or "spotted carriage dogs"—are thought to be very lucky if you see them in the course of your day. You can even make a wish upon seeing one, and since the lore isn't terribly specific, you could probably adopt one and it would be rather like having all your wishes come true. But then, we feel that way about adopting dogs in general.[1] Dogs also used to be employed in digging up magical ingredients like mandrake roots. It was thought that mandrakes screamed when first pulled from the ground, and the noise could paralyze or kill whatever removed them, so dogs were tied to the roots and then made to pull them loose in the hopes that any harmful effects would hit poor Fido first. *This seems awful, and we do NOT recommend it.*

The fur of a dog has a lot of folk magical uses, as well. If you've ever had a night of too much indulgence, you've probably also heard the phrase "hair of the dog" applied to a variety of sobering and soothing (and often somewhat disgusting) remedies. That axiom comes from an older folk belief that when one was bitten by a dog, especially a "mad" one or one infected with rabies, the best cure was to consume a bit of the dog's hair or bind some of its fur over the bite. That is absolutely NOT good medical advice, and modern medicine has a much better record of treating rabies than this folk method. Still, the concept has its uses, and making a little charm of shed dog fur as a ward against suffering ill effects from questionable life choices can be effective magic.

A dog's howl is also worth noting. We often used to work magical rites together, and we usually asked for a sign of some kind that our offerings to Underworld beings or our dispersals of magical intent had been accepted. We most commonly asked for a sign in the form of "the bark of a dog, the cry of a bird, or a gust of wind," and found that in most cases we could count on one of those things happening. A dog's bark or howl in the distance has been regarded as magical for a long time, although usually with less enthusiasm than we mustered. In most cases, a howling dog indicates that there is a death or other tragedy not far behind. Think also of the appearance of various spectral dogs, like the infamous "Black Shuck" of East Anglian English lore. Such tales inspired Sir Arthur Conan Doyle to pit his popular detective Sherlock Holmes against a supposedly spectral beast in "The Hound of the Baskervilles." Another eerie bit of lore says that a dog crawling on its belly is "measuring his master's grave."[2]

Does all of this mean that you should fret and worry every time your dog yowls or your neighbor's hound starts barking in the middle of the night? There are practical reasons to listen when your dog makes noise, as they are usually trying to communicate and may, in fact, be warning you of imminent danger. But it's far better to simply get to know the dogs in your life, carry a few extra treats in your pocket, and listen to what they have to say. Sometimes, they do seem smarter than the humans around them.

The Cackling Calico—Cat Witchery

Cats are intuitive, protective, and good at setting boundaries. They will let you know when they're done socializing or being touched. Use cat fur in your spells for when you need to stand up for yourself, such as when you plan to ask for a raise, or even in legal matters like divorce proceedings. Use the common superstition about black cats to your advantage—most people don't want to cross paths with one, so use the fur of a black cat in a spell for confidence and when you need to exude the energy of "don't cross me." There is an almost equal body of lore that says owning or petting black cats specifically brings luck, so you can have them do double-duty: give them a few scritches behind the ears to borrow their beneficial powers while also having them act as a barrier against enemies. We also love the idea of using a cat's collar in a binding spell, especially when you need to set specific boundaries with the person you are binding. Cats are frequently said to have "nine lives," too, meaning they represent resiliency and second chances. If you need to start over after something difficult, heavy, or bad, consider petting a cat (or even better, getting a cat, who will be a sympathetic, if demanding, companion).

One of the major threads of cat lore involves our feline friends' grooming habits. Cats frequently wash themselves, and the way in which they do so is sometimes observed to determine things like coming weather or other prognostications. A cat sitting with its tail pointing at the fireplace while it grooms is thought to be an indication of cool weather, frost, or snow. A cat licking its paws and using them to wash its face, particularly near a chimney or window, is believed to indicate rain coming soon. A cat cleaning behind its ears foretells of a visit from a stranger.[3]

It's normal for cats to routinely shed whiskers, and they can be great to collect for spells. Cats use their whiskers to gather information about their surroundings—whether that be finding any potential threats or seeing if they'll fit through a tight space. Do you need to navigate a delicate situation? Perhaps you need to have an awkward talk with a friend, or a difficult conversation at work. Incorporate shed cat whiskers into a spell to help you lithely maneuver through your own tight spot, whatever that may be. Laine likes to use a cat whisker like a quill, writing a few lines of her spells with it.

Whiskers also can be used for opening communication. Whisker follicles are packed with nerves and transmit information to the cat, working as a supplement to their other senses, so placing a whisker in a spell bag may boost your communication and intuition. This would also work well in protection spells, as the purpose of the whisker information is to keep the cat safe.

Another fact of owning cats is dealing with litter boxes. You can use your cat's litter box to banish something (or someone) negative from your life. Write out what you want to be rid of on a scrap of paper—something like biting your nails, unemployment, or the name of a person you no longer want in your life. Put the paper in the bottom the next time you change the litter. It will be peed on, pooped on, and scratched up. Then you can throw it away!

One place not to bring cats is on water. This isn't just because they don't typically like it—although there are obviously a number of cats who don't mind it. Cats on ships were sometimes seen as bad luck. Scottish maritime tradition held that even uttering the word "cat" on a sailing boat could bring misfortune and woe. Some sailors believed that bad weather was caused by someone keeping a cat shut up in a cupboard or under a bucket or other device, which could bring anything from becalmed conditions to outright gales and hurricanes.

A final bit of cat lore involves a delightful story of a family that adopted a big, strange cat. One day, the husband was out traveling, got caught in a rainstorm, and had to hole up in an abandoned house. While he was there, he witnessed a massive group of cats all carrying another large cat on something that looked a lot like a stretcher. One feline turned to the man and said, "When you get home, you let them know that old Kitty Rollins is dead!" The man couldn't believe it and ran from the house through the storm all the way home. After he had calmed down and warmed and dried himself by the fire, his family asked what had happened. He told the story of the cats in the old house, and when he got to the part about old Kitty Rollins being dead, their own cat jumped up from its place before the fire and did a little dance before crying out, "By the devil, that means I'm the new Queen of the Witches!" before it darted out the door and was never seen again. The family got a dog shortly after that.[4]

We share that tale because it's delightfully witchy and to remind you that you never know if a cat is just a cat—or if it's just biding its time, waiting to be crowned Queen of the Witches. Plan accordingly.

Enchantment Taking Wing—Bird-based Magical Lore

In general, feathers often represent the element of air. Creativity, travel, communication, and divination are all aspects of the element, and feathers are great to use when needing a spell in this area. One thing I love about using feathers is that there are so many kinds of birds! And their feathers all have different feelings and different properties for use in spellwork. Mockingbirds are common in the South and are well known for their ability to mimic. I once heard a cat meowing outside but couldn't find the cat, no matter how many "pssp pssps" I gave it. I finally realized that it was a mockingbird right outside my window. They also mock other birds or, rather, their calls. (There are no mockingbirds hopping into bird baths, saying, "lOoK aT mE i'M a cHicKAdEe! Shut up." Let's be honest—if any bird was saying that, it would totally be the blue jay.)

I love the idea of using different feathers for very specific reasons. The uses for feathers are varied—I often use one to simply waft incense around. But you could use a feather as a quill or a fan, or put it in a small pouch with other objects and make a mojo bag. Mockingbird feathers could be used for glamor magic, or when you're trying to "fake it till you make it." Canary feathers, due to the bird's history as an early indicator of danger, could be of use in protection magic. One of my favorite birds to spot is a bluebird! In many cultures bluebirds bring happiness and hope, plus it's so delightful to see a little pop of blue among the green and brown of my backyard. Use bluebird feathers as a way to count your blessings by taking three bluebird feathers and naming something that makes you happy for each one. Carry them with you as a reminder and to encourage more good things to come into your life.

There are lots of superstitions around crows and other corvid species (which includes birds like ravens, blue jays, and jackdaws). One of the best-known bits of lore involves the magpie, a corvid marked by white patches on its wings, which is famed for collecting shiny things. Many children in England and parts of the United States have grown up with a divinatory rhyme about these feathered fortune-tellers.

According to the number of magpies you see at the same time when on a journey, you may calculate your luck as follows:

> One for sorrow,
> Two for luck;
> Three for a wedding,
> Four for death;
> Five for silver,
> Six for gold;
> Seven for a secret,
> Not to be told;
> Eight for heaven,
> Nine for —,
> And ten *for the d—l's* [devil's] *own sell* [self]*!*[5]

I love to use the rhyme as a guide for how many feathers to use for certain goals. I might carry two feathers in my pocket when I need some luck, or perhaps wear a necklace that features two crows. If you need to stop gossip or a secret from getting out, try incorporating seven crow feathers into your spell. Maybe you're interviewing for another job but don't want that to get back to your boss, or perhaps someone overheard something they weren't supposed to, and you want to nip it in the bud before they start spreading that information.

Of course, finding any of these birds' feathers can be a rare treat, so collecting three bluebird feathers or seven crow feathers may take years of looking. Many feathers are illegal to buy or even possess due to the Migratory Bird Act Treaty, so we want to be sure we're procuring any feathers ethically and safely for the animal. Sometimes that means getting creative, which is the essence of junk drawer magic anyway. You could easily draw or paint the feathers of these birds based on the times you've seen them (or even take photos if you have a camera or camera-capable mobile phone handy). You might put out food for local corvids and get to be friends with them, in which case you could find discarded feathers near feeders. Or you might even find that they bring you shiny baubles to add to a charm necklace or bracelet.

Redbirds are often seen as good signs or omens, and they can even be used in wishing magic. A cardinal or similar bird is often greeted with the recitation "Redbird, Redbird, where, where?" If it responds with "Here! Here!" then you can expect to see someone dear to you soon, especially a lover. Similarly, if you see a redbird, make a wish and blow a kiss at it. If you can do so before it flies away, it will go and bring your wish back with it.

A few more bits of bird-based folklore have to do with specific species (please note some of these involve illegal harm to songbirds and migratory birds and are presented only as examples of folklore and not recommendations):

- Loons are considered to be bad luck when met on the water while rowing or sailing.
- Turkey eggs are thought to have restorative powers when consumed, but a turkey standing alone under a tree is considered a bad omen.
- Oil made from melted goose fat is sometimes used to "cure" everything from aches and pains to baldness.
- A bit of lore from Georgia says that consuming mockingbird eggs can help with stuttering.
- Roadrunners are sometimes killed as a proxy for sickness in a community.
- It is considered bad luck to kill a jay bird, which is thought to be either a messenger from the devil or a bird carrying the soul of someone who died in the woods, like a hunter or forester.
- Killing a goldfinch invites harm, usually in the form of broken bones or injuries.
- Hearing a whippoorwill at night can be a bad omen, and it's even worse if you hear one say your name. A similar tradition is true for hearing an owl outside your window or calling your name in the night.

One final bit of bird lore says that if a bird gets into the house, it is a sign of death soon to come. One story tells of a bird who flitted down a chimney through the fireplace and sat on the hearth. Soon after, the grandfather of the woman sharing the story passed away. Birds definitely belong outdoors in most cases, so we encourage you to help keep them there—or risk spooky consequences![6]

What the Groundhog Knows—Animals and Divination

Many people have heard of Punxsutawney Phil, the famed groundhog who can predict the coming weeks of winter based upon his shadow each February 2. Phil is one of a handful of famous groundhogs who are loved (and occasionally loathed) for their weather predictions. The Groundhog Day tradition of shadow-spotting derives from long-standing European traditions of watching hibernating animals during the waning days of winter. For example, there's the tradition of the "Candlemas Bear," a bear that was observed on February 1 (Candlemas Day) in England as a way of determining whether the winter would come to an early end. Over time, other animals such as groundhogs, badgers, and even skunks were substituted for the Candlemas Bear, largely because they are much more common (and less likely to eat the person observing them).

The tradition of using animal-based observations to learn a little something about our world and the hidden language it's speaking is nothing new. The Druids of Ireland were thought to engage in the practice of watching birds to determine future events, for example, and the Romans were known to bring chickens to the docks before a sea journey to determine whether they'd face rough sailing. In some cases, this took the form of *haruspicy*, or divination by entrails, but there are also accounts of the chickens being observed for their scratching and pecking behaviors.

In more recent times, entrail divination has gone the way of the dodo for most people, but we hold onto a remarkable number of folk beliefs about what animals can tell us about our near futures. A list of customary observations from West Virginia shows just how many species' actions might offer a glimpse of the seasonal forecast:

- "If the craw crabs throw up a mound around their holes, it will be a dry summer; if they do not throw up a mound around their holes, the summer will be a wet one.
- When the fur on the animals is unusually heavy, it means a hard winter.
- After you hear the first katydid, it will be six weeks until the first frost.
- When the squirrels put away many nuts, the winter will be severe.
- If the birds nest low, the river rises will be low that summer; if high, the rises will be high."[7]

A number of other animals can act as portents and omens. Animals like white deer, or rabbits and hares behaving oddly, are often thought to be witches in disguise—much like old Kitty Rollins in the story about the cats earlier. In the Ozarks through the Appalachians there is a tradition of "news bees," which are flower flies from the *Syrphidae* family. They are marked with bands of black and yellow, much like bees, but are harmless, although they do look an awful lot like the much more mean-spirited and sting-inclined sweat bees we get in the Southern summers. These news bees, sometimes also called "sand hornets," "sweat flies," or "Russian hornets," derive their folk name from the belief that these hovering insects watch the events of humanity unfold, then fly off to deliver their news to others.[8]

In all these cases, we can learn a lot by watching and observing the animals in our lives, who seem in the folklore we have to be more attuned to magic than many humans are. That brings us to a final note: a great deal of animal-based folklore involves harming them. We mention a few of these throughout the chapter, but we have tried to avoid the most egregious examples. There are rituals involving animals being sacrificed, sometimes in very gruesome ways, to gain magical bones or tokens or powers. Those are a part of the folk history and lore that makes up the legacy of magic. While we recognize this, and do not want to turn a blind eye to it, we also do not want to share most of those rituals. They are too easily repeated by people who don't understand just how brutal they are, and most of the magical outcomes people seek using those rites can be achieved in other ways. If you are truly determined to find those rituals, they are available in plenty of other places. Animals make wonderful companions, wise teachers, and sometimes very scary fellow travelers in this world. And that is enough for us.

NOTES:

1. The dalmatian lore is found in *A Dictionary of Superstitions*, by Iona Opie and Moira Tatem (Oxford Univ. Press, 1989), p. 115.
2. From *Folk-Lore From Adams County, Illinois*, by Harry M. Hyatt (Alma Egan Hyatt Foundation, 1935), pp. 361–62.
3. Opie and Tatem, *Dictionary*, pp. 58–60.
4. There are a number of versions of this story, but two good renditions that inspired this variation on the tale are "The Black Cat's Message," found in S.E. Schlosser's collection *Spooky Southwest* (Globe Pequot, 2017) and a version from Missouri recounted in Vance Randolph's *Ozark Magic and Folklore* (Columbia Univ. Press, 1947), pp. 236–7.
5. These superstitions and corvid lore examples are found in *A Collection of Proverbs & Popular Sayings Relating to the Seasons, the Weather, and Agricultural Pursuits*, collected by M.A. Denham, vol. 20 (Percy Society - London, 1846).
6. These tidbits are found in "Odds and Ends of North American Folklore on Birds," by W.L. McAtee, in *Western Folklore*, vol. 5, no. 3 (Autumn 1955), pp. 169–83. The redbird lore above is from *The Frank C. Brown Collection of North Carolina Folklore*, Vol. VI, pp. 530–32. The story about the bird getting into the house is from "Belief Tales and Superstitions," by Linda Lingle, 7 Nov. 1978 (in the Center for Pennsylvania German Studies archives, in a class collection project at Pennsylvania State University-Harrisburg with Dr. Yvonne Milspaw)
7. Found in *Witches, Ghosts, and Signs* (West Virginia Univ. Press, 2008), pp. 121–34.
8. This lore shared by Appalachian lore collector Dave Tabler on his site Appalachian History: https://www.appalachianhistory.net/2019/04/ever-talk-to-news-bee.html. News bees are also briefly mentioned in lore collected by Vance Randolph in his book *Ozark Magic and Folklore*.

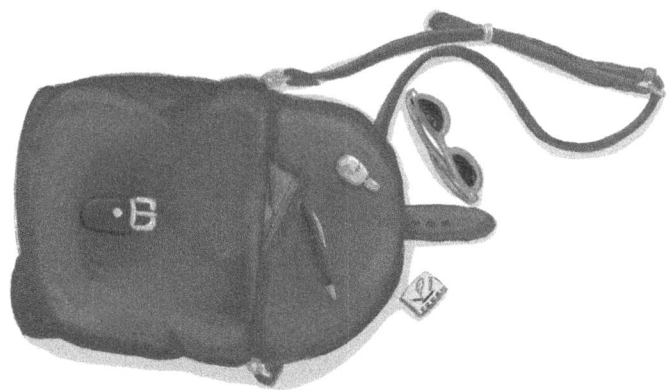

21. Purses and Wallets

Carrying the Magic with You

It's okay. We get it. Sometimes you don't so much have a junk drawer as just… junk. Heaven knows that we've been guilty of having countertops cluttered with mail, a car console full of ketchup packets, or a pocket full of old receipts. One of the places we see plenty of clutter pile up is in places like purses. On the one hand, it can feel mighty fine to dump out a purse and clean it up, reorganize it, and start anew. On the other hand, you never know just what kind of magic you have in there.

We go out into the world and carry a little bit of our domestic spaces with us, often in places like our pockets, purses, wallets, and more. This chapter will look at those portable magics that travel with us as we run our errands and go to work—and maybe offer you some good reasons to treat those crowded billfolds, overstuffed purses, and bulging pockets with a little bit more wonder.

Mary Poppins was on to Something—Digging in the Witch's Purse

Laine loves her purse. If she's out of the house, it's always with her. It collects little bits of ephemera from her life, and she loves being able to use the power that comes with that—with things that would otherwise be thrown away, left forgotten at the bottom for months, or used only for its mundane purpose. But what we can do, and what we hope to inspire you to do, is take the everyday things in your life and make them magical. By incorporating magic into mundane things, you're more likely to see enchantment in the everyday.

Some people like to carry small purses with their most essential items, while some like to carry huge tote bags filled with things that could come in handy for any situation. Laine was known among friends for her "Mary Poppins bag," so you can guess which side she comes down on. Anything a friend needed, she probably had in her purse. Pens? Do you need black, blue, or red ink? Or would you prefer a pencil? Band-Aids? Of course. Tampons? She's got you. Let's be honest, a large purse is just a portable junk drawer, so let's explore the magic at the bottom with the loose change, the old receipts, and that one random mint.

Speaking of mints, mint is often associated with prosperity and abundance, so keeping a mint where you keep money is a great way to draw more toward you. Altoid tins have been used by modern witches for years now as portable altars. They're the perfect size to keep a coin and a mint in for a quick, portable money drawing spell. You could also find an old bank deposit slip to fold up and put in the tin to encourage more deposits to your bank account.

Another minty item you often find in purses is gum. I used to fold and pick at the wrappers because I needed something to do with my hands, but lately I've been using them in my magic. Did you know that if you scrape your nail (or a penny would probably work) along the foil it will scratch off? Using this method, you can scratch a prosperity sigil on the wrapper, then put the gum back in it and save it for before you ask for a raise or haggle for an antique.

And don't worry, if you're more of a Big Red type than a fan of Double Mint, cinnamon can draw money too! It has other uses, too, of course—cinnamon is warm and spicy, and can kindle those feelings in a relationship. Save a piece of cinnamon gum for when you're swiping on Tinder or for your monthly date with your spouse.

Like many nowadays, another item I always carry is hand sanitizer. We use hand sanitizer as a shield of sorts—protection against germs and, we hope, protection against illness. You could add a few drops of protection oil to strengthen that shield or write a protective symbol on the bottle. You could do this with your packet of wet wipes as well.

As we dig around a bit more in our bags, another thing that tends to fall to the bottom is business cards. Business cards can be a great resource if you can't get your hands on something more personal (like hair), as they are personalized with someone's name and important information and they are an object that your "target" has touched. If you're having trouble with a coworker, you could sweeten them up by putting their card in a honey jar. Or maybe they're overly talkative and you can't get any work done? Put their card in the freezer to get them to chill out a bit.

I like to grab the business cards of my various doctors, as they usually have them sitting at the front desk. I like to put a sigil for good luck or anoint it with a drop of "Crown of Success" oil, because when it comes to doctor's offices, I often need to nudge things to go my way. If I need to squeeze in an appointment, talk to someone about billing, or get a quick call back from the nurse, I can grab their business card from my purse and help sway the outcome in my favor.

Another item often found in a large purse is makeup, which can be used for all kinds of magic. Mascara is often said to create the illusion that the eyes are wider and more open than they really are. With this in mind, enchant your mascara to enhance psychic abilities, opening up your third eye as well. Or, if a bold lipstick is more your thing, take inspiration from the unique names that cosmetic companies love to use. MAC has one that comes to mind, called "Breathing Fire," that you could apply when you need to light a fire under someone—or even yourself if you struggle with procrastination!

Eyeliner (the pencil kind) could also be used in a few ways. If there's an eyeliner pencil you won't be using again, use it to mark your tires with symbols to ensure safe travel.

Cash, Credit, or Conjuring? Enchantment in Your Wallet

If you're the type that only likes to carry a wallet, this chapter includes you too! Cory generally keeps a pretty trim wallet, with just a few essentials in it, but there's always a bit of magic. His billfold almost always contains a bay leaf, which is a symbol of luck and victory. He often will write a magical charm or symbol on the leaf and tuck it among the cards and cash to bring success in his day-to-day dealings. Giving it a light rub of olive oil or even whiskey can help to boost that effect, and as it deteriorates into crumbly fragments, he can dispose of them and add a new leaf. Bay isn't the only botanical item that winds up in wallets. Other herbs are thought to bring positive influences, including bayberry (for money), cinquefoil (also known as "five-finger grass," which is supposed to bring good favors from others), sassafras (money and business luck), and rosemary (intelligence, good memory, and wisdom). And there's always the famed four-leafed clover, which Cory has a strange knack for finding. He frequently has one of those in his wallet, too, although they don't last as long as the bay leaves. Some of the other things in his wallet include a prayer card depicting Mary (reflecting his Catholic upbringing, although he is not an orthodox follower of Catholicism in any way), a bit of currency from his time living in Prague (Czech Republic), and one of his most powerful tools: his voter registration card. (Seriously, vote when you can!)

Every person's wallet will be different. Some prefer a very slim sort of affair or even just a money clip, while others don't mind larger billfolds or even the pocketbook sort of wallets. Keeping currency may feel old-fashioned in the age of digital credit, but the precedent for keeping lucky money on hand is truly old, with special coins being minted for things like religious pilgrimages dating back to Ancient Roman times at least. In contemporary times, many people will carry uncommon currencies like a two-dollar bill in their wallets to attract more money, although there are some who believe such an odd piece of cash is bad luck. If you are inclined to think of it as bad luck, you can tear the corners of the bill to counteract it, or spend it and replace it often, which keeps the luck moving.[1] You should always put some money into a wallet before giving it as a gift, lest it lead to destitution.

Another way to use the currency is to write on it. Technically, you're not supposed to write on most currencies. In the United States it is considered "defacing" the currency and can even be treated as a criminal act. However, in most cases if you simply write in the margins of a bill, you're not going to incur the wrath of any government agencies. Many people do things like write blessings in those edge spaces around the printed portion of the currency. Sometimes these blessings are used like chain letters, with little instructions like: "You are now blessed! Write this blessing around the edges of six more dollar bills and give them to seven people and your prosperity will increase! + + +" (the three plus signs represent marking three crosses to "seal" the blessing). That's similar to a practice known as "St. Anthony's Bread," which involves blessing money in the name of St. Anthony of Padua and writing his name on the currency, then giving it away to those in need. Traditionally this was done with actual bread, marking it with a cross, but in contemporary times currency has filled in for baked goods.

Currency is also frequently anointed with oils to bless it and make it lucky. Some will use cinnamon or bayberry oils, both of which have strong associations with money and good business fortune. It's worth remembering, though, that your money will likely wind up in other hands, and those other hands may have allergies—so be as sparing as possible with this practice if you intend to circulate the currency. Keeping a small magnet can be a way to draw money to you, but magnets can interfere with some of the encoded strips on credit cards. Business cards are often collected in wallets, and they are frequently deployed in folk magic aimed at getting a good job or controlling someone who has influence over you, like a lawyer or judge (see our chapter "Desk Set" for more on these applications).

If you happen to hear a whippoorwill calling, or any other bird you consider lucky, you should turn your wallet over in your pocket to bring you a bit of luck or money.[2] You can use this method to "turn your luck around" by rotating your entire wallet in your pocket, or even going through and turning everything in your wallet around a different way.

One bit of magical protection involves inscribing the "INRI Cross" onto a piece of paper, folding it up, and carrying it in your wallet:

I.

N. I. R.

I.

Sanctus. Spiritus.

I.

N. I. R.

I.[3]

People often carry sentimental tokens in a wallet. One common example is a lock of hair. A little snip of a sweetheart's hair, or even the hair of one's children, can be a nice reminder of the bonds of love they share, but it can also be used magically to make them think of you (or think of you fondly, if you're not buying into the whole "absence makes the heart grow fonder" bit). Cory still carries a small paper sigil made for him by a friend years ago in his wallet, which has brought him good luck many times over.

What Have I Gots in my Pocketses? Other Portable Magics

In addition to our purses and wallets, we frequently find ourselves carrying all sorts of charms and baubles in our pockets. Some of these are things that seem to be put there by leprechauns or goblins and we have no idea why they're there, but many times we're toting magical items to have that little boost of love, luck, protection, or whatever we need. We're not alone in this, and the practice of carrying pocket charms is widespread. Here are some of the more interesting things people keep with them for magical purposes:

- One account from the Ozarks speaks of a man who carried an old bullet in his wallet and rubbed it with skunk oil from time to time to alleviate leg pain (which means it must have been a fairly large wallet).[4]

- A professional baseball infielder maintained a ritual of keeping a cheese sandwich in his back pocket to ensure that his performance would remain consistent throughout a game.[5]
- Carrying potatoes or onions in one's pockets can reverse bad luck (the onions might repel more than bad luck, though). Sulphur can also be carried to ward off bad luck, evil spirits, and disease (and, again, other people most likely).[6]
- Carrying a buckeye or "conker" in one's pocket is thought to prevent diseases, and especially to ward off rheumatism. Nutmegs are similarly carried to fend off illness and aches.[7]
- The *baculum* of a raccoon (its penile bone) is carried by gamblers in their pocket for good luck at games and is also believed to prevent cramps.
- Rattlesnake rattles are carried for good luck, to prevent headaches, and also to help improve musical performances for those who make their living at playing.
- Carrying the jack of spades or the queen of hearts stolen from someone else's deck is thought to bring good luck in gambling and gaming.
- The heart of a bat is sometimes carried in the pocket or pocketbook to bring good luck in games of chance or with money.[8]
- Carrying a rooster skull in one's pocket is thought to be a powerful love charm and can be used to win the affection of anyone the bearer chooses.
- A certain kind of bean known as a "mojo bean," "African wishing bean," or "St. Joseph's bean" can be carried in the pocket to help in situations where you need favors or to make a court case turn your way.[9]
- Peach pits can be carried for luck and love.
- There's always the famed lucky rabbit's foot, which many carry for good luck with all sorts of affairs, including gambling, looking for work, finding money or love, or just general good fortune.

We carry magic with us in a lot of ways. Sometimes that's more metaphorical, in the way we look at the world, listen for signs or omens, or just experience wonder. And sometimes, it comes down to having a little something in your purse, wallet, or pocket.

Whatever magic you're carrying, we hope it brings you good luck, happiness, and love! But if it's onions, we hope that you'll keep all that a good six feet away, please.

NOTES:

1. For more on the two-dollar bill superstitions, see *The Frank C. Brown Collection of North Carolina Folklore*, Vol. VI, pp. 454–56; and Harry M. Hyatt, *Folk-Lore From Adams County, Illinois* (Alma Egan Hyatt Foundation, 1935), p. 317.
2. See *The Frank C. Brown Collection of North Carolina Folklore*, Vol. VI, p. 442.
3. A good example of this can be found in the compilation of Pennsylvania German **braucher** lore entitled *The Red Church or The Art of Pennsylvania German Braucherei* (Pendraig Publishing, 2009), pp. 273–4.
4. See Vance Randolph's *Ozark Magic and Folklore* (Columbia Univ. Press, 1947), p. 158.
5. From George Gmelch's "Baseball Magic," in *Elysian Fields Quarterly*, vol. 11, no. 3, (1992), pp. 25–36.
6. Hyatt, *Adams County*, p. 25.
7. This lore has widespread currency, but you can find evidence of it in *Brown*, Vol. VI, pp. 111–12, among other sources. The lore about the raccoon baculum below is also from Brown, p. 164.
8. Hyatt, *Adams County*, p. 319.
9. From Zora Neale Hurston's "Hoodoo in America," in *Journal of American Folklore* 44, no. 174 (1931): 332.

22. Broken Things

Mending the Magic, and the Magic of Mending

There is a Japanese practice called Kintsugi that is the art of repairing broken pottery with a gold lacquer where the previous breakages are not hidden, but highlighted, bringing beauty to the so-called flaws. We love this for the practical side of reducing waste, but also the philosophy of embracing imperfections as part of the history of the object and as something to be celebrated, not hidden away.

Laine is a bit of a magpie, a collector of bits and bobs that might come in handy later. If a shirt is no longer wearable, she'll probably cut the buttons off and use the fabric as a cleaning rag. In the process of writing this chapter, one of her Pyrex dishes fell and broke, and she saved some of the pieces for later use. Our mindset is usually trying to fix what is broken, not simply tossing it out. We want to explore how an object being broken can often transform it from having one use to another. Let's find the magic in broken things.

In many traditions, the act of breaking an object can hold power. A Jewish wedding tradition has the couple smash a glass to represent the sorrows of the Jewish people, reminding them to take the good with the bad. The Greeks will break plates at joyous events, smashing them loudly to the ground, as it's believed the loud noises will ward off evil spirits that are attracted to the celebration. These practices are also thought to ward off the Evil Eye, which is a curse often unintentionally cast by someone jealous or envious of someone else's happiness.

When it comes to folk magic, there are many bits of lore about things breaking and what that signifies, often for common household objects or objects that you wear. Breaking a comb is bad luck, although you can counteract that by burying the pieces under your front porch steps. A girl's beads breaking indicates bad luck, and counting the beads on your necklace will cause it to break. And if they break at a party, you will never be invited back to that house. Breaking your watch (or even dreaming of breaking a watch) is an unfortunate omen for trouble coming your way. If a girl's shoestring breaks, it is said that her boyfriend "will soon be lost," or it can indicate a general disappointment.[1]

There is also a surprising amount of lore around dishes. Dishes spinning, falling, breaking, spontaneously shattering in your hand—anything you can think of happening to a dish usually means bad luck. There are variations on the theme, such as "whoever breaks a dish will soon break with a friend," "one of your secrets will become known after you break a glass," or "if in picking up a cup the handle comes off, it shows that someone hates you very much." But overall, it's not a good thing to break a dish—especially one you're using to carry some delicious chocolate cake or cherry pie. (Who wants to waste a perfectly good dessert?)

You can also work to prevent broken dishes using folk magic. According to lore from North Carolina, rubbing your hands with a shed snakeskin will ensure that you never break another plate. Servers, chefs, and home cooks can try carrying a small piece of snakeskin with them, warding off all that plate-breaking bad luck before it even happens.

Another common theme is that these tend to come in threes, so if you break a plate or dish, expect to break two more. From Hyatt:

- If a woman breaks a dish (in the morning say some), three dishes will be broken before she has finished or before the day is over.
- To break a dish signifies that three things will be broken before the end of the week.
- Break one dish and you will not stop breaking dishes until the whole set has been broken.[2]

Ain't Nothing Gonna Break My Stride: Breaking Dishes for Good (Luck)

If you find yourself standing among some shards of a broken dish, worrying about all the bad luck coming your way, don't despair! If you'd like to go the traditional way to stave off bad luck or misfortune, there's burying your broken dish to bury your troubles. For more dramatic flair, you can throw the broken pieces into a ravine. Some beliefs say that keeping your broken dishes in a pile in your backyard can do you some good, because they will stave off hunger and poverty.

If you're looking for a more modern solution, we've devised a ritual to help dispel all that bad luck. First, gather the pieces of the dish you already broke. Then, get two more intact dishes—whether you already own two you're willing to break, or you want to buy some cheap ones, we don't think it matters. You can often find them at thrift stores.

Take the broken dish that represents your unintentional bad luck, and set the pieces aside in something like a cloth or paper bag. Get the two pieces of dinnerware you're going to break and a grease pencil (something like an eyeliner pencil would work). Write down the possible misfortunes that you worry about the most on the two whole dishes. What's holding you back: A car with a tendency to stall out? Frequent minor injuries like rolled ankles or stubbed toes? A person who likes to flirt with your significant other? If you have detailed worries such as "paying the gas bill this month" or "student loan debt balance of $5,000," those work well. You can put as many as you want, or you could stay general and simply write things like "poverty" or "hunger" on them. The only real limit is the size of the plates or dishes you're using. Remember you can write on all sides of these.

If you find yourself standing among some shards of a broken dish, worrying about all the bad luck coming your way, don't despair! If you'd like to go the traditional way to stave off bad luck or misfortune, there's burying your broken dish to bury your troubles. For more dramatic flair, you can throw the broken pieces into a ravine. Some beliefs say that keeping your broken dishes in a pile in your backyard can do you some good, because they will stave off hunger and poverty.

If you're looking for a more modern solution, we've devised a ritual to help dispel all that bad luck. First, gather the pieces of the dish you already broke. Then, get two more intact dishes—whether you already own two you're willing to break, or you want to buy some cheap ones, we don't think it matters. You can often find them at thrift stores.

Take the broken dish that represents your unintentional bad luck, and set the pieces aside in something like a cloth or paper bag. Get the two pieces of dinnerware you're going to break and a grease pencil (something like an eyeliner pencil would work). Write down the possible misfortunes that you worry about the most on the two whole dishes. What's holding you back: A car with a tendency to stall out? Frequent minor injuries like rolled ankles or stubbed toes? A person who likes to flirt with your significant other? If you have detailed worries such as "paying the gas bill this month" or "student loan debt balance of $5,000," those work well. You can put as many as you want, or you could stay general and simply write things like "poverty" or "hunger" on them. The only real limit is the size of the plates or dishes you're using. Remember you can write on all sides of these.

Once you've finished transferring all your worries and bad luck possibilities to the dishes, stand and hold them. Try to feel if any part of you senses ill luck, and mentally push those feelings into the dishes. You should keep pushing that bad luck into them, and you can even say things like "Misfortune leave me, into this dish with you, and to me do not return." It is especially useful if you can feel yourself getting worked up—your body rocking, your hands feeling hot on the dish, your breath coming in short bursts, the dish trembling in your fingers. Finally, in one big motion, raise the dish over your head and fling it down onto the ground, preferably a rock or a hard surface that will shatter it (you may want to do this outside to avoid having to sweep up little shards all over your kitchen). Once both dishes are broken, gather up every bit of them you can and add them to your first dish in the cloth or bag.

Now, bury the broken dishes in your backyard, or in a flowerpot on a balcony, fire escape, back stoop, etc. if you don't have yard space. If you really want to finish it off, you can pour out some spring water with a pinch of salt added to it to make sure the bad luck stays down and away from you.

If you find yourself standing among some shards of a broken dish, worrying about all the bad luck coming your way, don't despair! If you'd like to go the traditional way to stave off bad luck or misfortune, there's burying your broken dish to bury your troubles. For more dramatic flair, you can throw the broken pieces into a ravine. Some beliefs say that keeping your broken dishes in a pile in your backyard can do you some good, because they will stave off hunger and poverty.

If you're looking for a more modern solution, we've devised a ritual to help dispel all that bad luck. First, gather the pieces of the dish you already broke. Then, get two more intact dishes—whether you already own two you're willing to break, or you want to buy some cheap ones, we don't think it matters. You can often find them at thrift stores.

Take the broken dish that represents your unintentional bad luck, and set the pieces aside in something like a cloth or paper bag. Get the two pieces of dinnerware you're going to break and a grease pencil (something like an eyeliner pencil would work). Write down the possible misfortunes that you worry about the most on the two whole dishes. What's holding you back: A car with a tendency to stall out? Frequent minor injuries like rolled ankles or stubbed toes? A person who likes to flirt with your significant other? If you have detailed worries such as "paying the gas bill this month" or "student loan debt balance of $5,000," those work well. You can put as many as you want, or you could stay general and simply write things like "poverty" or "hunger" on them. The only real limit is the size of the plates or dishes you're using. Remember you can write on all sides of these.

Once you've finished transferring all your worries and bad luck possibilities to the dishes, stand and hold them. Try to feel if any part of you senses ill luck, and mentally push those feelings into the dishes. You should keep pushing that bad luck into them, and you can even say things like "Misfortune leave me, into this dish with you, and to me do not return." It is especially useful if you can feel yourself getting worked up—your body rocking, your hands feeling hot on the dish, your breath coming in short bursts, the dish trembling in your fingers. Finally, in one big motion, raise the dish over your head and fling it down onto the ground, preferably a rock or a hard surface that will shatter it (you may want to do this outside to avoid having to sweep up little shards all over your kitchen). Once both dishes are broken, gather up every bit of them you can and add them to your first dish in the cloth or bag.

Now, bury the broken dishes in your backyard, or in a flowerpot on a balcony, fire escape, back stoop, etc. if you don't have yard space. If you really want to finish it off, you can pour out some spring water with a pinch of salt added to it to make sure the bad luck stays down and away from you.

Walking on Broken Glass

We know that witches love jars. I love to reuse spice bottles, candle holders, and pretty much anything with a lid. With all this dragonesque hoarding of glass, breakages are bound to happen. So what can we do with those broken pieces? Put them in more jars of course! We turn again to witch bottles. (See the chapter on Pins and Needles.)

Traditionally, witch bottles have contained objects like bent nails, pins, hair, urine, and blood. They were often created and then buried as a form of protective magic, the idea being that this will protect the witch's home and those inside it. But when looking through the lens of finding use for broken things, we suggest using small pieces of broken glass or even those pesky dishes we broke earlier. I find that using the pieces of a favorite coffee mug that cracked in the dishwasher, or a glass that slipped out of my hand, makes the home protection even stronger. There's something about including dishware from the kitchen—often called the heart of the home—that really strengthens the protection for me.

Laine's grandmother collected glass bottles, mostly in the popular colors of dark red and cobalt blue. She'd line her kitchen and dining room windows with them, and they always enchanted her. The sun would shine in, casting little patches of blue and red light everywhere. It was like being in a church filled with stained glass, but instead of pews and sermons, there was good food, laughter, and countless games of Spoons.

Blue bottles have other significance, traditionally being used as a means to trap spirits. The Gullah people, in particular, brought the concept of the bottle tree. A tree decorated with cobalt blue bottles stuck on the limbs is seen as a spirit catcher, the belief being that spirits will be attracted to the blue color of the bottles and become trapped. If you hear the noise of the wind humming across the opening of the bottle, you know you have caught a spirit.[3]

There is another tradition of hanging "witch balls" in the windows of homes, and these serve the same sort of purpose as a bottle tree.[4] We have an easy spell that combines all aspects of these bottle trees, witch balls, and broken glass that we'd like to share.

Witch "Bauble" Bottle Redux

You will need:
- A small bottle (preferably blue, but use whatever you have on hand).
- Something to hang the bottle with, such as yarn, twine, or fishing line.
- Broken glass

Pour the broken glass into the bottle. While you do, feel free to chant a few words or lines, or recite these lines three times:

The glass is broken,
All that's left is shards.
With these words spoken,
Please protect my home and hearth.

Next, tie your string securely to the bottle, or if you want to get a little fancy with it, you could macrame a hanger for the bottle. This would add in the benefit of having several knots to untie to keep an ill-intentioned spirit busy for a while. Hang it in your window for some extra protection, and have a beautiful sun catcher!

Another use for broken glass is to incorporate it into spells that seek to sever relationships you no longer want. That could be with a person or with something more abstract, like a bad habit. Perhaps a friend has asked for your help to stop drinking. Ask for the glass from their go-to alcohol bottle and use that in a spell to separate them from alcohol.

Before we move on from glass, we'd like to mention sea glass. Sea glass is glass found on beaches. It has been weathered and eroded by the sea, creating a smooth texture, often with a cloudy or frosted look. Sea glass is particularly special because it combines the four elements into one object. The sand comes from the earth, which is heated in fire, then the molten glass is blown into things like bottles and jars. After all this, the glass ends up in the ocean where it tumbles about for years, finally forming into sea glass. If you like to have representations of the elements on your altar but lack space, a single piece of sea glass can represent all four.

Your Own Personal Goblin Horde: Spirits and Shiny Baubles

Sometimes the broken things aren't beautiful bits of sea glass or a shard of an old dinner plate, but the weird little toys that come in children's fast food value meals, now missing a foot or a wheel. They could be a lone AAA battery that may or may not still have a charge in it, or a bundle of old twist-ties from bread bags that has taken on Cthulhu-like proportions over the years.

All of these lost objects have potential, though, for a role in magic. There's a trope in fairy tales that many otherworldly beings seem to enjoy collecting things from our world, no matter how bizarre or seemingly useless they might be to us. Some of this may be related to lore about gnomes, goblins, and dwarves and their interest in things like mines full of shiny gems, although the stereotype has spread more broadly to other fantastic beings (think of Disney's Ariel in *The Little Mermaid* and her cave full of human "treasures").

In many cultures, there is a belief in a form of "house spirit," a creature that dwells within the home and acts as its protector and a sort of police presence for the living there. It can bring misfortune when displeased with human action, or it can offer blessings and guardianship to those within the walls of the home. Many spirit beings seem to take on this role at different times and in different cultures: the Romans had their lares, while the Scandinavian peoples may look to the *nisse* or *tomte*, and Scots might see a brownie as a possible house spirit. These spirits are often treated with respect and can even be given little homes of their own within the house. They are sometimes thought to be responsible for objects going missing (so *that's* where your keys/library card/left sock went!). If that's the case, they may be looking for things to collect, so why not help them along?

A simple way to do this is to take something small, like an old Altoids tin or a mismatched bowl, and give it a designated place in your home. If you already have a sense of where your house spirit likes to be—maybe by the way things accumulate there or a feeling of being "with" something in certain spaces—you should probably set it up in that location. If not, you might be able to coax your spirit into a spot of your choosing. Simply place the "home" in the spot you've decided on, then write a letter of invitation to the spirit and let it know you mean it no harm. Take your various "shinies" and place them with the home, but do this one item at a time! See how things go in the house over the next few days—does luck generally improve, or are there good feelings and lots of laughter? Then you've probably found something your spirit likes and can build on that. If there's lots of tension and arguing, try replacing the object with a different one. You can also do divination to find out how the spirit feels about your little offerings.

Speaking of divination, broken items also can be a wonderful inclusion in a "bone throwing" style set, as we've mentioned in the chapters on buttons and toys and games. A battery could indicate a source of power or strength or motivation, for example (although you need to be careful about what you keep with the battery as they can leak a very corrosive acid). Maybe the kids' meal toy is about youthfulness and nostalgia, or perhaps it's about materialism and short-term happiness that fades quickly. There are lots of possibilities for the bits and bobs that have been used past their prime without simply throwing them away.

A final note, though, on accumulating "stuff." Stuff is just stuff, and we often wind up with a lot of it. For some of us, this stems from a mentality developed at some point in our lives when we experienced poverty. We might start keeping things "just in case," so that if we get something else and it breaks, we have the part we need to repair it. Or maybe we think it would go in a yard sale, or be useful to make into something else.[5] All of those are perfectly fine goals, but we can sometimes cross a line with that mindset and find ourselves hoarding things without real concern for what that does to our health and our lives. Hoarding can be incredibly disheartening when you see someone you love get lost in it, and if you're experiencing that kind of driving need to hoard, it's a good time to book an appointment with a mental or behavioral health professional. There's no shame in that, and it may help you clear your mind so you can clear your physical space.

And that is a final bit of magic to share: sometimes the real power in the junk drawer is cleaning it out. Finally saying goodbye to broken things means making space for something new. It's part of growing and changing over time in our lives. Cleaning a house can be a magical experience (as we mention in some of our earlier chapters on cleaning magic). And that moment when you've gotten rid of things you no longer need, with care and thought about what you keep, taking time to give things a home? Well, that is pure enchantment.

NOTES

1. See Harry M. Hyatt's *Folk-Lore From Adams County, Illinois* (Alma Egan Hyatt Foundation, 1935), pp. 360–64.
2. Most of the examples in these paragraphs are cited from Harry M. Hyatt's *Folk-Lore From Adams County, Illinois*, entries 11070–11670.
3. The Gullah people are a distinct ethnic group of African Americans who live in the Lowcountry regions of South Carolina and Georgia. They have a rich culture that has been preserved more than almost any other African American community in the United States. Blue is a common color associated with ghosts in the American South. Many a Southerner will have the ceilings of their porches painted a robin's egg blue sort of color, referred to as Haint Blue. This is thought to trick spirits, either by imitating the sky, which allows spirits to pass by your house without entering, or by imitating water, which spirits traditionally cannot cross. It has a more practical effect today by tricking wasps. They are less likely to build their nests on a porch painted with haint blue, as they prefer enclosed spaces.
4. Witch Balls are hollow glass orbs, much like Christmas ornaments, that are hung in windows to attract and trap evil spirits. While they are often presented as a very old phenomenon, folklorist and magical historian Owen Davies has indicated that he doesn't see them predating glass fishing floats from the late nineteenth and early twentieth centuries in general. That doesn't mean they aren't still useful tools for countering naughty imps, though!
5. We have a really wonderful discussion about this phenomenon in our podcast episode with author and podcaster Katrina Ray-Saulis, Episode 192 - Witches Crafting.

Conclusion

So what's left to say? We've taken a trip through the nooks and crannies of the house and looked for the folklore and fantastical in some of the strangest places. We've dumped out the junk drawer and seen buttons that bring good (or bad) luck, learned the history of the humble broom, and even found some creative (if rather unpleasant) uses for a bottle of milk.

The thing about magic in the home, though, is that there is no real end to it. Every person's home is unique, filled with the trappings of life that make it special to that individual or the group of people who inhabit that space. That means the possibilities for enchantment are endless! While our little book can introduce you to some of the wonders hiding in the sugar bowl or the backyard, all we can do is tell you about a small sliver of lore that exists regarding these spaces and objects. There's also the question of just what is a "home," and what do you do if yours isn't what we've assumed as "typical?" If your home doesn't feel safe, or you're in a temporary space that doesn't feel like *your* home, you can still use some of the folklore and history detailed here to help you feel safe. We hope a few of the protective charms will guard you, or that you'll find a spell or two that you can do without raising any alarms that might turn luck around for you. The greatest spell you can do, though, is seeking professional help: crisis intervention centers and hotlines, licensed therapists, and medical or legal experts all have extensive knowledge that can do you much more good than our book. The charms here are just to help tip the scales, at best, and we do want you to be safe.

Still others reading this may not have a distinctive sense of "home" where they live, or they may feel like some of the objects we've mentioned are far from "typical." How many people keep canning jars handy in contemporary times, for example? We've also overlooked so many objects that are part of modern life: we said virtually nothing of computers, televisions, mobile phones, or videogame consoles. In part, that is because we are trying to build a connection to existing lore from times when those devices were either very new or nonexistent. But that doesn't mean they don't have magic in them. There are already plenty of stories of people using "channel surfing" methods of divination to receive messages from the spirit world, or even using the static channels on a TV to induce trances ("They're heeeeeeeere!"). Computers offer us connections, like magical portals, to other people around the world, and a bevy of new folklore has been created in the online world. We are not neglecting these because they are invalid, but rather because there was already so much to say about the objects we have covered here.

You can probably look around your home and find plenty of things we didn't mention. In fact, that is our challenge to you: make a list, an inventory of your own space. What are your "typical" objects? Can you come up with half a dozen or more that we didn't list—maybe even just in your living room or kitchen? Once you have that list, start thinking about each object. Does it remind you of anything you've read about in this book? Does it have special connections for you that you can build upon, the way we've done with toys and games or even buttons and keys? Start keeping a log of your own everyday magical objects. After all, that's where our folklore comes from: you, one of the folk! Your choices, spells, traditions, and charms will be the folklore of the future, passed to a new generation, and what better way to do so than keeping track of the magic you're already weaving into your life?

If you want to go further with your magical research, we recommend looking at the books listed in our notes. Many of them have vast amounts of lore that might be useful to you. We can also recommend exploring folk magic through books like *Encyclopedia of 5,000 Spells*, by Judika Illes, or any of the books by authors like Jake Richards, Byron Ballard, Via Hedera, Laura Davila, J. Allen Cross, Roger Horne, Morgan Daimler, Brandon Weston, Luisah Teish, Mary-Grace Fahrun, Mhara Starling, Kelden Mercury, and Draja Mickaharic, among others. Check out your local library's collection of folklore and local history, and see what you can find there. And most importantly, talk to members of your folk community and find out just what they're doing with their salt and sugar, and how they're keeping their milk (or anything else they value) safe.

As you put this book down and close its cover, we hope you don't feel like you're shutting a door and leaving us behind. You're always welcome here. We've got magic, even if it is a little messy. Come home whenever you like.

Additional Notes, Resources, and Valuable Knick Knacks

If you've read this far, chances are you may be hoping to read further. To that end, we've got a few additional materials we thought it would be useful to toss in like some spare rubber bands or an old wooden spoon for you to sift and sort through at your leisure. Below we've got some reading selections that we think you might enjoy as companions or expansions upon what you've read here. We've also got a spell and magic concordance that will help you find the various spells in the book based on particular needs such as divination, love, or money.

Recommended Reading

At Home: A Short History of Private Life, by Bill Bryson. Bryson's books are known for their "microhistory" approach to the world. He frequently looks at everyday objects and asks, "Now why in the world is that there?" and then proceeds to peel back layer after layer of useful narrative that answer his query. In At Home, Bryson tackles the stuff of everyday living by walking you through his house and filling in the backstory of things like wallpaper, telephones, toilet paper, and throw pillows. His focus is not on the magical, but by making these items a narrative focus, they take on a sort of magical life of their own.

Folk Magic & Healing: An Unusual History of Everyday Plants, by Fez Inkwright. If the chapter on weeds excites you, well, this book will be a serious page-turner! In a similar vein to the older (but still quite good) The Folk-lore of Plants by T.F. Thiselton-Dyer, Inkwright's book looks closely at the herbs, flowers, brambles, and bushes growing out one's front door or along the local hedgerow. The history, story, and folk uses of plants such as daisies, dandelions, brambles, and even seaweed all create a well-rounded and thoughtful guide to the green world underfoot.

The Encyclopedia of 5,000 Spells, by Judika Illes. We turn to this book more than any other at this point. While it is a massive compendium of thousands of spells, Illes has done her homework and gathered lore about these practices and methods from around the world. You learn so much about the reasons behind different bits of magic, and you will never run short of inspiration for using everyday objects in magical ways with this book.

Jude's Herbal Home Remedies, by Jude Todd. This was one of the books that Cory spent hours learning from in his youth. Todd's remedies are simple and easy to understand, and they employ all sorts of everyday household items like cider vinegar or castile soap. Tinctures, scrubs, oils, and infusions all fill the pages, as well as a hearty bit of herbal lore for many commonly grown or foraged plants.

Spiritual Cleansing, by Draja Mickaharic. This slim little volume has so much wonderful information in it on how to keep your space magically clean. The ingredients are always ones that you'll have on hand, such as ammonia or cinnamon, and Mickaharic specifically draws on a deep knowledge of everyday folklore to make these magical workings come to life. It's practical, simple, straightforward, and frankly—wonderful!

The Tradition of Household Spirits, by Claude Lecouteux. If you want to know why your doorway is important to maintain, or just what could be lurking in your floors and ceilings, then crack open Lecouteux. He was a professor at the Sorbonne in Paris specializing in medieval knowledge and lore, and his work is often a bit dense and academic, but endlessly illuminating. Learning about the various spirits that have historically been associated with the household might open your eyes to the possibilities of just what's populating your lintels and hallways.

Thrifty Witchery, by Vincent Higginbotham and Martha Kirby Capo. This book covers some of the same principles we have here—the importance of working with what you have and the presence of magic in so many parts of our everyday lives. It also explores some of the underlying theories of contemporary magic and offers readers ways to think about the need fueling their work.

Panati's Extraordinary Origins of Everyday Things, by Charles Panati. This delightfully illustrated work details a number of objects we've missed (as well as some we've covered). You will learn all about the strange, wonderful, and frequently weird origins of potato chips, zippers, facial tissues, umbrellas, napkins, and even condoms! Many entries discuss the traditional lore associated with these objects, including their uses in marriage or funerary rites or the superstitions surrounding them.

Spell Concordance

Below the spells found within this book are categorized based on their particular need or use, as opposed to their components or place within one's home as the rest of the book is organized. We've primarily included the spells that are most complete, as opposed to the smaller "snippets" of lore, although we occasionally do include one of those.

Divination

- Bible-and-Key Method - p. 25
- Matchstick Love Divinations - p. 29
- "Dumb"/Silent Supper Love Divination - p. 47
- Tea Leaf Divination - p. 55
- Canning Jar Divinations - p. 72
- Bread-based Divinations - p. 81
- Broom-based Divinations - p. 102
- Calling Circle Divination - p. 122
- Button-box Oracle - p. 122
- Basics of Playing Card Fortune-Telling - p. 139
- Seed and Nut Divinations - p. 152
- Magpie Divination - p. 165
- Animal Weather Predictions - p. 166

Employment/Jobs

- Sweetening Jar - p. 70
- Job Success Jar Spell - p. 74
- Magic with Office Supplies - p. 134
- Business Card Success Spell - p. 170

Healing

- Buying Warts - p. 19
- Abracadabra Matchstick Healing - p. 31
- Rotting Rags Wart Cure - p. 37
- Plugging Trees for Illness - p. 146

Hexing

- Tongue Spell to Silence a Gossip - p.53
- Egg Hex - p. 63
- Souring Jar - p. 70
- Ammonia Punishing Spell (Hurston) - p.86
- Litter Box Hex - p.163

Law/Court-cases

- Sweetening Jar - p. 70
- Witness Silencing Spell - p. 114

Love

- Matchstick Love Divinations - p. 29
- "Dumb"/Silent Supper Love Divination - p. 47
- Trash Magic Breakup Spell - p. 97
- Jumping the Broom Wedding Custom - p. 103
- Remember-Me Dandelion Spell - p. 156
- Rose Syrup for Love - p. 158

Luck/Money

- Growing Fortunes Quarter Spell - p. 17
- Business Prosperity Packet - p. 129
- Chain Letter Magic - p. 130
- Money Boost Written Charm - p. 176
- Intentional Dish-Breaking Spell - p. 176

Protection/Defense

- Shield or Scout Pennies - p. 16
- Mercury Dimes - p. 17
- Singing Bowl Home Cleansing - p. 57
- Protective Pins and Nails - p. 114
- Witch Bottle Home Protection - p. 115
- Magical Scarecrow Guardian (Butzemann) - p. 150
- INRI Pocket Charm - p. 172
- Witch Bauble Bottle Redux - p. 179

Success/Fame

- Sweetening Jar - p. 70
- Knot Wishing Spell - p. 108
- Wallet Success Charms - p. 171

Index

A

abracadabra 31, 187, 201

acorns 152

alcohol 71, 72, 179

allspice 74, 75, 87, 129

ammonia 85, 86, 185

amulets 18; *See also* talismans

apple 46, 69, 78, 122, 139, 146, 148, 152, 153; *See also* trees

ash 146; *See also* trees

automatic writing 131, 132

axe 102

B

baculum 173, 174

badgers 166

bat 55, 173

baths 10, 164

bayberry 74, 75, 171, 172

bay leaf 74, 75, 129, 171

beads 175

beans 72, 79; *See also* peas

beds 148, 151

beech 147; *See also* trees

bees 155, 167, 168

Bible 25, 26, 125, 126, 129, 187

birch 147; *See also* trees

birds 69, 82, 108, 150, 164, 165, 166, 167

birthday candle 82

blackberries 69, 158

Black Pullet, The 63

blood 24, 26, 38, 39, 71, 73, 94, 149, 178; *See also* bodily fluids; *See also* menstrual blood bluing 89

bodily fluids 38; *See also* blood; *See also* menstrual blood; *See also* sexual fluid

bones 9, 87, 108, 126, 139, 166, 167

bone throwing 180

books 5, 12, 23, 25, 43, 55, 59, 67, 76, 80, 102, 129, 132, 136, 141, 155, 160, 161, 184, 185

bottles 69, 114, 115, 119

bottle trees 71, 178

bowls 35, 43, 56, 57, 59, 158

boxes 122, 124, 163

braucherei 28, 136, 174

bread 43, 47, 78, 81, 84, 172, 179

brick dust 88

brooms 101, 102, 104; *See also* sweeping

buckeye 152

bullets 44

business cards 170

butter 37, 65, 66, 75, 78, 81, 121, 122, 124

button 121, 122, 123, 124, 126, 187

C

cake 39, 56, 59, 80, 81, 82, 84, 87, 114, 124, 158, 176

canary 164; *See also* birds

candles 32, 73

candy 77

canning 69, 74, 183

cards, playing 76, 138, 139, 140

cash 21, 79, 98, 149, 171

cats 4, 9, 163, 164, 167

cayenne pepper 32, 63

cedar 147; *See also* trees

cheese 37, 65, 66, 173

chickens 40, 166, 167; *See also* birds

children 20, 23, 77, 78, 81, 82, 94, 101, 122, 124, 125, 128, 138, 139, 151, 152, 156, 165, 172, 179

chocolate 53, 176

chopsticks 48

Christmas 20, 32, 45, 182

cinnamon 61, 70, 80, 82, 129, 170, 172, 185

cinquefoil 74, 75, 171

citrus 64, 88; *See also* lemons; *See also* oranges

cleaning 13, 40, 64, 76, 85, 86, 87, 88, 89, 90, 94, 102, 163, 175, 181

cleansing 50, 63, 64, 85, 86, 88, 148, 150

clock 56, 65, 155

clothing 20, 38, 107, 116, 134, 139, 159

clover 33, 74, 75, 171

cloves 74, 75, 87

cobwebs 13, 93, 96, 98; *See also* spiderwebs

coffee 39, 44, 45, 46, 53, 54, 55, 56, 61, 150, 178

coins 15, 18, 19, 20, 71, 122, 171

cookies 64, 77, 80, 82, 83

corners 57, 93, 94, 104, 105, 115, 142, 171

coscinomancy 49

crabs 55, 167

crossroads 94

crossroads dirt 94

crows 165

cups 13, 49, 54, 158

cures 11, 26, 36, 37, 114, 148

currency 15, 18, 129, 171, 172, 174

curses 10, 11, 73, 80, 113, 137, 149, 158

D

daffodils 157

daisies 156

dandelion 155, 156, 157

death 19, 25, 32, 39, 40, 56, 62, 87, 96, 99, 126, 128, 137, 146, 148, 149, 162, 165, 166

deer 47, 167

desk 13, 125, 127, 134, 135, 147, 161, 170

devil 19, 57, 73, 78, 81, 152, 164, 165, 166

dill 79

dimes 94

dirt 13, 47, 63, 93, 94, 95, 97, 98, 99, 102, 105, 113, 115, 145

Discoverie of Witchcraft, The (Reginald Scott) 25, 51

dishes 35, 36, 40, 175, 176, 177, 178

dishes, broken 176, 177, 178

dishrags 36, 61

dish towels 37 *See also* towels

divination 25, 26, 29, 30, 55, 72, 73, 76, 122, 124, 126, 140, 141, 146, 148, 152, 156, 157, 164, 167, 180, 183, 185

dogs 161, 162

dogwood 147; *See also* trees

doll 33, 82, 90, 113, 114, 134, 138, 139, 143, 144; *See also* poppets

doors 24, 30, 38, 88, 89, 159

dreams 50, 78, 157

dumb supper 47; *See also* silent supper

E

eggs 62, 63, 64, 96, 166

eggshells 63, 102, 106

embroidery 53, 110

evil eye 57, 63, 78, 80, 104; *See also mal de ojo*

F

Fahrun, Mary-Grace 51, 84, 184

familiars 161

feathers 70, 108, 156, 164, 165

fire 9, 29, 30, 31, 32, 33, 66, 71, 81, 97, 98, 122, 131, 133, 146, 148, 152, 164, 170, 177, 178, 179

Florida Water 64

flying ointments 24

Folk-Lore From Adams County, Illinois (Harry M. Hyatt) 38, 51, 84, 111, 117, 119, 121, 126, 136, 154, 168, 174, 182

foot track dirt 95

forks 13, 43, 44, 45, 46, 51, 150

fortune-telling 54, 72, 79, 133, 156

frankincense 104

funeral 20, 55

fur, animal 161, 162, 163, 167

G

gambling 18, 79, 137, 173

games 11, 13, 50, 63, 72, 122, 133, 137, 138, 139, 141, 142, 156, 173, 178, 180, 184

garbage 98

garlic 69, 79, 84

geese 108

geomancy 122

ginger 158

glass 31, 48, 57, 62, 63, 70, 72, 73, 74, 75, 78, 83, 89, 95, 97, 175, 176, 178, 179, 182

glass, broken 178, 179

gold 63, 71, 165, 175

graveyard dirt 94

grimoire 63, 161

groundhogs 166

H

hagstone 151

hair 26, 31, 46, 64, 66, 70, 71, 81, 93, 97, 108, 114, 116, 131, 133, 134, 135, 139, 143, 146, 159, 162, 170, 172, 178

Halloween 80, 82, 102, 113, 122, 152

hand sanitizer 170

hares 161, 167; *See also* rabbits

hawthorn 147; *See also* trees

healing 10, 38, 44, 47, 62, 95, 104, 113, 138, 148, 151, 155 herbs 30, 33, 74, 78, 80, 87, 134, 171, 185

hexes 11, 50, 137

himmelsbriefen 131

holly 147, 157, 158, 159; *See also* trees

honey 53, 65, 70, 88, 95, 129, 170

hornets 167; *See also* wasps

horseradish 79

hot peppers 114

house spirit 180

I

ice 43, 61, 62, 64, 158, 161

iceboxes 61

INRI cross 172

iron 23, 24, 26, 50, 79, 85, 86, 89, 94, 102, 103, 115, 124, 159

J

jars 69, 70, 71, 72, 73, 85, 88, 97, 122, 178, 179, 183

jasmine 88, 89

jinx 104

jumping the broom 103

juniper 147; *See also* trees

K

keys 13, 23, 24, 25, 26, 27, 86, 146, 151, 180, 184

keys, skeleton 23

kintsugi 175

kitchen 12, 13, 37, 40, 45, 46, 49, 54, 57, 61, 64, 69, 74, 79, 80, 82, 86, 88, 89, 161, 177, 178, 183

knitting 4, 109, 110, 113, 117

knitting needles 113, 117

knives 12, 45, 46, 47, 49, 51

knot magic 107

knots 107, 109, 111

L

lamps 12, 73, 74

laundry 13, 39, 71, 85, 89, 90

laundry bluing 89

lavender 80, 88, 89

leaves 13, 53, 54, 55, 56, 63, 80, 139, 147, 148, 152, 156, 157, 171

lemons 64, 65

letters 10, 26, 97, 128, 130, 131, 132, 136, 140, 144, 171

limpia 50, 63; *See also* eggs

litter boxes 163

locust 147, 148; *See also* trees

Long Lost Friend 86, 136

loons 166

luck 18, 19, 20, 24, 32, 33, 36, 39, 40, 44, 46, 47, 48, 50, 56, 64, 69, 70, 72, 78, 79, 80, 81, 83, 86, 87, 96, 103, 104, 105, 110, 113, 117, 121, 123, 127, 128, 129, 130, 131, 133, 134, 139, 140, 147, 148, 149, 151, 157, 163, 164, 165, 166, 170, 171, 172, 173, 175, 176, 177, 178, 180, 183

M

Magical Spells of the Minor Prophets (Draja Mickaharic) 25, 28

magnets 172

magpies 165; *See also* birds

mail 110, 129, 130, 142, 169

makeup 170

mal de ojo 63, 104; *See also* evil eye

maple 145, 148, 152, 157; *See also* trees

marriage 10, 30, 44, 48, 51, 55, 56, 81, 82, 97, 103, 106, 124, 133, 147, 186

matches 13, 29, 30, 31, 32, 33, 34, 152

May's Eve 48

meat 61

menstrual blood 38, 39; *See also* bodily fluids; *See also* blood

mercury 79

mercury dime 19, 79; *See also* dimes

Midsummer 48, 96

milk 10, 37, 38, 65, 66, 72, 183, 184

mint 169, 170

mirror 40, 56, 114

mockingbirds, *the smuggest* 164; *See also* birds

molasses 70, 88

money 18, 19, 20, 21, 33, 56, 72, 79, 87, 95, 117, 123, 128, 133, 134, 151, 170, 171, 172, 173, 185

monthly cloths 39

moon 21, 82, 83, 101, 146, 148, 150

mops 35

mudroom 9, 89

mugs 45, 54

mustard 32, 79, 84, 85

mustard seeds 32, 79, 85

N

nails 72, 86, 115, 116, 139, 159, 163, 178

names 10, 25, 61, 93, 110, 128, 130, 159, 170

necklaces 151

needles 70, 113, 114, 115, 116, 117, 121, 122, 124, 148; *See also* knitting needles

New Year's 48, 87, 90, 105

nickels; *See also* coins

nutmeg 79, 84

nuts 115, 139, 152, 167

O

oak 145, 146, 148; *See also* trees

oil 12, 30, 45, 69, 72, 74, 75, 85, 86, 88, 95, 96, 97, 99, 104, 170, 171, 173

"One for Sorrow" rhyme 165

onions 173

oracle 122, 123, 126

oranges 64

Ouija board 132

Ozark Magic and Folklore (Vance Randolph) 21, 41, 46, 51, 59, 65, 67, 76, 84, 99, 111, 154, 168, 174

P

paper 33, 57, 61, 62, 63, 65, 66, 74, 75, 82, 86, 87, 95, 98, 114, 117, 125, 127, 128, 129, 132, 133, 134, 135, 141, 147, 163, 172, 176, 177, 185

peach 148, 173; *See also* trees

peaches 69

peas 62, 72, 79; *See also* beans

pencils 133, 135

pennies 19, 20, 21, 94, 99, 151; *See also* coins

pens 127, 133

pepper, black 86

peppers, hot 114

peppers, red 79

petitions 128, 129

pine 56, 86, 88, 131, 148; *See also* trees

Pine-Sol 86, 148

pins 45, 70, 113, 114, 115, 116, 117, 118, 121, 124, 134, 139, 178

place settings 48

plates 35, 49, 175, 176, 177

poplar 145, 146, 148; *See also* trees

poppets 90, 113, 114, 138, 158; *See also* doll

poppy seeds 70

potatoes 173

purses 169, 170, 172

Q

quarters 75, 123; *See also* coins

R

rabbits 109, 150, 155, 167; *See also* hares

rags 35, 38, 39, 40, 113, 139

ravens 165; *See also* birds

redbirds 165; *See also* birds

Red Church, The (Chris Bilardi) 25, 28, 136, 174

ribbons 9, 108, 124

ring 20, 25, 26, 55, 57, 81, 122, 124

rocks 150, 151, 152

rooster 18, 173

rose 55, 87, 88, 150, 157, 158, 159

rosemary 171

rowan 148, 149. *See also* trees

S

sage 80, 139

salt 30, 36, 66, 78, 79, 80, 84, 88, 90, 103, 105, 114, 124, 177, 178, 184

Samhain 48

sassafras 149, 171; *See also* trees

scissors 47, 49, 50, 51; *See also* shears

scrying 56

Secret Garden, The (Frances Hodgson Burnett) 23, 26, 27

sewing 9, 13, 109, 113, 116, 118, 121, 125, 134

sexual fluids 107, 124; *See also* bodily fluids

shears 49, 50; *See also* scissors

sieve 49, 50

sigils 33, 74, 128, 134, 136, 158

Signs, Cures, & Witchery (Gerald C. Milne) 66

silent supper 47, 48

silver 19, 20, 21, 43, 44, 65, 66, 71, 79, 124, 141, 148, 165

Silver Bullet, The (Hubert J. Davis) 21, 28, 65, 67, 76

silverware 43, 44, 45, 49; *See also* forks; *See also* knives; *See also* spoons

sixpence 20; *See also* coins

smoke 31, 32, 40, 70, 80, 117, 150

soap 63, 86, 87, 149, 185

souring jars 70, 85

Southern Cunning (Aaron Oberon) 97

spiders 95, 96, 97, 98

spiderwebs 96, 99, *See also* cobwebs

spinning 4, 15, 46, 49, 89, 107, 175

spoons 9, 13, 43, 44, 45, 46, 51, 61

sporks 45

squirrels 150, 167

St. Agnes' Eve 48

sticky notes 134

St. John's nuts 152

stones 13, 33, 126, 150, 151

string 9, 10, 11, 25, 26, 40, 79, 80, 107, 109, 117, 124, 125, 129, 179

sugar 37, 70, 77, 78, 79, 80, 83, 86, 88, 158, 183, 184

sweat 167; *See also* bodily fluids

sweeping 87, 88, 102, 103, 104, 105; *See also* brooms

T

Taboo, Magic, Spirits (Eli Edward Burriss) 102, 106

talismans 95, 128; *See also* amulets

talking boards 132, 144; *See also* Ouija board

tape, measuring 124

tasseomancy 54

tea 40, 53, 54, 55, 56, 63, 110, 146

tea leaves 54, 56, 63

teeth 20, 57, 82, 95, 96, 151

thimbles 124

thorns 158

tins 122, 170

tokens 18, 82, 102, 138, 141, 167, 172; *See also* coins

tongue 44, 57, 61, 62, 114

tooth 20, 122, 123, 124

towels 35, 37, 38, 40, 64, 110; *See also* dishrags; *See also* dish towels toys 13, 137, 138, 139, 142, 143, 179, 180, 184

trash 32, 97, 98

trees 13, 20, 71, 82, 96, 115, 146, 148, 149, 150, 154, 156, 157, 159, 178

turkey 166

twigs 147, 148, 149, 152

U

urine 70, 71, 85, 88, 114, 115, 178; *See also* bodily fluids

V

vinegar 63, 65, 66, 70, 72, 79, 85, 86, 96, 114, 116, 129, 185

voodoo dolls 114; *See also* poppets

W

wallets 169, 171, 172

walnuts 149, 152; *See also* trees

wasps 69, 96, 97, 182; *See also* hornets

water 20, 31, 36, 38, 54, 56, 62, 63, 72, 73, 74, 76, 78, 83, 86, 87, 88, 89, 103, 104, 106, 114, 116, 119, 122, 124, 147, 149, 150, 151, 158, 163, 166, 177, 178, 182

weather 72, 83, 96, 97, 99, 148, 163, 164, 166

weddings 103

weeds 155, 185

whippoorwill 166, 172

willow 149, *See also* trees

wine 48, 53, 83, 84, 150

wishing wells 20

witch balls 178

witch bottle 70, 71, 115, 116

Witches, Ghosts, and Signs (Patrick W. Gainer) 51, 65, 99, 154, 168

witch's ladder 108

worms 97, 109

Y

yarn 33, 107, 108, 109, 110, 124, 179

yew 146, 149. *See also* trees

Also from 1000Volt Press

Changing Paths
Yvonne Aburrow

The Voices of the Dead Series:
Who By Water
Our Lady of the Various Sorrows
Like a Pale Moon
Strange As Angels

Renegade Tea Cookbook
Victoria Raschke